Social Cognition
and the
Acquisition of Self

Social Cognition and the Acquisition of Self

Michael Lewis
and
Jeanne Brooks-Gunn

Institute for the Study of Exceptional Children
Educational Testing Service
Princeton, New Jersey

PLENUM PRESS · NEW YORK AND LONDON

Library of Congress Cataloging in Publication Data

Lewis, Michael, 1937 (Jan. 10)-
  Social cognition and the acquisition of self.

  Bibliography: p.
  Includes index.
  1. Self. 2. Social perception. 3. Personality. 4. Infant psychology. I. Brooks-Gunn, Jeanne,
joint author. II. Title. [DNLM: 1. Self concept. BF697 L675]
BF697.L46   155.4'22   79-12070
ISBN 0-306-40232-7

Plenum Press, New York
A Division of Plenum Publishing Corporation
227 West 17th Street, New York, N.Y. 10011

Printed in the United States of America

To Rhoda
who has given my mind a place to rest
and an opportunity to grow

Michael Lewis

To my parents

Jeanne Brooks-Gunn

Preface

It is always enlightening to inquire about the origins of a research endeavor or a particular theoretical approach. Beginning with the observation of the mental life of the infant in 1962, Michael Lewis has contributed to the change in the view of the infant as an insensate mass of confusion to a complex and intellectual being. Anyone fortunate enough to have participated in the infancy research of the 1960s knows how exciting it was to have discovered in this small creature such a full and complex organism. More central to the origins of this work was the perception of the infant as an interactive, not a reactive, organism, and as one who influenced its social environment and constructed its cognitive life, not one who just passively received information. Other areas of psychology had already begun to conceptualize the organism as active and interactive, even while developmental psychologists still clung to either simple learning paradigms, social reinforcement theories, or reflexive theories. Even though Piaget had proposed an elaborate interactive theory, it was not until the late 1960s that his beliefs were fully implemented into developmental theory and practice. A concurrent trend was the increase of concern with mother–infant interactions (Ainsworth, 1969; Bowlby, 1969; Goldberg & Lewis, 1969; Lewis & Goldberg, 1969) which provided the impetus for the study of social and emotional as well as cognitive development.

About this time, Michael Lewis made an interesting observation of his daughter, Felicia, who was then about eight months old. Although the approach of adult strangers produced "stranger fear" as expected from the infancy literature, the approach of child strangers, friends of her three-year-old brother Benjamin, elicited no such response. Fear was absent, yet greeting and approach were not. The current or subsequent theories concerning fear were not adequate in offering an explanation for the observation, nor did they adequately address the interface between emotional expression and cognition. It was at this point that the notion of similarity, of "like me", was formulated. The empirical literature on self development was practically nonexistent. Discussing this problem with Jeanne Brooks-Gunn, then a student at the University of Pennsylvania, we decided to test this observation. In the study originating out of this observation (Lewis & Brooks, 1974) and in several subsequent studies (Brooks & Lewis, 1976; Lewis, Young, Brooks, & Michalson, 1975), we confirmed that young infants are more wary and frightened of adult strangers than child strangers. In the original Lewis and Brooks study, we decided to observe the child's response to other social objects besides strangers and, to this end, a mother- and a self-approach procedure were observed. In the self-approach, the infants were moved toward a mirror in which they could see only their own image during the approach. From our observations in this study, our interest in self recognition and the development of self was born. For her dissertation, Jeanne Brooks-Gunn studied self recognition in a mirror and a still-picture situation. The results of this labor are Mirror Study I and Picture Study I. The other studies reported in this volume have been run since, confirming our belief that self knowledge has its origins in infancy. Moreover, as our interest in social cognition and affect development has deepened, the central role of the self as a mediating construct has become increasingly relevant. Fortunately, the work of others has guided us: Gallup with nonhuman primates, the personality theory of Kelly, and the social theories of Mead and Cooley. Even more, their insights have encouraged us, sometimes in the face of skepticism of our colleagues, to continue our work. Although self knowledge is widely discussed in the personality, social, clinical, and philosophical literature, its place in developmental psychology is sadly precarious. Since we have begun our work, a few empirical papers have appeared and a few developmental psychologists have begun to discuss the self. Our hope is that this volume and the theoretical approach that we present will encourage others to approach the problem of self knowledge and development. For us, the problem of the self remains a vital consideration in any theory of social cognition and motivation. It is necessary to reintroduce the organism into psychology, somewhere between the stimulus and the behaviors we observe.

MICHAEL LEWIS
JEANNE BROOKS-GUNN

Princeton, New Jersey

Acknowledgments

We would like to express our gratitude to the many people who provided assistance and support. Christine Brim, Susan Lee-Painter, Eileen Scott, Linda Michalson, Gina Rhea, and Sherrill Lord all gave generously of their time during data collection and data coding. Erik Holme designed our original mirror apparatus and provided invaluable technical help during all the studies. Al Rogers and Allan Yates lent their statistical expertise to the data analysis. Jeannette Haviland assisted us in the study presented in Chapter 8 in her design of a system for coding emotional expressions. Marsha Weinraub deserves special mention as she contributed to early conceptualizations of the problem and early behavioral coding systems.

Picture Study I and Mirror Study I were conducted as part of Jeanne Brooks-Gunn's dissertation at the University of Pennsylvania, and special mention should be made of the faculty members who served on the thesis committee. Dr. Joanna Williams, Dr. Gail Zivin, and Dr. Erling Boe's encouragement and advice were extremely helpful.

Special thanks are due to the many mothers from the Princeton area who participated in our studies with their infants, who were usually cooperative and always interesting subjects, and to Gloria Weiss and Claire Montagna who typed the many drafts of this book.

Support for this research was generously provided by a grant from the National Institute for Mental Health (MH-24849-01). The writing of the volume was funded by a grant from the Foundation for Child Development. Our personal appreciation goes to Orville Brim, who supported our work.

Contents

LIST OF FIGURES xv
LIST OF TABLES xvii

Chapter 1
THE ORIGINS OF SELF 1
Social Cognition 7
Duality of Self 8
Theoretical Accounts of the Origins of Self 11
Self Knowledge and Self Awareness 26
Plan of This Volume 27

Chapter 2
MIRROR REPRESENTATIONS OF SELF 29
Mirror Study I 29
Mirror Study II 46

Chapter 3
VIDEOTAPE REPRESENTATIONS OF SELF AND OTHERS 69
Videotape Study I 71
Videotape Study II 87

Chapter 4
PICTORIAL REPRESENTATIONS OF SELF AND OTHERS 115
Picture Study I 116
Picture Study II 123

Chapter 5
VERBAL LABELING OF SELF AND OTHERS 141
  Labeling Study I 142
  Labeling Study II... 150

Chapter 6
INDIVIDUAL DIFFERENCES IN THE EXPRESSION OF SELF RECOGNITION 165

Chapter 7
SELF RECOGNITION AND EMOTIONAL DEVELOPMENT 184
  A Definition of Emotion 185
  The Ontogenesis of Emotional Experience and Self Knowledge 189

Chapter 8
THE DEVELOPMENT OF SELF RECOGNITION 198
  Representational Forms of the Self 199
  Criteria for Self Recognition 212
  The Ontogeny of Self Recognition 214
  Individual Differences in the Development of Self Recognition 219

Chapter 9
TOWARD A THEORY OF THE DEVELOPMENT OF SELF 222
  Self Development 222
  Self, Interaction, and Other: The Onset of Social Cognition ... 228
  Three Principles of Social Cognition....................... 230
  Social Dimensions and the Categorical Self 233

Chapter 10
THE USES OF A THEORY OF SELF 241
  The Ontogeny of Thought: A Sociobiological Approach 241
  The Role of Self in Cognition 246
  The Self–Other Distinction 249
  Self and Interaction 257

REFERENCES 273

AUTHOR INDEX 289

SUBJECT INDEX 293

List of Figures

2-1   Nose-directed behavior: Percentage difference between No Rouge and Rouge 1 Conditions by age   41

2-2   Body-directed behavior: Percentage difference between No Rouge and Rouge 1 Conditions by age   43

2-3   Mark-directed behavior in Rouge 1, Mirror Study I and Condition B, Mirror Study II   56

2-4   Percentage of subjects exhibiting mark recognition in the present study and in Amsterdam's (1968) study by age   64

2-5   Percentage of subjects in the Rouge 1 Condition by age who exhibited other- and self-directed behavior   68

3-1   Mean percentage of subjects who smiled, concentrated, imitated the tapes, and played with the contingencies   76

3-2   Contingent play: Mean proportion of trials by stimulus condition and by age   79

3-3   Imitates tape: Mean proportion of trials by stimulus condition and by age   80

3-4   Mean difference scores for the three comparisons for contingent play and imitates tape   81

3-5   Mean difference scores for smiling for the three comparisons.   84

3-6   Mean proportion difference scores for the three comparisons for target turns by age   95

3-7   Mean proportion difference scores for the three comparisons for contingent play by age   102

9-1   Schematic representation of social objects utilizing three social categories: age, gender, and familiarity   239

10-1   The relative influence of complex social reflexes and complex social cognitions upon behavior expression in the first year of life   243

List of Tables

1-1   Mirror Test Items in Five Infant Tests   22

2-1   Behaviors Observed in the Mirror Conditions   32

2-2   Percentage of Subjects Responding in the No Rouge Condition by Behavior and by Age   36

2-3   Percentage Change Scores between the No Rouge and Rouge 1 Condition by Behavior and by Age   40

2-4   Number of Subjects Exhibiting Mark Recognition in Rouge 1, Mother Rouge, and Rouge 2 Conditions   45

2-5   Percentage of Subjects Exhibiting Each Behavior in Trials 1 and 2 of Condition A in Mirror Study II (No Rouge Trials) and in the No Rouge and Rouge 1 Condition in Mirror Study I   52

2-6   Percentage of Subjects Exhibiting Each Behavior in Trial 2, Condition B in Mirror Study II by Age   54

2-7   Percentage of Subjects Exhibiting Each Behavior in Trial 2 of Conditions B and C in Mirror Study II and in the Rouge 1 and 2 Conditions in Mirror Study I   55

3-1   Measures Used in Videotape Study I   73

3-2   Mean Proportion of Trials and Number of Subjects Exhibiting Contingent Play and Imitates Tape by Stimulus Condition   78

3-3   Mean Proportion of Trials in Which the Infants Smiled, Moved toward, and Vocalized Positively to the Stimulus Condition by Age and Sex of Subject   82

3-4   Mean Proportion of Trial Spent Looking, and Mean Proportion of Trial in Which Infants Exhibited a Concentrate Expression to the Stimulus Conditions by Age and Sex of Subject   86

3-5   Measures Used in Videotape Study II 91
3-6   Mean Proportion of Trials in Which Subjects Turned Right
        and Left by Age, Sex, and Stimulus Condition 94
3-7   Mean Proportion of Trials in Which Infants Exhibited Posi-
        tive Affect and Contingent Play by Age, Sex, and Stimu-
        lus Condition 99
3-8   Mean Proportion of Trials in Which Subjects Turned Right
        and Left by Stimulus Condition and Turning Group dur-
        ing Training 103
4-1   Behaviors Observed and Scores Assigned to Each Behavior
        in the Picture Procedure 118
4-2   Mean Amount of Affect and Fixation for the Age of
        Stranger Comparison 120
4-3   Mean Amount of Affect and Fixation for the Self–Peer
        Comparisons 124
4-4   Mean Amount of Positive Affect and Visual Fixation for the
        Stranger Comparisons 128
4-5   Mean Amount of Positive Affect and Visual Fixation for the
        Self–Peer Comparisons 131
5-1   Number of Subjects and Frequency with Which Different
        Labels Are Applied by Baby Picture and by Age of Sub-
        ject.. 148
5-2   Picture Sets for the Verbal Comprehension Task Labeling
        Study II 152
5-3   Number of Infants Using Their Own Name and Personal
        Pronouns 154
5-4   Number of Infants Using "Boy" and "Girl" 156
5-5   Percentage of Subjects Who Pointed at Least Once during
        the Comprehension Task by Stimulus Group 158
6-1   Correlations between the Mirror and Videotape Measures
        of Self Recognition 171
6-2   Correlations between Self Recognition and Cognitive Mea-
        sures 173
6-3   Correlations between Self Recognition and Social Measures 176
6-4   Summary of Multiple Regressions for Self Recognition
        Combinations 177
7-1   Percentage of Subjects Exhibiting Self-Directed Behaviors
        and Facial Expressions 195

7-2   Relationship between Self Recognition and Facial Ex-
        pressions (Number of Subjects) 196
8-1   Self Recognitory Representations 218
9-1   Development of Self Knowledge, Emotional Experience,
        and Cognitive Growth 227

The Origins of Self

The phenomenon which we have chosen to study is easily observed in the everyday situations of children and infants. The theories we construct must allow us to observe the necessary events. Make no mistake—we cannot watch everything that the child does. Our observations themselves are determined by the assumptions we bring to the observation. There is no end to the things the infant does, nor is there any easy way to reconstruct the myriad of events we do watch or to place them into a coherent and meaningful whole. That is the function of theory. Our task, then, is not unlike that of the infant who, awake and alert, attempts to make sense out of the enormously large and complex set of events that surround him. Indeed, the infant's task may be a bit easier than our own since a caregiver helps structure the infant's world; we have only our intuitions and theories. The infant must observe, form hypotheses, and test them against the action of the world, just as we must observe, hypothesize, and test.

> Susan is 16 weeks old. She is lying on her back in her crib looking at a brightly colored mobile above her. She kicks her foot and the mobile rattles. Within seconds she kicks her foot again and again the mobile moves. She watches the moving objects with great interest without kicking. Finally, 20 seconds after the mobile is perfectly still, she kicks her foot again while watching it.

Piaget (1936/1963) has described this series of events carefully, describing them as a circular reaction. An accidental action of the child is observed to result in another interesting action, and the child quickly repeats the original action. Action X (foot kick) results in Action Y (mobile movement), and Action X is repeated. In this way, associations between events are built up; relatively little mental apparatus is necessary for this process, especially given the short latency between the two events. But notice, Susan did something else: after a long, 20-sec pause in which Susan did not kick her foot nor did the mobile move, she kicks her foot and watches the mobile. The long latency of 20 sec has broken the simple chain of foot kick–mobile move as the foot kick occurred in the absence of the mobile movement and signals that a major developmental milestone may have occurred. Susan has demonstrated a tentative plan, a course of action, holding the association as a mental image or a memory and acting on the basis of this memory and plan: an intentional act. These internal processes—memory, action plan, and intentionality—are not visible and may only be inferred from the infant's behavior. A more mechanistic view could explain Susan's behavior without postulating such processes. Although we realize that internal processes are only one way to explain Susan's behavior, we find that these observations fit our notion of agency: the child's foot kicking after a long latency represents the beginning of representation and plans, the beginning of self actions predicated on some internal processes. These processes have an executor, whose intentions can best be explained, we believe, by the notion of self.

> Gregory is also about 3 months old. Lately, he has begun to coo loudly during those moments between waking and calling his mother by crying. One morning, Gregory's mother walks quietly into his bedroom and finds him awake, on his back, with his right hand extended above him and to the right; his head is turned toward his hand and he is watching his fingers move with considerable interest. He continues to do this for a while longer, then lowers his arm and finally gets the fingers of his right hand into his mouth.

Around this age, infants begin to explore their hands (White, 1971). These moving objects, of moderately high contrast, are of considerable interest to the 3-month-old infant because of these salient stimulus dimensions. Although there is no doubt that stimuli with these dimensions have the capacity to draw and hold the infant's attention, why are infants not attentive to their hands at younger ages? Certainly the motoric ability to move one's hands and fingers into the field of vision occurs before this. Observation of infant's motoric behavior indicates that this is the case. However, an alternative explanation to motoric maturation is possible and relies on the development of means and ends or early circular reactions. Rather than the action taking place inside the body and the reaction taking place outside the body (as in the example of the mobile), both events involve the self. Intentions, memory, and plans play a part in the exploration of the child's own body. Thus, in some sense, the means and ends relationships being established have both as a subject and object the same locus in space. Moreover, the proprioceptive feedback from the two events and actions (looking and moving one's hands and fingers) are both located in the same nervous system. This example differs markedly from the first since the child can operate on *both* events, rather than just one event being external to the organism. The infant, having control of both actions, can turn to look at the object *or* have the object move into the field of vision. This duality of subject and object must represent the beginning of the self as distinct from other, the knowledge of different classes of events, those internal to the self (located somewhere "here" in space) and those external to self (located "there" in space), and the perception of self as having a specific location in space. Parenthetically, we have often thought it interesting that when we are attended to, people look at us, at the one locus in space we cannot see—ourselves. This same process occurs for the infant with the perception of the duality of subject–object having some relationship to spatial knowledge and to self knowledge. Depending on our model of development, Gregory's moving his hand and fingers before his eyes may reflect simple attentional behavior elicited by salient stimulus dimensions or may reflect his earliest exploration and discovery of his own body in relation to other classes of events.

> Robert is 37 weeks old and enjoys banging on his high chair with a hard rubber toy. It is well worn, having been bitten and sucked on for many months. Today, while he is banging on it, it falls to the ground. It is a bit out of sight, having fallen below his seat. Robert starts to whine, which brings his mother to his side. Seeing the fallen object, she replaces it. Off it goes again, and again she retrieves it. The fourth time Robert throws it to the ground, his mother picks it up, but, instead of replacing it, she places it behind a pile of dishes and returns to her kitchen task. From the high chair, Robert can no longer see the toy; nonetheless, he continues to whine and bang, expressing his displeasure over the missing object.

Robert is now able to remember objects which are no longer present. Several months earlier, he was easily distracted and quickly forgot the missing object. Robert has acquired an early form of object permanence (Piaget, 1936/1963): the knowledge that objects exist independently of the perceiver and that objects have permanence independently of our sensory experience of them. This permanence has become one of the most studied phenomena in the sensorimotor period, and its emergence has been heralded as one of the markers of the first year of life. Person permanence has been studied as well (Bell, 1970; Décarie,

1965) and its development parallels that of object permanence. Self permanence has not been subject to scrutiny even though it is logically impossible that infants know an object exists independent of their own existence, without also postulating that infants also have a concept of self. Moreover, since person and object permanence emerge more or less at the same time, it is hard to imagine that infants can achieve person permanence, especially of family members, without having self permanence. This milestone, occurring in the last quarter of the first year, must have significance for self as well as other people and objects. Since most of the scientific inquiry of early development in the first two years has focused on object knowledge, little attention has been paid to the child's emerging social cognition. Since we believe that social and object knowledge are similar, object permanence has implications for social and self knowledge.

> Maude is 8 months old and loves to sit up in her high chair by the table. During dinner she looks at Ben, her 3-year-old brother, most of the time. Even when her mother feeds her, her attention is drawn to him. When he makes funny faces, she smiles and laughs; everyone thinks she likes him best. Earlier in the day, Ben's new friend from nursery school came home. Maude approached the strange child immediately, and all three played for over an hour. After dinner, Maude loves to play a tickle game with her father, but tonight Dad had an office worker come over. Unlike her behavior toward her brother's friend, she refused to meet the strange adult and when carried to him, began to cry.

The social objects that exist in the life of the young child are multiple and varied. From the beginning of life, the child is embedded in a social network made up of different people (Lewis & Rosenblum, 1979). Moreover, these different people have different and overlapping functions in the child's life (Edwards & Lewis, 1979; Lewis & Feiring, 1979). Although functions and people are not equivalent (e.g., "mothering" is a function not a person), it is the case that people have traditionally assumed different roles. The mother has been assigned the caregiving role; she is the primary caregiver. Fathers, although often not very involved in their young children's lives, appear to have a supportive role. In addition, because they leave and return to the house each day, many fathers have an important role in the child's cognitive development (Lewis & Weinraub, 1976). Parsons and Bales (1955) have distinguished between these roles labeling the caregiving one as affective and the supportive one as instrumental. Siblings also have different functions which include education and socialization of peer behavior (Zajonc,

1977). Peers and friends are relatively rare in the first year of life, but even so, appear to be important in terms of their role in the social development of children (Harlow & Harlow, 1965; Lewis, Young, Brooks, & Michalson, 1975; Mueller, 1979). Even strangers are responded to differentially, with children strangers eliciting less fear and more approach behavior than adult strangers (Brooks & Lewis, 1976; Lewis & Brooks, 1974).

In short, data from a variety of sources suggest that complex social behavior is present very early and that social knowledge is well established by the last quarter of the first year (Brooks & Lewis, 1976; McGurk & Lewis, 1974). Some believe that these early responses are controlled by a limited set of social stimuli, specifically, that the infant is attached to the mother through imprinting and fearful of all strangers through biological processes (Bowlby, 1969). We believe that the view of the infant as already possessing a primitive model of its social world fits the data better than this more evolutionary view. From our viewpoint, the infant interacts with many people who have multiple and overlapping functions. Within each function, different behaviors are directed toward people by the child and toward the child by others. These behaviors constitute a complex perceptual, cognitive, and affectual organization, in which the child perceives these behaviors as differentiated by function and person (child as object) and the child produces these behaviors by function and person (child as subject). By the time the child is 8 months of age, it has a complex set of social cognitions and behaviors. The infant's place within the differentiated world as a function of his behavior and how others behave in return, begins to emerge. The self as an element within this complex social matrix of objects and functions must start to have meaning.

> David, at 15 months, loves to run around and pretend he is a cowboy. Today he has been playing in the kitchen while the housekeeper has been baking. His hands are covered with flour and some of it has gotten on his cheek and nose. Having been told to go and wash up, David goes to the bathroom sink and, while washing his hands, notices his image in the mirror. Seeing the flour on his nose, he laughs and then, still looking at his own image, wipes the flour off with his hand.

Children's interest in mirror reflections was reported by Darwin (1877) and Preyer (1893) before the turn of the century. This interest in mirrors may be related to the concept of the self, although interest in the reflection that one sees in the mirror can be nothing more than interest in the reflection of another. David's behavior, however, was more than noticing his reflection in the mirror; what David did was to use the mirror to guide his behavior, in particular to guide his behavior in removing the flour from his own nose. It appears as if David recognized that the reflection was himself. We believe this to be true, since David had not only to respond to the image in the mirror but had to engage in self-directed behavior; he had to demonstrate that he knew that the image there (in the mirror) represented the object here (his own flour-marked nose).

But more importantly, self recognition implies to us that David has a notion of self, a notion that he has existence in a particular point in space and that this existence has characteristics or features, i.e., when he looks or talks he is treated in a certain way by others. The ability to identify the reflection "that's David" may be nothing more than learning to apply a label to a set of stimuli. However, the self-directed movement must represent his knowledge that the image there represents something here (here being the space occupied by David). Such evidence represents David's knowledge of self. In the work to follow, we will make use of this procedure and the results generated by it to show the early acquisition of self recognition.

> At 24 months, Leah loves to play with dolls, especially Sarah, the one with long yellow hair. Her younger sister also likes to play with the doll. This morning, Leah could not find the doll and so went into her sister's room, where she found it lying on the bed. Leah grabbed the doll from the bed, brought it toward her body and said, "That's my doll, it's mine."

Here, finally, is the use of a personal pronoun. By this age, Leah has acquired and correctly uses noun references which refer to herself. Although Leah's behavior could be interpreted in terms of the acquisition of a referent, a substitution for the proper name that she had learned almost a year before, we believe her behavior represents the first clear language demonstration of self knowledge. The use of "mine" or "me" and "I" constitutes the flowering of early self knowledge into linguistic symbolic representation. Although the concept of self continues to change throughout the life cycle, the use of these personal pronouns represents the end point in our study of the origins of self, the first truly symbolic representation.

Taken together, these various examples of early behavior can best be explained by a developing sense of self. While other interpretations are possible, the model of an organism who is active and interactive from the beginning of life necessitates the postulation of a concept of self. Further, these examples suggest that the self must be incorporated into a social cognitive view of development.

SOCIAL COGNITION

Our discussion of the role of self in social cognition will occupy much of the discussion of Chapters 8, 9, and 10, and so we will save most of our comments for that time. Nonetheless, a brief discussion of social cognition is necessary to understand how important a role the concept of self and the knowledge of others plays in the child's development. While social cognition has been defined in a variety of ways—for example, in the recognition of various emotions exhibited by others or the reasons persons act as they do—our definition of social cognition includes three major aspects: (1) knowledge of self, (2) knowledge of others, (3) and knowledge of one's relationship to others. In order to understand these three aspects of social knowledge, it is necessary to study the relationship between them. For us, the child's knowledge of self and others is developed through one's interaction with these others, and that social interaction is the basic unit out of which social cognition derives. As Merleau-Ponty (1964) states:

> If I am a consciousness turned toward things, I can meet in things the actions of another and find in them a meaning, because they are themes of possible activity for my own body. (p. 113)

While, as interactionalists, we have been in accord that knowledge of the world is derived through interaction with it, we have only considered knowledge of others. We have not considered that knowledge of others gained through interaction must inform us about ourselves. Because we have failed to attend to this parallel development between self and other, we have failed to understand social cognition. The reason for this is that our studies of cognition have concerned themselves with attributes of the physical world which, in general, have little bearing on people. The acquisition of knowledge of these physical properties, such as weight, height, and time, also tell us something about ourselves, but their relationship is far less tenuous. Although these attributes of objects are acquired early, the attributes of the social world, because the child needs to adapt to its social world in order to survive, are learned as early if not earlier. Lest you feel that the infant is intellectually unable to deal with such complex issues, remember the infant is considerably more cognitively advanced and capable than we thought even ten years ago (Stone, Smith, & Murphy, 1973). We hold to a model of an active and competent organism, one who at an early age already shows signs of planning and of intentional behavior (for example, in primary and circular reactions, Piaget, 1936/1963), and one who derives information from its interactions with its world. Such an organism does possess the perceptual-cognitive ability to acquire early social cognitions, as the studies in this volume attest.

DUALITY OF SELF

Most psychologists, phenomenologists, and philosophers have emphasized the duality of the self and have distinguished between the self as subject and the self as object (Wylie, 1961). The first aspect is the existential self or the self as subject. The self as subject is seen as distinct from others and from the world and is thought to involve such active processes as thinking, remembering, and perceiving in the mature organism (Hall & Lindzey, 1970). The self as object is the second aspect of the self. We will call it the categorical self. The composite of attitudes, abilities, and values that comprises one's self concept is synonymous with self as object. These two aspects of self have been considered separately in the research as well as the philosophical literature and have led to different types of research. These two aspects of self—subject and object—are referred to throughout literature, as we shall see in the following section.

The Self as Subject: Existential Self

The basic premise of the existential self is that the self is distinct from others. Awareness of this distinction is thought to occur very early, and there have been many attempts to describe the process by which one comes to know oneself. The ego psychologists emphasized the infant's incessant desire for oral gratification and the tempering of these needs through the gradual differentiation of self and mother (Freud, 1965; Spitz & Wolf, 1946). Sociologists such as Mead (1934) and Cooley (1912) were concerned with the growing awareness of self as distinct from, but in relation to, other persons. Genetic epistemologists, following the lead of Piaget (1936/1963) and Wallon (1949), concerned themselves with the child's changing cognitive strategies which enable him to see the invariances in the world (and in himself).

The basic notion of existence separate from other (both animate and inanimate) develops as the infant differentiates self from other persons. The first social distinction probably involves the mother or caregiver, a position advocated by psychoanalytic theorists (Erikson, 1937; Spitz & Wolf, 1946). This primitive self develops from birth and therefore exists in some form in the early months. In fact, 3- and 4-month-old infants are able to differentiate between mother and female stranger, as measured by a variety of infant responses (cardiac deceleration—Banks & Wolfson, 1967; vocalization—Rebelsky, 1971; Turnure, 1971; wariness—Bronson, 1972; differential reinforcing properties—Wahler, 1967). It is not unreasonable to assume that the self–other differentiation also occurs by this time.

This nonevaluative, existential self is developed from the consistency, regularity, and contingency of the infant's action and outcome in the world. The mechanism of reafferent feedback provides the first contingency information for the child; therefore, the kinesthetic feedback produced by the infant's own actions forms the basis for the development of self. For example, each time a certain set of muscles operates (eyes close), it becomes black (cannot see). The action of touching the hot stove and the immediacy of the pain tells me it is my hand that is on the stove. This self is further reinforced if, when I remove my hand, the pain ceases. These kinesthetic systems provide immediate and regular action–outcome pairings.

Such contingent feedback is also provided by the environment. Infants' interactions with objects provide consistent information (a round object always rolls while a square object does not). In addition, social stimuli (especially the caregiver) provide extensive feedback and are potent reinforcers. Indeed, social reinforcement may be the most effective behavior-shaping mechanism in infancy. Wolff (1963), in his intensive study of infant behavior in the first weeks of life, has found that social stimuli (such as vocalizations and facial movement) elicit smiling responses more readily than do nonsocial stimuli. Social reinforcers (an adult smiling, talking, patting an infant) can also be used to condition smiling and vocalizing by the age of three months (Brackbill, 1958; Rheingold, Gewirtz, & Ross, 1959). Since social stimuli are such potent reinforcers, it is not surprising that differentiation between familiar and unfamiliar persons occurs early. The caregiver is the person who provides the bulk of social reinforcement in the first year of life.

The contingency feedback given by the primary caregiver probably provides for generalized expectancies about the infant's control of his world. Such expectancies would also help differentiate the infant's actions from others' actions. The generalized expectancy model (Lewis, 1977; Lewis & Goldberg, 1969) proposes that a mother's responsiveness to her infant's cues determines the infant's expectations. The consistency, timing, and quality of the mother's responses create expectancies about control and competence. If the infant's demands (defined as his behavioral repertoire) are reinforced, he is, in a sense, controlling his environment. Thus, his actions may produce outcomes in the social as well as in the kinesthetic realm. Such contingencies should relate to the development of self–other differentiation. Moreover, since self–other interaction always involves the other's relating to a specific locus in space, the interactive nature of self–other should facilitate a schema for self. For example, action by the other directed toward self is always space specific. Thus, not only is there interactive reciprocity in time, but reciprocity in space as well.

The development of self may also be related to the general issue of permanence. Permanence deals with the recognition that objects and people exist even when perceptually absent. Self permanence may exist when the infant is aware that the existence of other objects is not contingent on his presence. That the self is distinct from other environmental events is a necessary condition for later development of self-identity (Guardo & Bohan, 1971). The concept of self as identity is elucidated by Guardo (1968), who defines self "from the point of view of the experiencer as a phenomenological feeling or sense of self identity" (p. 139). If object permanence and person permanence exist by 8 months, it may be reasonable to suppose that self permanence also exists and that these phenomena develop simultaneously. Thus, the early differentiation of self and other should take place at the same time the child is differentiating its mother from others and is acquiring object permanence.

The Self as Object: Categorical Self

The self as object has been discussed as the empirical self (James, 1892/1961), the social self (Cooley, 1912), and me (Mead, 1934). More recently, psychologists have termed this self concept (Wylie, 1961). It is thought that self concept, unlike the existential self, can be operationalized and measured.

In the specific area of early childhood development, attempts to measure self concept are numerous. Coller (1971), after reviewing 50 techniques for assessing self concept in preschool to third-grade children, also found no consensus in definitions. At one point, he suggests that we define self concept "as that construct or set thereof assessed by the set of so-called self concept instruments" (p. 73). Self concept, like intelligence, seems to be impervious to consensual definition.

The development of self concept or the categorical self is somewhat different than the development of the existential self or the self as subject. Referring to the categories by which the infant defines itself vis-à-vis the external world, the categorical self is subject to many lifelong. changes. Ontogenetically, it should change as a function of the child's other cognitive capacities, as well as with changing social relationships. Some categories, like gender, remain fixed; others, like size, strength, and competence, change either by being added to or altered entirely. While in adolescence ability in sports and clothes were important, in adulthood competence and creativity may take their place. Historically and socially, the categorical self changes. For example, different cultures have different requirements for their members. In one case the male is expected to be a good hunter, while in another, being a good scholar is important. Given these different values, different categories of self should emerge and disappear over time. If this conceptualization is at all valid, it becomes necessary to consider what categories are available to the infant, which ones are acquired, and how these change with time.

THEORETICAL ACCOUNTS OF THE ORIGINS OF SELF

Early Sociological Theories

Mead and Cooley both believed that knowledge of self and other developed simultaneously. Indeed, neither could exist without the other, since both originated through social interaction. Cooley (1909/ 1962; 1912), in developing a theory regarding the social nature of man and social organization as a whole, posited a reflective or "looking glass" self. The self is reflected through others; thus, other people are the "looking glass" for oneself. The development of self is therefore dependent upon interaction with others and the world. In fact, Cooley stressed that self and society are a common whole, with neither existing in the absence of the other.

Cooley believed that the infant is not conscious of the self or the "I" nor of society or other people. Infants experience a simple "stream of impressions," impressions that gradually become discriminated as the young child differentiates self or "I" and society or "We." After "I" and "We" are separate, knowledge, attitudes, abilities, values, and feelings become incorporated into the self concept. Although discussing the origins of self, Cooley did not explicate the process of the development of self (Deutsch, 1965).

Mead (1934), drawing upon Cooley's theory of a "looking glass" self as well as James's distinction between the "Me" (self as known) and the "I" (self as knower), provided the first systematic description of the development of the self. Mead, heavily influenced by Darwin, believed that the human infant is active rather than passive, selectively responding to stimuli rather than responding to all stimuli that impinge. Mead further believed that the infant actively constructs the self. As he states:

> The self has a character which is different from that of the physiological organism proper. The self is something which has a development; it is not initially there at birth but arises in the process of social experience and activity, that is, develops in the given individual as a result of his relations to that process as a whole and to other individuals within that process. (p. 135)

For Mead, self development was dependent upon the development of language. Gestures and language provide the infant with the means to interact with others, to anticipate others' reactions, to take the *role* of the other person, to perceive the self as an object, and to differentiate between self and others. Play and games constitute the actual mechanisms by which roles are learned and the self is differentiated. Like Cooley, Mead thought knowledge of the self was dependent upon knowledge of others, since knowledge of others (and the world) is necessary to differentiate between self and other and to perceive self as an object. Consequently, the self is a cognitive structure that arises out of interaction with the world.

Cognitive Theory

Cognitive psychology, arising out of gestalt psychology, can be represented by Heider (1958). Like others, Heider was concerned with the "balance" of cognitive structures. When an imbalance is introduced (i.e., from environmental stimuli dissonant with the present cognitive structure), then a tendency to resolve that imbalance will result. According to Heider, the resolution of the imbalance is accomplished in one of two ways: "moving away" from the source of the balance or, if movement is not possible, a change in the cognitive structure, the cognitive structure being akin to the self. Imbalance theory, then, could explain changes in one's self concept.

Heider also addressed the question of self more directly. Like Cooley and Mead, he believed that the self was the result of social interactions. Heider suggested that events in one's life were attributed either to one's own actions or to forces outside the self. To make this determination, a person must have knowledge of self and others, as well as the ability to compare oneself with others. Again, others, or society, are necessary to know oneself. Although acknowledging the necessity of self and specifying the way in which the self arises, Heider did not discuss the origins of self nor developmental changes.

Psychoanalytic Theory

Freud thought that the acquisition of a notion of self was crucial for normal, healthy development. In addition, Freud discussed the mechanisms involved in self development and placed this development in the opening months of life. According to Freud, the infant's primitive sense of self arose out of the differentiation of the inner and outer worlds, of sensations inside the body and stimulation provided by the world.

This distinction formed the basis for the development of ego functions in the infant. Ego functions mediate between instinctual needs and external realities. As the infant's instinctual needs (or Id) come into contact with reality, the ego aids in the gratification of instincts while restraining or transforming the needs so they do not conflict with social reality. Ego functioning does not require conscious comparison of self and other, although it does require knowledge of the social world and its constraints and differentiation of self and other. Indeed, the ego arises out of the awareness that the self and the mother are not one unit and that the mother does not gratify the infant's every need. Without this knowledge, an independent and autonomous self could not develop.

Following Freud, several psychoanalysts developed even further the notions of ego and self. Sometimes called ego psychologists, they detailed the process by which the infant developed a self identity. The most extensive and thorough description of this process has been provided by Mahler (1968). Mahler observed that autistic persons had not developed a sense of individuation, whereas the symbiotic person had no sense of separation of self and other. These observations led her to study how an independent and autonomous sense of self normally developed (cf. Mahler & Gosliner, 1955; Mahler, 1968; Mahler, Pine, & Bergman, 1975).

For Mahler, the child acquires a sense of separateness along with a sense of relatedness to the world through a process Mahler labeled as separation–individuation. Both cognitive and affective in nature, this process is characterized by the child's emergence from the symbiotic relationship with the mother (separation) and the child's acquisition of individual characteristics (individuation) during the first three years of life. At the end of this period, an independent and autonomous sense of self has been formed.

The developmental timetable for this process is specified by Mahler. The newborn child is in an autistic stage in which no contact with the outside world has been established. Mahler likens this phase to a chick in an egg who has no need for or awareness of the world. After the first few weeks of life, the infant becomes dimly aware of the fact that his or her needs are being met by another person, not the self. This awareness marks the end of the autistic stage, as the infant is aware of the mother but believes mother and self to be one, to have a common boundary. Both Spitz (1954) and Mahler believe that "I" and "not I" are not differentiated during this period.

The symbiotic phase begins at the end of the first half of the first year. At 4 to 5 months of age, the self–other differentiation occurs, with the advent of smiling to the mother thought to be indicative of this budding awareness (Spitz, 1954). At 6 months of age, the infant experiments with the knowledge that his or her own body and that of the mother are separate, as evidenced by increased play and exploration of the mother's body parts. At 7 to 8 months, the mother is compared to others, as the infant tries to figure out what mother actually *is*. Thus, at the end of the first subphase of the symbiotic stage, the infant has differentiated self from other, established a body boundary, and begun emotionally separating from the mother.

In the next subphase, which occurs from 1 to 1½ years of age, the infant further refines the knowledge acquired earlier, spending much time exploring the world and disentangling self from the mother. The last half of the second year brings increased awareness of what it means to be separate and autonomous and an expansion of emotional experience, the beginning of empathy. The knowledge that he or she is small, sometimes helpless and separate, leads to a vulnerability and a need to share experiences with the mother.

From 2 to 3 years, individuality is consolidated, separation from mother easier to bear, love for the mother more mature and more of a "give and take," all of which results in a stable self identity (Mahler, Pine, & Bergman, 1975). Thus, self identity develops gradually, as the infant learns to differentiate self and other. Like Freud, Mahler believes that this process involves the infant's relationship with the mother, which is the prototype for all other relationships and forms the basis for the first self–other distinction.

Epistemological Theory

Epistemology, which involves both philosophical and psychological disciplines, also considers the origins of self. The writings of the epistemologists are best exemplified by Merleau-Ponty (1964), Wallon (1949), and Piaget (1936/1963; 1937/1954; 1947/1960; 1970). Merleau-Ponty and Wallon both discuss the origins of self, although they are primarily concerned with the child's early relationships with others. For Piaget, knowledge of self and of other people as independent from object knowledge is not thought to occur until the end of the sensorimotor period. We shall return to consider these theories in more detail later (see Chapters 9 and 10).

Empirical Evidence on the Origins of Self

Visual self recognition, or at least facial recognition, due to repeated exposure to mirrors and pictures, is almost universal in our society. The only adults who have difficulty recognizing their faces visually are persons suffering from certain central nervous system (CNS) dysfunctions, severely mentally retarded children and adults (Cornielson & Arsenian, 1960; Frenkel, 1964; Harris, 1977; Shentoub, Soulairac, & Rustin, 1954), as well as some psychotic patients.

Clinicians report that psychotic patients do not respond to mirrors with self-directed behaviors and do not recognize themselves in pictures, presumably because of a loss of the sense of self (Delmas, 1929; Faure, 1956; Frenkel, 1964). This distortion of the self is readily seen in schizophrenics, who have been reported to gaze into mirrors for long periods of time without recognizing themselves (Abely, 1930; Delmas, 1929). More than one investigator has suggested that such mirror behavior might aid in the diagnosis of schizophrenia (Gallup, 1968; Ostancow, 1934).

Research utilizing distorted mirrors also indicates that psychotics have difficulty realistically assessing their mirror images. Traub and Orbach (Orbach, Traub, & Olson, 1966; Traub & Orbach, 1964) have devised a situation where the subject may manipulate the amount of distortion present in a mirror. When asked to adjust the mirror so that no distortion was present, schizophrenics were unable to do so while normal subjects had no such difficulty. To see whether the psychotics' inability was specific to self reflections, the schizophrenics were asked to manipulate the mirror in order to obtain a distortion-free representation of a door, which they were able to do. In addition, mirrors, pictures, and videotapes of the patient have been used in therapy to increase self awareness (Cornielson & Arsenian, 1960; Frenkel, 1964; Stoller, 1967).

As the review of the self recognition in clinical populations suggests, the self may be visually experienced in different representational mediums, including mirrors, pictures, movies, and videotapes. The most common medium—mirrors—presents contingency cues as well as movement and feature cues. By using picture and videotape representations, such cues can be systematically manipulated in order to better understand what cues are necessary for self recognition and if cue salience varies developmentally. In fact, a developmental study of self recognition almost demands such a manipulation of cues, as we shall see in later chapters.

Unfortunately, most of the research on visual self recognition has focused primarily on mirror-image stimulation. Procedures involving pictures and videotapes are just being introduced to study self recognition development. Therefore, the following review focuses primarily on the mirror literature.

Before going on, we must emphasize that self recognition involves more than a simple discrimination of body features, however. To determine that the person in a picture is oneself, that a mirror reflection is oneself, and that the self cannot exist in two places simultaneously—all requirements of self recognition—knowledge of one's own identity as continuous through time and space is necessary. Thus, recognizing oneself presupposes a knowledge of one's identity. As Gallup (1977) has suggested, "The capacity to correctly infer the identity of the reflection must, therefore, presuppose an already evident identity on the part of the part of the organism making this distinction" (p. 334).

Mirror Images and Self Recognition

Phylogenetic Trends

Reactions to self reflections in mirrors have been studied extensively in a variety of species. Gallup has presented a comprehensive review of this literature on several occasions (1968, 1973, 1977); therefore, this literature will only be summarized here.

Gallup has defined mirror-image stimulation as "situations in which an organism, human or otherwise, is confronted with its own reflection in a mirror" and self-recognition as "behavior in which the self rather than the mirror is the referent" (1973, p. 2). Using these definitions, reactions to a mirror may be divided into two categories: mirror-directed and self-directed behaviors.

Mirror-Directed Behavior. The social nature of mirror-image stimulation, as inferred by the stimulus properties of mirrors, inevitably leads to social behavior on the part of many organisms. This is evidenced by the fact that many species act differently in the presence of a mirror than they do in isolation. For example, Tolman (1965) reports that chickens characteristically eat more in the presence of conspecifics and in the presence of mirrors than they do when alone.

Not only do animals react as if the mirror were a social object, but they act as though it were a conspecific. The most well-known and widely verified example involves aggressive displays toward a mirror image. These displays may be reliably elicited in fish (Lissman, 1932), birds (Ritter & Benson, 1934), and primates (Schmidt, 1878). The fact that human infants (Amsterdam, 1972) and primates (Goodall, 1971) will search behind a mirror, presumably for the reflected image, is also thought to be an example of socially appropriate conspecific behavior. A further social discrimination is made by some species as the mirror image is usually seen as an unfamiliar rather than a familiar conspecific. Gallup (1973) reports that male macaque monkeys, when confronted with a mirror, exhibit a facial gesture that is only elicited by unfamiliar male macaques. This expression is not exhibited toward familiar male conspecifics, such as other colony members.

Thus, many species act as though the mirror were another organism. Furthermore, not only is the reflected image seen as another being, but is treated as a conspecific, and usually an unfamiliar one. The lack of self-directed behaviors and the preponderance of mirror-directed or conspecific-directed behaviors suggest that a concept of self does not exist in many species (Gallup, 1977). This idea is further reinforced by the nature of the behavior exhibited to the mirror. Very often mirror-image stimulation elicits such high interest that it may be used as a reward in a learning paradigm and has been for fish (Melvin & Anson, 1970; Thompson, 1963) and monkeys (Gallup, 1966; Gallup & McClure, 1971; McLean, 1964). Gallup (1973) suggests that this interest may be related to the relatively rigid social behavior of fish and birds, not specifically to an awareness of the contingent nature of mirror feedback. These species may be so stimulus-bound that they cannot escape from the contingent feedback, although they are not actually aware of or actively experimenting with the contingency itself.

Self-Directed Behavior. While mirror-directed behavior has been observed in many animals, self-directed behavior has been observed only in primates. The transition from other-directed to self-directed behavior is illustrated by the following two points. First, monkeys have been shown to react to their own reflections as if they were other unfamiliar conspecifics, although their behavior is not as inflexible as that of fish and birds. Normally reared rhesus monkeys have been shown to prefer viewing conspecifics rather than mirrors (Gallup & McClure, 1971). Thus, although the contingent action of the mirror image elicits high interest and some conspecific-appropriate behavior, it is not as interesting as the noncontingent action of another. Presumably, this is due to the importance of reciprocal interaction for primates. Second, monkeys are able to use mirrors to manipulate objects (Brown, McDowell, & Robinson, 1965) and to look at objects and persons indirectly (Tinklepaugh, 1928). However, they do not seem to understand the nature of a reflective surface as it pertains to themselves.

The first demonstration of self-directed behavior in subhuman primates occurred in 1970, when Gallup observed four wild-born preadolescent chimpanzees' reactions to mirrors. The chimpanzees began to use the mirror to examine and to groom visually inaccessible parts of their bodies after only three days of experience with mirrors (30 h). As the incidence of self-directed behavior increased, other-directed behavior decreased. To further investigate the occurrence of self-directed behavior, Gallup anesthetized and placed red, odorless dye on each animal (on an eyebrow ridge and on the opposite ear). After the animals had recovered from the anesthesia, they were placed in front of the mirror again. All four chimpanzees directed their actions toward the marks on their faces, rather than the mark on the mirror image. Not only did they touch their marked faces, but they spent more time observing themselves in the marked condition than they had previously. Interestingly, two other marked chimpanzees, who had no prior exposure to mirrors, did not exhibit self- or mark-directed behaviors. These findings strongly suggest that chimpanzees are able to recognize themselves in mirrors and that this recognition does not occur without some exposure to mirrors (Gallup, 1970).

These findings have been replicated with chimpanzees (Gallup, McClure, Hill, & Bundy, 1971; Hill, Bundy, Gallup, & McClure, 1970; Lethmate & Dücker, 1973) and extended to orangutans (Lethmate & Dücker, 1973). Interestingly, no primate species other than the great apes has been found to exhibit self recognition, even after thousands of hours of mirror experience (Gallup, 1970, 1979). Macaques, rhesus monkeys, and java monkeys (Gallup, 1979; Lethmate & Dücker, 1973), spider monkeys, capuchins, baboons, and gibbons (Benhar, Carlton, & Samuel, 1975; Pribram as cited in Gallup, 1973) have all failed to recognize themselves in mirrors. This phenomenon is one of the few striking discontinuities between great apes and lower primate species.

An interesting sidelight of the findings on self recognition in primates deals with the effects of social experience on the notion of self. Gallup suggests that social interaction with other conspecifics is a necessary precondition for self awareness in chimpanzees (see Cooley, 1912; and Mead, 1934; for a similar statement concerning humans). Therefore, he postulated that isolate-reared chimpanzees would not exhibit self-directed behavior as did the feral animals tested previously. This expectation was confirmed (Gallup & McClure, 1971). Anecdotal evidence about chimpanzees reared by humans also suggests that social experience with humans rather than chimpanzees may lead to a distortion in self identity. When asked to sort pictures of humans and chimpanzees, Viki, the chimpanzee reared by the Gardners, did so, although she placed her picture with the humans (Hayes & Nissen, 1971).

In summary, the transition from other- to self-directed behavior follows a phylogenetic trend—the lower, more stimulus-bound species, such as birds and fish, exhibit only socially-appropriate and other-directed behavior to a mirror; the lower primates, i.e., monkeys, recognize the duality of mirrors for others but not for themselves and discriminate between mirror images and conspecifics; and the higher primates, i.e., chimpanzees and man, exhibit self-directed behavior and may be said to recognize themselves.

Ontogenetic Trends

The topic of mirror-image stimulation in infancy has been of interest since the time of Darwin, although only recently have more "scientific" studies of infants' responses to mirrors appeared and more "objective" measures of self recognition developed. Three different sources of information on mirror-image stimulation will be reviewed: diaries of infant development, infant intelligence tests, and experimental studies.

Early and Anecdotal Accounts of Self Recognition. The potency of the mirror for the young is undisputed. Mothers often report that their infants enjoy mirror play and that they sometimes use a mirror to soothe a fussy infant. Social scientists have also made this observation and have realized that the mirror may be used to measure self recognition. Almost a hundred years ago, Preyer (1893) and Darwin (1877) both observed that mirror-image stimulation elicited great interest and curiosity in their children. Darwin observed what he thought was self recognition in his 9-month-old son, as his son would turn toward a mirror when his name was called. Of course, today this observation would be attributed to learning, not self recognition. However, Darwin's recollections of his son's social and mental development were the first to include reactions to a mirror as a significant event *and* as a measure of self recognition. More recently, Zazzo (1948) observed his child's self recognitory behavior in pictures, mirrors, and home movies. He reported that self recognition did not occur until the third year of life. Recognition in all three situations occurred between 2½ and 3 years of age.

Infant Intelligence Tests. The infant intelligence test developers were also interested in early mirror behavior, and all of them included mirror items in their scales. Table 1-1 presents the mirror items and age ranges for these items for five of the major infant intelligence tests (Bayley, 1969; Buhler, 1930; Catell, 1940; Gesell, 1928; Gesell & Thompson, 1934; Griffiths, 1954). The large range of items presented in Table 1-1 are representative of the diverse reactions mirrors typically elicit. The test items may be divided into five different categories: (1) regards own image, (2) social responses, (3) searching behavior, (4) other-directed behavior, and (5) verbal self reference. The first two categories are included in all of the tests, while the last three are not, suggesting that the importance attributed to age-related behavior changes in mirror-image stimulation and in self-directed referent varies among tests. Only Buhler (1930) and Gesell (1928) included mirror-related behavior that occurred after the first year of life and that may be indicative of self recognition. Unlike the other tests, Buhler's is seen to follow a developmental sequence. By 8 months of age, infants regard their image with interest and smile at their reflection; by 12 to 14 months, infants are likely to touch and feel the mirror image as well as to grasp at the mirror reflection when an object is placed behind them; by 15 to 17 months of age, infants respond with "astonishment" and turn around when seeing another person in the mirror (presumably, the properties of the reflective surface are being understood for the first time); by 18 to 20 months of age, searching behind the mirror is seen, although one might expect this behavior to occur before appropriate turning toward a person.

Another interesting and somewhat surprising aspect of the infant intelligence tests is the lack of consensus as to when various mirror items occur. Remember that Table 1-1 presents the normative ages at which the items are expected to be passed. For example, regarding one's own image in the mirror "typically" occurs at either 5 or 8 months, smiling at the image at either 5, 7, 8, or 10 months, and searching behind the mirror at 10 or 18 months of age.

A few items in Table 1-1 are indicative of visual self recognition, specifically, Gesell's items in the second and third years of life. Stutsman (1931) also included a self recognitory measure in the Merrill-Palmer Scale. In the standardization of this scale, two-thirds of the 2-year-olds recognized or labeled themselves when seeing themselves in mirrors.

In summary, the infant intelligence tests shed little light on visual

TABLE 1-1

Mirror Test Items in Five Infant Tests

Test items							Age in months at which item occurs										
	4	5	6	7	8	9	10	11	12	13–14	15–17	18–20	21–23	24–26	27–29	30–32	36
Approaches image	Bayley																
Regards own image		Gesell			Buhler Griffiths												
Smiles at image		Gesell		Cattell	Buhler		Griffiths										
Vocalizes to image		Bayley	Gesell Bayley	Cattell Gesell													
Pats, feels image			Bayley						Buhler								
Leans forward							Gesell										
Plays with image			Bayley				Griffiths										
Searches							Griffiths	Gesell	Buhler			Buhler					
Reaches toward mirror for object																	
Reaches toward adult, not reflection											Buhler						
Refers to self by name														Gesell		Gesell	
Refers to self by pronoun																Gesell	
Refers to self by sex																	Gesell

self recognition since: first, there are few items measuring behaviors indicative of self recognition; second, there are large discrepancies in the type and number of mirror items included in each scale; and third, there is no indication that the designers, except Gesell and Stutsman, had even considered the issue of self recognition.

Experimental Studies. Until the last few years, little experimental evidence on infants' responses to mirrors has been collected. Two of the earliest investigators (Amsterdam, 1968; Dixon, 1957) systematically studied the development of self recognition in terms of mirror-image stimulation. Both Dixon and Amsterdam observed different-aged infants in front of a mirror and postulated age-related stages of mirror behavior. Dixon outlined four stages: (1) "Mother," (2) "Playmate," (3) "Who do dat when I do dat?" and (4) "Coy." In the "Mother" stage (4 or 5 months of age), the infant enjoys observing mother's movement in the mirror; in the "Playmate" stage (5 to 6 months of age), the infant responds playfully to his own image (as if it were a peer); in the "Who do dat when I do dat?" stage (6 to 12 months), the infant is interested in observing the actions performed by himself; and in the "Coy" stage (12 to 18 months), the infant acts coy, shy, or fearful in front of the mirror. Dixon believes the "Coy" stage to be indicative of self recognition. Amsterdam's stages are similar; the first involves social responding to the mirror (smiling at, vocalizing to, approaching, and patting the mirror); the second indicates the beginning of self awareness (acting self conscious, fearful, and coy); and the third involves self recognition (self-directed rather than other-directed behavior as inferred through a mark-on-the-face technique similar to that of Gallup's). The social stage is prevalent from 6 to 12 months of age, the transitional stage from 12 to 18 months of age, and the self recognition stage from 20 to 24 months of age. Amsterdam also reports little overlap between stages.

More recently, Schulman and Kaplowitz (1977) observed infants' responses to distorted and flat mirrors, finding sociable behavior in the second half of the first year, puzzled and avoidance behavior in the first half of the second year, and self conscious behavior in the second half of the second year. Dickie and Strader (1974) found interest in the mirror to be most pronounced at one year of age, body exploration at 16 months.

Although these studies are informative, they must be viewed with some caution. First, the sample sizes are small and the age ranges are restricted [Amsterdam's (1968) study being the notable exception, as she observed infants at each month from 3 to 24 months of age]. Second, procedural difficulties in several studies allowed the infants to see their mothers and the observer in the mirror. Thus, the infants may have been responding to their mothers rather than to their reflections. Third, criteria for the existence of stages in the first two mirror studies could be more rigorously defined and observations could be better standardized. For example, Dixon did not systematically control time spent in front of the mirror and Amsterdam placed her infants in a playpen for a 7½ min observation. Fourth, the operational definitions of visual self recognition need to be specified. Most of the behavioral indices—observing one's movements in the mirror (Dixon, 1957), turning to the mirror as one's name is called (Darwin, 1877), and recognizing one's mother in the mirror (Preyer, 1893)—are interesting but certainly not rigorous or convincing. Fifth, using a mark on the face may have methodological problems. The act of wiping the face or nose may increase nose-touching, olfactory cues from the rouge may affect mark-touching, and rouge may be seen by the infant if placed on certain parts of the nose (Gallup, 1977).

Pictorial and Videotape Representations

The self may be represented visually in many different ways, the most obvious being mirrors (contingent, immediate representations), pictures (static, nonimmediate representations), and movies (moving, noncontingent, and nonimmediate representations). The advent of videotape systems allows a fourth type of representation. Although the mirror representation has generated the most interest, almost 30 years ago Zazzo (1948) observed his son's reaction to mirror self reflections, pictures, and movies of himself. Although Zazzo's self recognition criteria were verbal, making them inappropriate for the early years, he was the first to consider self recognition in various representational forms.

Movies and videotapes have recently been suggested as a means of isolating the effect of contingency on mirror-image stimulation. Three studies need to be mentioned in this regard: Amsterdam and Greenberg (1977), Papoušek and Papoušek (1974), and Rheingold (1971). In the Rheingold study, 5-month-old infants were shown a number of different stimuli, including a mirror, a moving picture of another infant, and static representations of social and nonsocial stimuli. Infants were most likely to smile at the mirror condition, suggesting that the infants were responding to the contingency provided by the mirror rather than the movement. In the Papoušek and Papoušek study, two factors which are inherent in mirror representations were systematically varied, using a videotape system. These two factors were eye-to-eye contact and contingency. They report that 5-month-old infants differentiated between the two factors and responded more to eye-to-eye contact than to contingency. In the Amsterdam and Greenberg study (1977), a small number of 10-, 15-, and 20-month-old infants received simultaneous self images, past self images, and a control child as seen on a TV monitor. No differences between conditions were found.

Pictorial self recognition has received little interest, although infants' responses to pictures of social and nonsocial stimuli, of normal and distorted faces, of two- and three-dimensional forms, and of different facial expressions has (e.g., Bond, 1972; Brooks-Gunn & Lewis, 1979a; Lewis & Brooks, 1974).

Self Recognition as a Measure of Self

Before leaving our empirical review of early self development, we must mention that self recognition is only part of the self construct, one that is easy to define. Although there is usually a high degree of correspondence between the general concept of self and self recognition, we recognize that these two constructs are not synonymous. However, the demonstration of self recognition may give us insights on the general concept of self. It is to be noted that visual self recognition is only one aspect of self recognition, one which in fact may be the last to develop. For example, proprioceptive recognition of self may occur much earlier. This being so, visual self recognition may not be demonstrable in infants who do, in fact, already have some self recognition and concept of self.

Our concern for clear measures of self recognition, which invariably reflect categorical as well as existential knowledge of the self, provides an age frame for our studies which include infants from 9 to 36 months of age. Given that children under 8 to 9 months of age may not have the needed motoric ability to demonstrate recognition, and that children from 24 to 36 months are able to demonstrate personal pronoun usage, this age range seems appropriate. That is not to say that we do not believe in the continual and early development of self, nor that self development stops abruptly at the onset of personal pronoun usage. In

Chapter 8, where our findings are summarized and integrated, our theoretical discussion of the acquisition of self points to its continuous development from the opening months through the life cycle.

SELF KNOWLEDGE AND SELF AWARENESS

In any discussion of self knowledge the issue of self awareness becomes important to consider. When subjects are preverbal, it is impossible to test for awareness, since the child cannot be easily questioned. This means we need to make clear that we are referring to knowledge of the self, not the epistemological issue of knowledge of the knowledge of self. It is our belief that the former can exist prior to the latter. For example, by 9 months infants know—that is, will search for—a hidden object, but cannot tell us if they have knowledge of the knowledge of object permanence. We accept their behavior as demonstrating knowledge but do not ask about knowledge of knowledge. In the same way, we may speak of a cat's knowledge of spatial properties when it goes around an object rather than trying to go through it. We cannot be sure what form this knowledge takes; in fact, it may be reflexive behavior, but we do infer that the cat has knowledge of objects.

When dealing with self awareness, we are making the same point, namely, that self awareness is equivalent to knowledge of the knowledge of self. Reference to adult behavior in this regard may be informative. We would agree that adults have knowledge of themselves. We use as evidence their use of self referents, their ability to describe themselves as different from or the same as others, their ability to recognize themselves, and their use of self-directed behavior. We also know from introspection and observation that, although we adults have self knowledge, we do not always have self awareness. Many of our thoughts and actions do not involve any consideration of ourselves, and much of our behavior is often quickly done. Only during those times of inactivity, when action does not have to be quick, or when we have made an error and need to rethink an action, does self awareness become more prevalent. We would not use the typically low level of self awareness to disregard the importance of self action, but only to point out that the role of self knowledge is to guide us at an executive level, leaving for other processes the mechanics of action. The self sets goals, has intents, and does evaluations, while the scripts are executed through more simple processes of associations, learning, and overlearned response patterns (see Abelson, 1976, and Schank & Abelson, 1977). These more simple processes guide behavior without evoking self awareness or knowledge as long as the action is taking place. Given the occurrence of errors or completion of the script, awareness becomes immediately present.

Other models also consider the role of self awareness. Freud (1900/1954) proposes an unconscious self which mediates the organism's behavior at all times. In this way, self knowledge and self awareness are two aspects of the same process which are always operating on the organism. Whether this is indeed the case is unclear; however, the function of slips of the tongue, accidents, and dreams would suggest that another level—we can call it unconsciousness—is a useful concept to explain some individual behavior (Freud, 1900/1954).

Whether infants have self awareness or an unconscious is totally unexplored, nor will we consider this issue again. For the sake of our exposition we wish only to draw the distinction between self knowledge and self awareness. It is our belief that the set of infant behaviors which we will examine, having to do with self recognition and social behavior, lead to the conclusion that self knowledge develops early and is a central focus to the study of social cognition.

PLAN OF THIS VOLUME

The contents of this volume are arranged so that we shall consider the history of self recognition in research, examine the findings from our own studies, integrate these with other findings, describe the course of self recognition in the first few years, look at the role of self in social cognition, and present a theory of social cognition incorporating the self. Chapters 2, 3, and 4 deal with our empirical studies which have concerned themselves with different modes of representations of the self. In Chapter 2, we report on three studies using mirror images. Mirror images have the distinction of being both contingent, "they do what I do," which taps into our notion of existential self, and they also possess physical features, "they look as I look," which taps into our notion of categorical self. Picture representations, described in Chapter 4, involve only the categorical self since "they look as I look" but do not act contingently. Recognition of self pictorially is more difficult, as we shall see, and infants' self recognition is delayed under these conditions. The third mode, videotape representations described in Chapter 3, combines both pictorial and mirror representations providing categorized and contingency information and makes possible the separation of these features. It must be pointed out that we have been unable to work out a representation in which the representation "does what I do" but does not "look like I look," which would be the best test of the existence of the existential self. Imitation, however, may satisfy our requirements as it possesses reciprocity, contingency, and consistency. Our own work on imitation (Lewis, 1979; Waite & Lewis, 1978, 1979) and that of Piaget (1962) suggest that infants, as young as two weeks, may be capable of imitating adult models.

Three further sets of self recognition data were collected. Chapter 5 looks specifically at language development and self recognition. In Chapter 6, we explore the relationship between self recognition and individual differences from a cognitive point of view and from a social personality point of view. Chapter 7 deals with the relationship between self recognition and emotional experience. James (1890/1950), in discussing emotional behavior, draws the distinction between emotional expression (some somatic change) and emotional experience (the interpretation of that change). In our analysis, we attempt to show how the concept of self is important in the latter issue and the relationship of the level of self recognition and one emotional experience—fear.

The results of the work of others and our own are integrated in Chapter 8. Using these data, a theory of the development of self is presented. Chapter 9 extends this theory to include social cognition and to explicate how the role of the self is essential to any theory of general cognitive development. The final chapter incorporates the discussion of social cognition and the development of self into a still broader perspective. In this chapter, the role and uses of a theory of self are expanded. In its general form, it is an argument that the organism must be brought back into the study of psychology, as well as a demonstration of how theorists such as Kelly (1955) have done so. Finally, it offers more specific ways in which a theory of self fits into the more general problems of empathy, peer relations and friendship, and sex role development.

It is our aim, then, to move from setting the stage in Chapter 1, to the empirical data in Chapters 2 through 7, to the theoretical and practical issues in Chapters 8, 9, and 10. We hope that the study of the origins of the self will convince you that the emerging self exists; if not, we can only hope that it provides you with the incentive to study this issue yourself.

CHAPTER 2

Mirror Representations of Self

Infants' reactions to mirrors were observed by modifying an ingenious technique that was independently developed by Gallup (1968) and by Amsterdam (1968). Sixteen infants in each of six age groups were observed in the following mirror situations. Infants were first placed in front of a large mirror and observed. Then, a dot of rouge was placed on the infants' noses by their mothers, and they were again observed in front of the mirror. Following this procedure, the experimenter applied a dot of rouge to the mothers' noses, and the infants' reactions to their mothers' marked faces were noted. After they had seen their mothers, the infants were placed in front of the mirror for a third time. This design was used in order to: (1) provide a standardized observation procedure; (2) provide a descriptive account of infants' responses to mirrors at different ages; (3) study the effect of rouge application on self-directed behavior, using an unmarked condition as a baseline; (4) compare infants' ability to recognize a mark on their mothers' noses as well as their own, in order to test the salience of this specific facial distortion; and (5) see whether maternal mark recognition facilitates subsequent self-directed behavior, since noticing the rouge on the mother may "prime" the child for noticing it.

MIRROR STUDY I

EXPERIMENTAL PROCEDURES

SUBJECTS

Ninety-six Caucasian infants were observed in the mirror situation. Sixteen infants (8 males and 8 females) in each of six age groups (9, 12, 15, 18, 21, and 24 months of age) were seen. The mean ages for the six groups were 9.17, 12.27, 15.27, 18.33, 21.23, and 24.10, respectively. All infants were full-term and had no congenital defects. Six other infants were dropped from the sample because of extreme fussiness. All these untestable infants were over 18 months of age, and five were female.

The demographic data indicate that the parents of the sample were in their late 20s or early 30s, were well educated, and had one or two children. Fourteen percent of the mothers had attended graduate school, 40% had an undergraduate degree, 24% had attended but not graduated from college, and 21% had no college experience. Socio-economic status of the family (as determined by father's occupation and education, Hollingshead, 1957) was also high: 34% of the families were in Class I, 43% in Class II, 16% in Class III, and 7% in Class IV. Approximately half of the infants were firstborn and half later-born.

STIMULUS CONDITIONS

The mirror was a 46 cm × 89 cm one-way mirror mounted in a large 1.22 m × 2.44 m piece of plywood. The entire structure fit between two walls and formed a triangle with the walls and corner of the room. A camera was placed inside this triangle and was covered with a black cloth to reduce the amount of light on the back of the one-way mirror. Thus, the front, but not the back, of the one-way mirror reflected light, and the camera could not be seen. There were lights on either side of the one-way mirror since the natural light contrast between the two sides of the mirror was not enough for reasonable video resolution. The mirror was situated in a pleasantly decorated room that contained two chairs, a table, and wall posters.

The four mirror conditions were as follows:

1. *No Rouge Condition:* Infants first observe themselves in front of the mirror without their faces being marked. The infants must look in the mirror at least three times. Trial length was approximately 90 sec (±10).

2. *Rouge 1 Condition:* Infants' faces are marked with rouge. They must look at themselves in the mirror at least three times. Trial length was approximately 90 sec (±10).

3. *Mother Rouge Condition:* Infants are observed with their mothers, who have rouge on their noses. Infants must look at their mothers' faces. Trial length was variable, as the trial was terminated after infants had looked at their mothers' faces.

4. *Rouge 2 Condition:* Infants are placed in front of the mirror a third time. They must look in the mirror at least once. Trial length was approximately 30 sec (±10).

Procedure

Infants were brought to the laboratory by their mothers; and the following instructions were given:

We will observe your child's behavior in front of a mirror. I will take you and your child to another room where a large mirror has been placed on the floor. There is a camera behind the mirror which will record your child's mirror play. After I have left the room, please encourage your child to go to the mirror. You may place him in front of the mirror, tell him to go to the mirror, sit beside the mirror, or place the small chair in front of the mirror. *Do not sit in front of the mirror yourself.*

After I have observed your infant in front of the mirror from the observation window, I will reenter the mirror room. I will give you a cloth which has rouge on it. Please wipe your child's nose with the rouge so that his nose is noticeably red. Tell the child that you are wiping his/her face because it is dirty. *Do not mention* the child's *nose* or the *rouge.* I will then leave the room and go to the observation window. I will knock on the window three or four times. Each time, try to get your child to look at himself in the mirror. Again, do not mention the child's nose or the rouge and do not sit where your image would reflect in the mirror.

After your infant has observed himself, I will come back into the room and apply rouge to *your* nose. Then I will leave and knock two different times on the observation window. At the first knock, get your child to look at you by sitting next to him or by picking him up. Talk to him but *do not mention your nose, his nose, or the rouge.* On the second knock, please have your child go to the mirror alone again. Are there any questions?

The mirror procedure was reviewed and the infant and mother were taken into the mirror room. The experimenter left the room, only reentering prior to the rouge applications. The mother applied the rouge to the infant, the experimenter to the mother. The ruse of wiping the infant's face was effective, as only one of the 96 infants touched his nose immediately after the rouge was applied and before looking in the mirror. The rouge was applied to the mother's face when the child was not looking; no infant saw the application.

Although the instructions for the mirror procedure were lengthy, the mothers, in general, were able to follow them. Confusion was evident only in the last condition, as approximately 5% of the mothers did not complete it. Mothers did not mention the rouge or the nose in the first three conditions, although they were less careful in the last condition. After the infants touched or pointed to their mothers' noses, many of the mothers could not refrain from talking about the rouge. However, as will be seen, maternal vocalizations about the rouge did not seem to influence the child's behavior.

MEASURES

The mirror conditions were videotaped, and coding was done from the tapes by observing the absence or presence of a number of behaviors which are presented in Table 2-1. These behaviors may be classified as follows: (1) facial expressions, (2) vocalizations, (3) attention, (4) mirror-directed behaviors, (5) self-directed behaviors, and (6) imitative behaviors. The listing in Table 2-1 gives an idea of the large range of behaviors exhibited toward the mirror by the infants.

Facial expressions were coded by attending to the configuration of the mouth and forehead–eye area. A smile was coded when the corners of the mouth turned upward and the eyes widened and brightened; a

TABLE 2-1
Behaviors Observed in the Mirror Conditions

Facial expression	Self-directed behaviors
Smile	Body-directed
Concentrate	(touches face, touches body, hands in mouth)
Frown	Nose-directed
	(touches nose, wipes nose repeatedly)
Vocalization	Points to self
Laugh, squeal	Verbally refers to nose, rouge, or self
Coo, babble, talk	
Whimper, whine, fret	Attention
Cry, scream	Number of brief looks
	Number of moderate looks
Mirror-directed behaviors	Number of sustained looks
Points to mirror	Number of total looks
Touches, pats mirror	
Touches own image in mirror	
Kisses, mouths mirror	
Hits, kicks mirror	
Imitation	
Rhythmic body movements	
(bounces, claps, waves, skips)	
Facial movements	
(makes faces, sticks tongue out)	
Acts silly or coy	

frown when the corners of the mouth turned downward, the eyes narrowed, and the forehead tensed; a concentrate face when the lips were shaped like an ellipse or a square, the eyes were wide, and eyebrows raised. Three types of *vocalizations* were coded—laugh/squeal, talk/babble, and fret/cry. The last behavior occurred only when an infant was attempting to leave the room and/or actively resisting his mother's attempts to interest him in the test situation. *Mirror-directed behaviors* were behaviors that were directed to the mirror image instead of the self—pointing, kissing, touching, or hitting or kicking the mirror. *Imitative behaviors* were behaviors that were performed in front of the mirror and subsequently watched. Three types were coded—rhythmic body movements (bounce, clap, wave, skip), facial movements (makes faces, sticks tongue out), and body and facial movements (clowns, preens, acts silly, coy). *Self-directed behaviors* were behaviors that were directed toward one's own body instead of the mirror image. These included specific responses to the mark (touching the nose, wiping the nose repeatedly, and saying "nose" or "red") and general body-directed behavior (touching the face and touching the body). Pointing to oneself was also considered self-directed behavior. The incidence of some of the specific behaviors in the imitative and self-directed categories was low, and these behaviors were combined as indicated above. Bouncing, making faces, and acting silly account for the majority of responses in their respective imitative categories, as did touching the nose (or mark) in the mark-directed category.

Although all infants were required to look at the mirror three times in the No Rouge and Rouge 1 Conditions, they often looked many more times. Therefore, number of looks was coded. In addition, length of look was coded; any look of less than a few seconds' duration was coded as *brief*, a look of 5 to 15 sec as *moderate*, a look of over 15 sec as *sustained*.

The infant's response to the Mother Rouge Condition was coded for facial expression, vocalization, self-directed, and mother-directed behaviors. The last category included touching the mother's nose and touching the mother's face.

Interobserver Reliability

The mirror conditions were videotaped, and behavioral coding was done from these videotapes. Presence or absence of each behavior for each condition was coded. Two observers coded the tapes, and eleven subjects were randomly selected for reliability purposes after half of the coding had been done. Interobserver reliabilities for all but the looking data were calculated by the following formula: number of agreements/ number of agreements and disagreements. The reliabilities for the look ing data were calculated by using the number of looks as the denomina- tor and the number of agreements as the numerator (if the two observers recorded four and five looks for a condition, the percentage of agree- ments would be 80%). The interobserver reliabilities for the behaviors were all over 85%, with the exception of concentrate face (70%). Coding the length of each look was more difficult, and these reliabilities were somewhat lower (number of brief looks, 65%; number of moderate looks, 70%; and number of sustained looks, 85%).

DATA ANALYSIS

Since the presence or absence of each behavior was coded, the re- sults are presented as percentage of subjects exhibiting each behavior. Chi-square statistics (chi-square for between-subject comparisons; Mc- Nemar test for the significance of changes for within-subject compari- sons) were used for data analyses.

A descriptive picture of the infants' responses to the mirror in the unmarked condition was first examined in order to get a "feel" for the typical responses. To date, no data base gives a complete picture of infants' responses to mirrors nor of the changes over age. Age dif- ferences were tested using the chi-square statistic. Due to the expected cell frequency requirement of the chi-square, the six age groups some- times had to be collapsed; when this was necessary the 9- and the 12-, the 15- and the 18-, and the 21- and the 24-month-olds were combined to form three age groups.

Three comparisons among the stimulus conditions were made: (1) the effect of rouge application on self-directed behavior, (2) the rela- tionship of maternal and self mark recognition, and (3) the effect of maternal mark recognition on subsequent self-directed behavior. First, the central issue of the study was whether or not the infants noticed the rouge on their noses. In order to observe mark recognition, a baseline of behavior in front of the mirror prior to the rouge application was ob- tained, and responses to the unmarked and marked conditions were compared. Second, to test the salience of a mark on the face for eliciting self recognition, rouge was applied to the mother's nose as well as to the child's. Whether some infants did not touch their noses because they did not recognize themselves in the mirror or because the rouge was not sufficient to elicit recognition was investigated by observing the infants' reactions both to themselves and to their mothers. In addition, the relationship between maternal and self recognition was examined to see whether infants who touched themselves in Rouge 1 were more likely to touch their mothers' noses in Mother Rouge than those who did not, and vice versa. Third, noticing the rouge on the mother might facilitate subsequent mark recognition. Infants who did not notice the mark in the Rouge 1 Condition but did notice it on their mothers might be more likely to notice the mark on themselves in the Rouge 2 Condition.

The three comparisons were made using chi-square statistics to test the effects of stimulus condition (McNemar test), age of subject (independent chi-square test), and age and condition interaction (independent chi-square test, using three age groups and two condition groups, i.e., change from one condition to the next and no change). Again, recombination was sometimes necessary due to expected cell frequency requirements.

RESULTS

DESCRIPTION OF RESPONSES TO A MIRROR

No Rouge Condition

Table 2-2 presents the percentage of subjects exhibiting each of the behaviors for each age group and for the total sample in the No Rouge Condition. All but one of the infants looked in the mirror at least three times during this condition, and only one other infant was fussy, suggesting that infants do not resist looking in the mirror.

Attention. The infants' looking behavior was characterized by many brief glances, with occasional looks of longer duration. Total number of looks did not vary with age, although the number of moderate and sustained looks decreased with age [$F(5,89) = 2.33$, $p < .05$, and $F(5,89) = 7.59$, $p < .001$, respectively]. These differences were most pronounced between infants over and under one year of age.

Table 2-2
Percentage of Subjects Responding in the No Rouge Condition by Behavior and by Age

Behavior	Age in months						
	9	12	15	18	21	24	Total
Number Ss	16	16	16	16	16	15	95
Facial expression							
Smile	81	94	88	56	63	60	75
Frown	0	0	6	6	6	0	3
Concentrate	31	25	19	25	25	27	25
Vocalization							
Laugh, squeal	20	0	22	0	20	20	13
Coo, babble, talk	80	50	78	62	80	80	71
Fret, cry	0	0	11	0	20	0	4
No vocalization	0	50	11	38	0	10	21
Mirror-directed behavior							
Point	19	25	0	25	56	13	23
Touch	88	100	69	56	81	67	77
Touch image	50	69	25	25	38	33	40
Kiss	38	31	6	6	0	7	15
Hit	50	25	31	25	38	27	33
Imitation							
Rhythmic	38	19	19	6	0	13	16
Facial	13	13	13	25	25	13	17
Coy, silly	0	0	31	13	13	27	14
Self-directed behavior							
Body	25	0	19	6	44	33	21
Nose	0	0	0	0	7	7	2
Fussy	0	0	0	0	6	0	1
Number of looks							
brief	2.56	2.75	3.63	4.38	3.06	3.33	3.28
moderate	1.75	1.13	1.13	0.63	0.88	0.80	1.05
sustained	0.69	0.13	0.06	0	0.06	0	0.16
Total looks	5.00	4.00	4.81	5.00	4.00	4.13	4.49

Affect.　　Three-quarters of the infants smiled at their reflections. In contrast, few infants (only 3%) frowned. Although more of the younger infants smiled than the older ones (80% of the 9- to 15-month-olds and under 63% of the 18- to 24-month-olds), this trend was not significant.

The vocalization data present a similar pattern, with positive rather than negative vocalizations being elicited by the mirror. Seventy percent of the infants cooed or talked when seeing themselves in the mirror, 13% laughed or squealed, and only 4% cried.[1]

Mirror-Directed Behaviors. The infants also exhibited a variety of behaviors toward the mirror itself. Not surprisingly, the most frequent response for the total sample was touching or patting the mirror (approximately 75% did so). In addition, approximately one-half of the infants who touched the mirror also touched their own image in the mirror. One-third of the sample hit the mirror, and 15% kissed or mouthed the mirror. There were age trends for some of the mirror-directed behaviors. Touching the mirror [$\chi^2(2) = 8.96$, $p < .05$], touching the image in the mirror [$\chi^2(2) = 8.27$, $p < .05$], and kissing the mirror [$\chi^2(2) = 14.92$, $p < .001$] all decreased with age; the infants under one year of age were most likely to exhibit these behaviors. There were no significant age differences for hitting or pointing at the mirror.

Imitation. Sixteen percent of the infants bounced, clapped, waved, or skipped; 14% clowned or acted coy; and 17% made faces in the mirror. Although there were no overall age differences, infants under and over a year of age responded somewhat differently. Bouncing was characteristic of the infants under a year of age ($\chi^2 = 5.22$, $p < .05$), while acting silly or coy was characteristic of infants over a year of age ($\chi^2 = 6.00$, $p < .02$).

Self-Directed Behaviors. Only 2% of the infants touched their noses in the No Rouge Condition whereas one-fifth of the sample touched their body or their face. Body-directed behavior increased with age [$\chi^2(2) = 8.62$, $p < .02$], with the 21- and 24-month-olds being most likely to touch themselves.

Summary. In general, then, the infants were quite interested in the mirror, as evidenced by the large number of infants who smiled, vocalized, and touched the mirror and the relatively few who frowned, cried, and fussed. Approximately one-fifth of the infants also touched themselves, made faces, or bounced in front of the mirror. However, only 2% of the infants touched their noses spontaneously.

The different-aged infants reacted somewhat differently to the mirror, with the major differences occurring at one year of age. The infants under one year were most likely to exhibit sustained attention, smile at, kiss, touch the mirror and/or their image, and bounce in front of the

---

[1]Since only one-half of the videotapes could be accurately coded for vocalization (due to mechanical difficulties), the age trends in vocalization were not analyzed.

mirror than were the older infants. In addition, they never exhibited silly or coy behaviors as did the older infants. Thus, the 9- and 12-month-olds were more likely to interact with the mirror and seemed to find the mirror more interesting and enjoyable than did the older infants.

Although the infants under one year were more likely to look at, smile at, and interact with the mirror, the older infants were more likely to act silly or coy and touch themselves. The differences between the younger and older infants suggest that other-directed behavior was more characteristic of the infants in the first year, self-directed behavior of the infants in the second year.

Rouge 1 Condition

After the mother applied rouge to her infant's face, the infant's attention was directed back to the mirror. As in the preceding condition, all but one infant completed the procedure by looking in the mirror at least three times. However, 12 infants became fussy during this condition. Only two behaviors (body-directed and mark-directed behaviors) will be mentioned here, as the responses to this marked condition are discussed in comparison to the unmarked condition in a later section. Mark-directed behavior was exhibited by one-third of the sample and was greatly influenced by age. Of the 30 infants who touched their marked noses, none were 9- or 12-, three were 15-, four were 18-, 11 were 21-, and 12 were 24-month-olds $[\chi^2(5) = 40.04, p < .001]$. More general body-directed behavior was observed in 44% of the sample, with no age differences occurring.

Mother Rouge Condition

After the Rouge 1 Condition, the mother's nose was marked with rouge, and the infant's reaction to the mother's marked face was observed. Recognition of the rouge on the mother was widespread. Fully two-thirds of the infants noticed the rouge on their mothers' noses, as inferred by their touching, wiping, or mentioning their mothers' noses (there were two infants who did not touch their mothers' noses but said "mommy's nose" and "fix it, it hurts"). Mark-directed behavior also increased with age: 31% of the 9-, 50% of the 12-, 64% of the 15-, 92% of the 18-, 82% of the 21-, and 69% of the 24-month-olds exhibited maternal mark recognition $[\chi^2(5) = 13.88, p < .05]$. Touching the mother's face, but not specifically her nose, was exhibited infrequently and was not related to age (19% of the sample).

Touching one's own nose also occurred in the Mother Rouge Condition, with 11 infants (all of whom had also noticed the rouge on their mothers' noses) doing so. These infants were equally distributed among the three oldest age groups. Although age differences could not be tested due to low expected cell frequencies, the difference between the three groups who did exhibit mark-directed behavior and the three who did not was highly significant ($\chi^2 = 11.34$, $p < .001$). Remember that the infants could not see their own faces during the Mother Rouge Condition and, therefore, were touching themselves without the benefit of visual feedback. More general self-directed behavior occurred rarely.

Rouge 2 Condition

After the infants had seen their mothers' marked faces, they were placed in front of the mirror again. Each infant only had to look in the mirror once. Even with this brief requirement, 18% of the sample did not complete the condition and another 11% became fussy. This lack of interest in the mirror is reflected in the overall decrease in responding from the Rouge 1 to the Rouge 2 Condition. Only 9% of the sample touched their noses, 22% other parts of their bodies. As in the Rouge 1 Condition, the infants who touched their noses were over 12 months of age and were somewhat more likely to be in the two oldest age groups. Body-directed behavior was exhibited by infants in all six age groups and tended to increase with age.

Comparisons between the Stimulus Conditions

The Effect of Rouge Application on Self-Directed Behavior

The central issue of the study—whether or not different-aged infants would respond to a dot of rouge applied to the nose—was tested by observing infants' mirror behavior prior to and following mark application. The frequency of occurrence of various behaviors in the No Rouge and Rouge 1 Conditions were then compared. Table 2-3 presents the percentage differences between the two conditions by age and by behavior. These percentages reflect the magnitude and the direction of the change, with a positive percentage indicating more infants respond-

TABLE 2-3

Percentage Change Scores between the No Rouge and Rouge 1 Condition by Behavior and by Age[a]

Behavior	Age in months						Total
	9	12	15	18	21	24	
Number Ss	16	15	16	16	16	15	94
Facial expression							
Smile	13	−20	0	19	18	0	5
Frown	16	17	−16	−16	0	27	14
Concentrate	25	50	31	25	25	53	33
Mirror-directed behavior							
Points	−13	0	19	−16	0	27	16
Touch	0	−17	19	19	0	13	17
Touch image	16	−17	19	13	31	20	14
Kiss	16	−13	0	17	6	−17	0
Hit	13	20	17	0	13	−14	12
Imitation							
Rhythmic	16	−17	−16	0	13	0	11
Facial	16	−17	18	−12	19	0	15
Coy, silly	0	0	0	25	16	16	16
Self-directed behavior							
Body	19	33	25	25	16	34	24
Nose	0	0	19	25	63	66	29
Fussy	0	16	13	31	13	6	12
Number of looks							
brief	0.57	2.67	1.00	0.87	1.07	0.20	1.07
moderate	1.31	0.86	0.55	0.62	1.06	1.20	0.94
sustained	0.12	0.20	0.19	0.00	0.25	0.54	0.16
Total looks	2.00	3.73	1.75	1.50	2.38	1.94	2.17

[a] A positive percentage indicates more responding in the Rouge 1 Condition; a negative percentage indicates more in the No Rouge Condition.

ing in the Rouge 1 Condition, a negative percentage indicating more responding in the No Rouge Condition.

Nose-Directed Behavior.   The nose-directed responses, the most obvious measure of self recognition, were directly affected by the rouge application. Figure 2-1 presents the percentage of difference scores for each age group between the No Rouge and Rouge 1 Conditions for nose-directed behavior. As can be seen in Table 2-3 and Figure 2-1, nose-directed behavior increased dramatically from the No Rouge to the Rouge 1 Condition, occurring only twice in the former but 30 times in the latter. The main effect of stimulus condition was highly significant ($\chi^2 = 25.04$, $p < .001$). The age of subject × stimulus condition interaction was also highly significant [$\chi^2(2) = 32.63$, $p < .001$], as the increase in nose-touching from the unmarked to the marked condition only occurred in infants over one year of age. In addition, this increase was

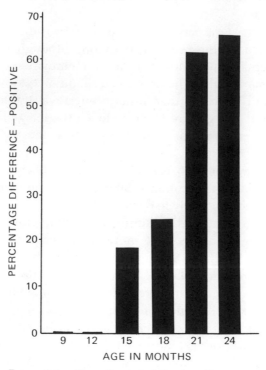

Figure 2-1.   Nose-directed behavior: Percentage difference between the No Rouge and Rouge 1 Conditions by age.

linear, that is, each group always had a higher number of nose touchers than did the preceding age groups.

Attention. The number of looks increased dramatically after the rouge application. Age and condition differences were analyzed using a 6 (age) × 2 (condition) analysis of variance. As can be seen when looking at the change scores in Table 2-3, one and one-half as many looks occurred in the Rouge 1 as in the No Rouge Condition $[F(1,77) = 39.25, p < .001]$. The condition differences were significant for all three types of looks [brief: $F(1,77) = 7.18, p < .01$; moderate: $F(1,77) = 31.64, p < .001$; and sustained: $F(1,77) = 5.16, p < .03$].

Concentrate expressions, another measure of attention, also increased after the rouge application ($\chi^2 = 21.95, p < .001$). As can be seen in Table 2-3, there were no age differences with respect to this increase.

Affect. Smiling and pleasant vocalization remained at a high level over the two conditions and no significant stimulus effects were found. The negative behaviors, frowning and crying, were also very similar in the two conditions.

Mirror-Directed Behaviors. In general, mirror-directed behaviors were not affected by the rouge application, although there was one interesting exception: more infants touched their own image in the mirror during the marked than the unmarked condition ($\chi^2 = 4.36, p < .05$). As can be seen in Table 2-3, this stimulus effect was influenced by age, with older infants being more likely to touch the image in the marked than the unmarked condition than the younger ones $[\chi^2(2) = 7.87, p < .05]$.

Imitation. The imitation behaviors were not likely to change as a function of the rouge application. Making faces, bouncing, and acting silly or coy were equally likely to occur in the two conditions. There was one significant age of subject × stimulus condition effect, as the older, but not the younger, infants were more likely to act silly or coy in the marked condition $[\chi^2(2) = 6.84, p < .05]$. This was because none of the 9- to 12-month-olds acted silly or coy in either condition and thus had a zero change score whereas the older infants were more likely to act silly or coy in the marked than in the unmarked condition.

Body-Directed Behavior. General body-directed, as well as specific nose-directed, behavior also increased dramatically after the rouge application ($\chi^2 = 15.75, p < .001$). This increase was seen in all age groups (see Figure 2-2). It is interesting that body-directed behavior increased

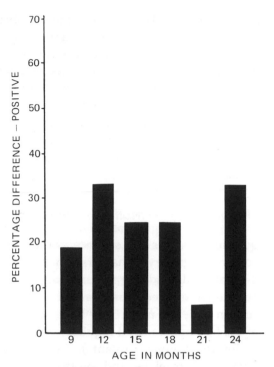

FIGURE 2-2.   Body-directed behavior: Percentage difference between No Rouge and Rouge 1 Conditions
by age.

after the rouge application in *all* age groups, even in those who did not
exhibit mark recognition.

Summary.   The infants responded very differently prior to and following the mark application. The most dramatic change was in nose-
directed behavior, as only two infants in the unmarked and 30 in the
marked condition touched their noses. The ability to direct behavior
toward the mark was also age-specific; mark-directed behavior was
never seen before 15 months of age and was not the modal response
until 21 months of age. Body-directed behavior also increased significantly from the unmarked to the marked condition, as infants not only
explored the mark but explored their bodies and faces as well. This
increase was seen in all age groups, even in the younger infants who did
not exhibit mark-directed behavior.

Self-directed behaviors were not the only responses to change after

stimulus conditions; only those infants who completed all three conditions are presented ($N = 70$). When the data were examined in terms of the absence or presence of mark recognition in Rouge 1, interesting relationships between Mother Rouge and Rouge 2 mark recognition appeared. Of the 22 infants who touched their noses following the rouge application, 77% also touched their mother. Of these infants, only a small number (three) also touched their noses in the Rouge 2 Condition. Thus, only three infants exhibited mark-directed behavior in all three conditions. Nose-touching in both the Rouge 1 and Mother Rouge Conditions did not result in nose-touching in the Rouge 2 Condition.

What of the infants who did not exhibit mark recognition in the Rouge 1 Condition? Would maternal mark recognition facilitate self recognition in these infants? No such facilitation effect was found. Of the 26 infants who did not touch their noses in the Rouge 1 Condition, but touched their mothers' noses in the Mother Rouge Condition, only one subsequently touched his nose in the Rouge 2 Condition.

MIRROR STUDY II

EXPERIMENTAL PROCEDURES

Although the findings from Mirror Study I were quite clear, especially with regard to the age-related nature of mark-directed behavior, they may have been affected by the particular design of the study. Two possibilities are of concern. First, the act of wiping the face and nose may have influenced the increase in mark- and face-directed behavior. Second, the effect of time spent in front of the mirror may also have influenced the increase in nose- and face-touching. That is, given a long enough mirror observation period, infants may spontaneously touch their faces and noses. To test these possibilities, the following study was designed, the purpose being to see whether our original results were affected by either the amount of time spent in front of the mirror or the act of wiping the child's face. In other words, could mark-recognition in Mirror Study I be accounted for by methodological considerations rather than self recognition?

In addition to the methodology question, we were interested in whether or not mark recognition could be facilitated by a training technique. In Mirror Study I, infants observed their mothers' marked faces and then observed themselves with marked faces in a mirror. Of the 26 infants who did not originally exhibit mark-directed behavior, but did notice the rouge on their mothers' noses, only one subsequently noticed the rouge on his own nose. (Table 2-4). Unfortunately, these findings may have been influenced by situational factors. First, the manipulation may not have been powerful enough to allow for generalization from other to self, as the mothers only asked their infants to look at them and did not point to or verbally refer to the mark. Second, a high degree of disinterest and fussiness was evident by the time the infants saw themselves in the second rouge condition; one-quarter of the infants did not look or were fussy. Therefore, disinterest rather than inability may have accounted for the low incidence of responding to the mirror and, specifically, the low incidence of mark recognition in the Rouge 2 Condtion. In order to overcome these difficulties, a new training technique was designed that reduced the length of the experimental session and referred more pointedly to the mothers' marked faces. Infants saw their mothers' marked faces immediately upon entering the testing room and then observed their own marked faces in the mirror; this was done to increase interest and reduce fussiness. The mothers were instructed to draw attention to the rouge in order to insure that the infants were aware of the rouge; this was not done in Mirror Study I. In short, the purpose of this part of Mirror Study II was to see whether facilitation was possible when the training technique was more forceful and the infants were more interested.

Infants were randomly divided among three different mirror conditions, each of which had two 2-min trials. In Mirror Condition A, infants observed themselves in a mirror during Trial 1, had their faces and noses wiped (but no rouge applied), and observed themselves again during Trial 2. In Mirror Condition B for Trial 1, infants were placed in the mirror room (where the mirror was covered) and for Trial 2, rouge was applied to their faces by their mothers, the mirror uncovered, and responses to the mirror noted. In Mirror Condition C, infants observed their mother's marked nose through face-to-face contact in Trial 1, had rouge applied to their faces, and observed themselves in the mirror in Trial 2. The first condition tests the effects of wiping the face and mirror exposure on subsequent self-directed behavior, the second tests the effect of no immediately previous mirror experience on self recognition, and the third tests the effect of seeing another person marked with rouge on self recognition.

SUBJECTS

Fifty-four infants divided evenly among three age groups (9 to 12, 15 to 18, and 21 to 24 months of age) were seen. The mean ages and age ranges of the three groups were 10.7 (8.87 to 12.30), 16.57 (14.53 to 18.10), and 22.70 (20.70 to 24.40) months. There were equal numbers of males and females in each age group. Forty percent of the infants were firstborn, 60% later-born. The sample was primarily middle to upper-middle class; one-half of the subjects were in Hollingshead's Social Class I, 29% in Social Class II, and 12% in Social Class III. The sample was very similar to that seen in Mirror Study I. One-third of each age group was randomly assigned to each of the three conditions, resulting in 18 infants in each age group, 18 infants in each condition, and 6 infants in each condition by age group.

PROCEDURE

The following instructions were given to the mothers for each of the three conditions:

CONDITION A

Mirrors offer a unique learning experience. The information provided by the mirror can be used to visually recognize oneself. We are interested in the relationship between mirror play and self recognition.

Your child will be observed in the following situation. You and your child will be taken to another room where a large mirror has been placed on the floor. There is a camera behind the mirror which will record your child's mirror play. The experimenter will go into the next room and observe through a one-way mirror. The experimenter will knock on the one-way mirror three different times. After each knock, please encourage your child to go to the mirror. You may place him in front of the mirror, tell him to go to the mirror, sit beside the mirror, or place the small chair in front of the mirror. *Do not sit in front of the mirror yourself.* There will be two X's on the floor; please try to stay behind these marks during the mirror procedure.

Then, the experimenter will reenter the mirror room and will give you a cloth (tissue). Please wipe your child's nose with the cloth. Tell the child that you are wiping his/her face because it is dirty. Do not mention the word *nose*. The experimenter will leave the room, go to the observation window, and will knock on the window three separate times. Each time, try to get your child to look at himself in the mirror. Do not mention the child's nose and do not sit where your image would reflect in the mirror. The experimenter will return to the room after the three knocks.

Please do not bring any toys or food into the room.

If at any time you feel that you wish to stop participating in our study, please say so and the researcher will simply stop the experiment.

CONDITION B

Mirrors offer a unique learning experience. The information provided by the mirror can be used to visually recognize oneself. We are interested in the relationship between mirror play and self recognition.

Your child will be observed in the following situation. You and your child will be taken to another room where a large mirror has been placed on the floor. When you first enter the room, the mirror will be covered. *Please do not uncover it.* The experimenter will go in the next room and observe through a one-way mirror. We will observe the child in the room for about 2 minutes.

Then, the experimenter will reenter the mirror room and will give you a cloth which has rouge on it. Please wipe your child's nose with the rouge so that his nose is noticeably red. Tell the child that you are wiping his/her face because it is dirty. *Do not mention* the child's *nose* or the *rouge.* The experimenter will uncover the mirror, leave the room, and go to the observation window. The experimenter will knock on the one-way mirror three different times. After each knock, try to get your child to look at himself in the mirror. You may sit beside the mirror, or place the small chair in front of the mirror. Do not mention the child's nose or the rouge and do not sit where your image would reflect in the mirror. There will be two X's on the floor; please try to stay behind these marks during the mirror procedure. The experimenter will return to the room after three knocks.

Please do not bring any toys or food into the room.

If at any time you feel that you wish to stop participating in our study, please say so and the researcher will simply stop the experiment.

CONDITION C

Mirrors offer a unique learning experience. The information provided by the mirror can be used to visually recognize oneself. We are interested in the relationship between mirror play and self recognition.

Your child will be observed in the following situation. You and your child will be taken to another room where a large mirror has been placed on the floor. There is a camera behind the mirror which will record your child's mirror behavior. When you first enter the room, the mirror will be covered. *Please do not uncover it.* The experimenter will give you a cloth which has rouge on it. Please wipe the child's nose with the rouge so that his/her nose is noticeably red. Tell the child that you are wiping his/her face because it is dirty. *Do not mention* the child's *nose* or the *rouge.* Then, a dot of rouge will be placed on your nose. The experimenter will leave the room and go to the observation window and will knock on the one-way mirror three different times. After each knock, try to get your child to look at your face. You may pick him up or kneel beside him. First, let your child look at your face without comment. Then, whether or not your child spontaneously noticed the rouge, tell him to look at the rouge on your nose and point to it. *Do not mention the rouge on your child's nose, however.*

The experimenter will reenter the room, uncover the mirror, and return to the observation window. The experimenter will knock on the one-way mirror three different times. After each knock, try to get your child to look at himself in the mirror. You may sit beside the mirror or place the small chair in front of the mirror. Do not mention the child's nose or the rouge and do not sit where your image would reflect in the mirror. There will be two

X's on the floor; please try to stay behind these marks during the mirror procedure. The experimenter will return to the room after three knocks.

Please do not bring any toys or food into the room.

If at any time you feel that you wish to stop participating in our study, please say so and the researchers will simply stop the experiment.

The infant was taken to a pleasantly decorated room in which a 46 cm × 89 cm one-way mirror was mounted in a large 1.22 m × 2.44 m sheet of plywood. The structure fit between two walls, and a camera was placed inside the triangle formed by the plywood wall and corner of the room. The camera side of the mirror was covered so that only the front of the one-way mirror reflected light. Lights were mounted on the front of the plywood structure to allow for reasonable video resolution.

The rouge was applied to the infants by their mothers, to the mothers by the experimenter. None of the infants touched their noses immediately after the rouge was applied and none of the infants saw the rouge applied to their mothers. In the mirror conditions, the infant was placed in front of the mirror by the mothers upon signal; if the infant left, the mother attempted to interest him or her in the mirror by sitting beside it (but not in front of it), by tapping on it, or by placing a small chair in front of it. Mothers were instructed to persuade their infants to interact with the mirror at least three times. In the training condition (C), the mothers first silently showed their marked faces to their infants and then referred to the mark (by pointing at, touching, and verbally referring to the rouge). This procedure was repeated three times.

MEASURES

The coded behaviors were identical to those in Mirror Study I and included five different categories of behavior: (1) facial expression, (2) vocalization, (3) mirror-directed, (4) self-directed, and (5) imitative behavior (see Table 2-1, Mirror Study I).

The infant's response to the training condition (C) was coded for face-directed and for mark-directed responses to the mother and to the self. Mark-directed responses included touching, wiping, pointing to, or verbally referring to the mark. Face-directed responses included all other gestures or verbalizations involving the face. Coding was done from videotapes, with the absence or presence of each behavior being noted.

Interobserver Reliability

The observer for Mirror Study I trained the observer for Mirror Study II. Ten subjects were randomly chosen from the first half of the subjects coded for reliability purposes. Reliabilities were calculated as the number of agreements/number of agreements and disagreements. The interobserver reliabilities ranged from .77 to .95, with the lowest reliabilities (those under .80) being reported for acts silly and coy and for frowns.

Results

Three issues were of interest: (1) the effect of repeated mirror exposure on self-directed behavior (Condition A), (2) the effect of previous mirror exposure on self-directed behavior (Condition B), and (3) the effect of training, in this case the observation of the mother's marked face, on self-directed behavior (Condition C).

Data analyses involved the McNemar test for the significance of changes for within-subject comparisons and chi-square tests for between-subject comparisons.

Condition A: Effect of Repeated Mirror Exposure on Self-Directed Behavior

Three comparisons were made. In Comparison I, infants' responses to Trial 1 in Condition A, Mirror Study II and the No Rouge Condition, Mirror Study I were compared; the two conditions, being identical, presented a picture of different-aged infants' responses to mirrors. In Comparison II, the number of subjects responding to Trials 1 and 2 in Study II were compared, the expectation being that, unlike Mirror Study I, there would be no significant differences since no rouge was actually applied in Study II. In Comparison III, the change scores from Trial 1 to Trial 2, Condition A, Mirror Study II and from the No Rouge to the Rouge 1 Condition, Mirror Study 1 were compared; it was expected that the change scores would be greater in the first study. Table 2-5 presents the percentage of subjects exhibiting each behavior in Trials 1 and 2, Condition A, Mirror Study II and in the No Rouge and Rouge 1

TABLE 2-5

Percentage of Subjects Exhibiting Each Behavior in Trials 1 and 2 of Condition A in Mirror Study II (No Rouge Trials) and in the No Rouge and Rouge 1 Condition in Mirror Study I

Behavior	Study II			Study I		
	Trial 2	Trial 1	Difference score	Rouge 1	No Rouge	Difference score
Facial expression						
Smile	50	56	−6	79	75	5
Frown	22	11	11	7	3	4
Vocalization						
Laugh	17	22	−5	29	13	16
Coo	89	94	−5	76	71	5
Fret, cry	22	17	5	10	4	6
Mirror-directed						
Point	33	28	5	26	23	6
Touch	83	83	0	84	77	7
Touch image	50	67	−17	53	40	14[b]
Kiss	22	17	5	16	15	0
Hit	67	39	28	35	33	2
Imitation						
Rhythmic	28	11	17	17	16	1
Facial	17	0	17	21	17	5
Silly	22	17	5	22	14	6
Self-directed						
Point	6	22	−16	[a]	[a]	[a]
Body-directed	22	17	5	44	21	24[b]
Nose-directed	6	6	0	32	2	29[b]

[a] Behavior not measured.
[b] Significant difference.

Conditions, Mirror Study 1, and the percentage difference scores between trials for each study: all three comparisons are in Table 2-5.

Comparison I: No Rouge Conditions in Studies I and II

As stated previously, Trial 1 and the No Rouge Condition were methodologically similar and should, if our original findings are to be replicated, be identical. These two conditions were compared using chi-square statistics. As can be seen in Table 2-5, no significant differences for the total sample were found. No individual age group differences were found, except that 9- to 12-month-olds were more likely to act silly or coy in Mirror Study II than in Mirror Study I ($\chi^2 = 5.56$, $p < .05$).

Comparison II: Trial 1 versus Trial 2

As can be seen in Table 2-5, the infants responded very similarly to Trial 1 and Trial 2, with no significant differences appearing between the two trials for the total sample (McNemar tests). Of most interest was the fact that there were no increases in body-directed behavior, nose-directed behavior, touching one's own image, or acting silly or coy, behaviors that all increased in Mirror Study I.

With regard to the specific age groups, responses to Trial 1 and Trial 2 were highly similar. For the 9- to 12-month-olds, there were no differences; for the 15- to 18-month-olds, there was a 50% increase in number of subjects pointing to the mirror; for the 21- to 24-month-olds, there was a 50% increase in number of subjects hitting the mirror but a 50% decrease in touching the mirror and the mirror image. These differences could not be tested due to the small number of subjects in each age group and are not presented in tabular form. However, it is clear that there was little effect of nose-wiping and repeated mirror exposure on infants' responses for any age group.

Comparison III: Change Scores in Mirror Studies I and II

The change scores from the first to second trials for both studies were of interest, with the changes being significant in Mirror Study I but not in Mirror Study II. Table 2-5 presents the percentage change scores for both studies. There were significant increases in Mirror Study I for mark-directed behavior, body-directed behavior, acts silly or coy, and touches image (see Table 2-3). No such increases occurred in Mirror Study II.

Condition B: Effect of Prior Mirror Exposure on Self Recognition

To see whether the increase in behaviors from the No Rouge to the Rouge 1 Condition in Mirror Study I was due to the inclusion of a mirror condition prior to marking the face, the infants observed their marked faces without a preceding marked condition in Condition B. It was expected that there would be no differences between marked conditions with and without a preceding unmarked condition. In order to test this hypothesis, the results from the present study were compared to those of the Rouge 1 Condition in Mirror Study I. Table 2-6 presents the percentage of subjects exhibiting each behavior in Trial 2 (the marked trial), Condition B, Mirror Study II by age. Table 2-7 presents the percentage of subjects exhibiting each behavior in Trial 2, Condition B, Mirror Study II, and in the Rouge 1 Condition, Mirror Study I.

Description of Responses to Condition B

To control for time spent in the room, the infants in Condition B spent two min in the testing room with the mirror covered. The infants explored the room, interacted with their mothers, and/or looked at the

TABLE 2-6

Percentage of Subjects Exhibiting Each Behavior in Trial 2, Condition B in Mirror Study II by Age[a]

| Behavior | Age in months | | | |
	9–12	15–18	21–24	Total
Facial expression				
Smile	83	83	83	83
Frown	50	0	0	17
Vocalization				
Laugh	17	67	33	39
Coo	100	100	100	100
Fret, cry	50	0	0	17
Mirror-directed				
Point	33	50	67	50
Touch	33	100	83	72
Touch image	33	83	83	67
Kiss	17	33	0	17
Hit	50	100	0	50
Imitation				
Rhythmic	33	33	0	22
Facial	0	17	17	11
Silly	0	17	0	6
Self-directed				
Point	0	0	0	0
Body-directed	17	50	0	22
Mark-directed	0	33	67	33

[a]Rouge Trial.

TABLE 2-7

Percentage of Subjects Exhibiting Each Behavior in Trial 2 of Conditions B and C in Mirror Study II and in the Rouge 1 and 2 Conditions in Mirror Study I[a]

	Mirror Study I		Mirror Study II	
Behavior	Rouge 1	Rouge 2	Trial 2 Condition B	Trial 2 Condition C
Facial expression				
Smile	79	62	83	67
Frown	7	9	17	22
Vocalization				
Laugh	29	10	39	22
Coo	76	51	100	78
Fret, cry	10	24	17	22
Mirror-directed				
Point	26	15	50	28
Touch	84	67	72	78
Touch image	53	32	67	67
Kiss	16	11	17	18
Hit	35	14	50	56
Imitation				
Rhythmic	17	13	22	22
Facial	21	11	11	28
Silly	22	6	6	17
Self-directed				
Body-directed	44	22	22	44
Mark-directed	32	9	33	28

[a] All four are Rouge Trials.

posters on the wall during the no-mirror trial (Trial 1). None of the infants uncovered the mirror or spontaneously touched their noses.

Viewing oneself with rouge on the face elicited a great deal of pleasure. As can be seen in Table 2-6, all the infants vocalized positively, 83% smiled, 72% touched the mirror, 67% touched their own image, and 50% pointed to and kissed the mirror. At the same time, few (17%) infants frowned or cried. In terms of imitative and self-directed behaviors, one-third of the sample touched the mark on their faces. One-fifth made rhythmic movements and touched their bodies, while fewer infants exhibited silly or facial imitation behaviors. Interestingly, none of the infants pointed at themselves.

Trial 2, Condition B versus Rouge 1 Condition

Table 2-7 presents the percentage data for Trial 2, Condition B, Mirror Study II, and the Rouge 1 Condition, Mirror Study I (as well as two other conditions that will be discussed in the next section). The responses to the two were very similar, with only one significant difference: infants were more likely to coo and talk in the second than in the first mirror study ($\chi^2 = 4.08$, $p < .05$). Thus, the original results cannot be accounted for by the inclusion of an unmarked condition preceding the marked condition.

Age differences between the marked conditions with and without a preceding unmarked condition were also examined. Again, responses to the two conditions were very similar. The most striking similarity was found for mark-directed behavior as one-third of each sample noticed the mark. None of the 9- to 12-month-olds in either study, one-quarter and one-third of the 15- to 18-month-olds, and three-quarters and two-thirds of the 21- to 24-month-olds in Mirror Studies I and II, respectively, noticed the rouge on their noses; this is illustrated in Figure 2-3.

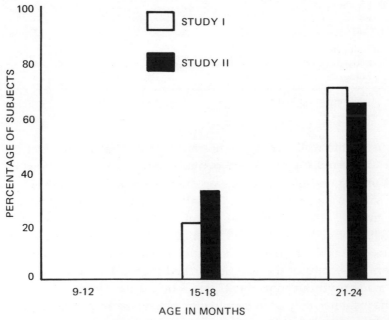

FIGURE 2-3.   Mark-directed behavior in Rouge 1, Mirror Study I and Condition B, Mirror Study II.

Thus, no effect of a preceding unmarked condition on mark recognition was found, either for the total sample or for the different age groups.

CONDITION C: EFFECT OF TRAINING ON SELF-DIRECTED BEHAVIOR

Two comparisons were of interest. First, the effectiveness of the maternal training condition in Mirror Studies I and II was examined to see whether maternal mark recognition occurred with the same frequency in the two studies. Would the more direct training technique employed in Mirror Study II result in a higher incidence of maternal mark recognition than the less direct technique in Mirror Study I? Second, the incidence of self mark recognition as a function of the training was examined. Specifically, the incidence of mark recognition in Trial 2, Condition C was compared to the incidence of mark recognition in Trial 2, Condition B, to the Rouge 1 Condition, Mirror Study I, and to the Rouge 2 Condition, Mirror Study I. If the facilitation were effective, then more infants would have noticed the rouge in the present condition than in the other three. This effect would be especially prevalent at 15 to 18 months of age, the age at which mark-directed behavior first appears. Table 2-7 presents the percentage of infants exhibiting each behavior for the four conditions.

Description of Responses to the Mothers' Marked Faces (Trial 1)

Of the 14 infants who looked at their mothers' faces (out of 18 tested), 64% touched their mother's nose, 43% touched her face, 50% touched their own face, and 43% touched their own nose. There were age trends such that touching the mother's nose increased with age, the largest increase occurring between the 9- to 12- and 15- to 18-month-old age groups. Touching one's own nose also increased with age, with the largest change occurring between the 15- to 18- and 21- to 24-month-old age groups.

The responses to the mothers' marked faces in Studies I and II were similar for some behaviors but not for others. Approximately equal numbers of subjects in each condition looked at their mothers' faces (86% in Study I, 78% in Study II). Of those who looked, 64% in both studies touched their mothers' marked noses. However, 43% touched their mothers' faces in Study II as compared with 17% in Study I ($\chi^2 =$ 3.48, $p < .10$). Approximately one-half of the subjects in the present study touched either their own face or their own nose, while less than 15% did so in the previous study (touches own face, $\chi^2 = 15.38$, $p < .001$ and touches own nose, $\chi^2 = 5.36$, $p < .05$). In short, the infants in the Mirror Study II were more likely to touch their mothers' faces, their own faces, and their own noses than in the Mirror Study I, although equal numbers of infants touched their mothers' marked noses, the criterion for maternal mark recognition. Although the present study seemed to facilitate touching the mothers' faces, it had no effect on maternal mark-touching.

Interestingly, maternal mark-directed behavior was somewhat less prevalent in the 9- to 12-month-olds in the present study than in the first study (20% versus 41%), and somewhat more prevalent in the 15- to 18-month-olds (100% versus 78%). However, these differences were not significant.

Description of Responses to Trial 2

The infants exhibited much interest in and positive affect toward their marked mirror images when they finally were placed in front of the mirror in Trial 2, Condition C. Two-thirds to three-quarters of the infants smiled at, vocalized to, touched the mirror, and touched the image in the mirror. Imitative behaviors were exhibited by one-quarter of the sample, body-directed behaviors by 44% of the sample, and mark-directed behaviors by 28%. As was expected, mark-directed behavior increased with age, as none of the 9- to 12-, one-third of the 15- to 18-, and one-half of the 21- to 24-month-olds touched their marked noses. Body-directed behavior did not change as a function of age.

There was also no relationship between touching the mother's nose in Trial 1 and touching one's own nose in Trial 2 when age was taken into account. Although 20% of the 9- to 12-month-olds touched their mothers' noses, none of them touched their own noses. All of the 15- to 18-month-olds touched their mothers' noses, but only 33% touched their own. And the 21- to 24-month-olds who touched their mothers' noses were not more likely to touch their own noses than those who did not.

Comparison of Condition B with Condition C, Rouge 1 and Rouge 2 Conditions

Table 2-7 presents the percentage data for Trial 2 of Conditions B and C, Mirror Study II and Rouge 1 and 2 Conditions, Mirror Study I. First, responses to the present condition were compared with those in the Rouge 2 Condition, as both of these conditions were preceded by a training condition. As was expected, there was somewhat more mark-directed behavior in this condition than Rouge 2 Condition in the first study (28% versus 9%, $\chi^2 = 3.25$, $p < .10$). In addition, touches images and hits mirror were seen more in Study II than in Study I subjects ($\chi^2 = 6.21$, $p < .05$ and $\chi^2 = 12.63$, $p < .001$). However, these differences were, in all likelihood, due to the general fatigue effects seen in Study I. Therefore, a second set of comparisons was made. If the training technique were effective, then the incidence of mark recognition would be higher in the present condition than in Condition B or the Rouge 1 Condition, both of which had no preceding training condition. However, no significant differences between the present condition and Condition B or between the present condition and the Rouge 1 Condition were found, nor were any age differences found.

DISCUSSION

Infants' responses to mirror-image stimulation prior to and following rouge application were observed, allowing for an examination of the development of visual self recognition in the first two years of life. Visual self recognition, when defined as behavior directed to a mark on the face, exhibited dramatic age trends. Self recognition, at least as measured by mark-directed behavior, did not occur in the first year of life, as some theorists have suggested (Darwin, 1877; Dixon, 1957; Preyer, 1893). At the same time, it was not delayed until the onset of speech, as others have thought (Ames, 1952; Gesell & Thompson, 1934). Instead, mark-directed behavior first appeared at 15 months of age and was seen in most infants by 21 months of age.

The present study reflects on three issues: (1) how do infants usually respond when seeing themselves in a mirror and do their responses change with age; (2) how do infants respond to the mirror after a mark of rouge has been applied to their faces and do their responses vary as a function of age; and (3) are there any individual differences that are related to or will in part predict mark recognition.

INFANT'S RESPONSES TO MIRRORS

What do infants typically do when they see themselves in reflective surfaces? Their responses may be divided into pleasureful responses, interest and attention, mirror-directed behaviors, imitation, and self-directed behaviors.

Pleasureful Responses

The overwhelming response to the mirror was one of pleasure and interest. There were few infants who did not smile, vocalize, or touch the mirror, and few who cried or frowned.

These pleasureful behaviors have been likened to sociable responses directed to a playmate by Amsterdam (1972), Dixon (1957), and Gesell and Thompson (1934) and have been called other-directed behavior by Gallup (1968, 1973). Smiling, vocalizing and approaching are thought to be typically elicited by playmates in the first year and a half of life. No direct test of the assumption has been made as no sample of infants has been systematically exposed to both peers and mirrors. However, infants' reactions to other infants have been studied and have been shown to be pleasureful (e.g., Bronson, 1975; Eckerman, Whatley, & Kutz, 1973; Lenssen, 1973; Lewis, Young, Brooks, & Michalson, 1975; Mueller & Lucas, 1975). All these studies report that infants do smile and approach same-age peers, but these behaviors occur relatively infrequently. In comparison, the mirror is much more likely to elicit smiling and approach.

Pleasureful behaviors have been thought to drop out as self recognition develops (Amsterdam, 1968; Dixon, 1957; Schulman & Kaplowitz, 1977). However, this was not the case in our sample, since the modal response of all infants in the present study was smiling at, touching, and vocalizing to the mirror, and since even the infants who did touch their noses were not less likely to smile and touch the mirror than those who did not. Instead, positive affect seems to be coupled with different behaviors at different ages. For example, smiling, touching, and vocalizing were coupled with sustained looking, kissing, and hitting in the 9-month-olds, but with touching the body, touching the mark, and acting silly or coy in the 24-month-olds. This coupling suggests that there may be a pleasure component which is independent of or interactive with other classification systems, such as other-directed to self-directed behavior, or that smiling and other positive affectual responses may be in the service of different motives—pleasure or excitement in the 9-month-old, recognition in the 24-month-old. The least we can say is that smiling and vocalizing are not direct and exclusive components of either other- or self-directed behavior.

Interest and Attention

The mirror image elicited a great deal of attention as well as pleasure, as others have also reported. Interestingly, the youngest infants looked at the mirror for the longest periods of time, a finding also reported by Dickie and Strader (1974). Was this because they were less mobile or because they became passively trapped by the contingent feedback of the mirror, like the fish and birds Gallup (1968) studied? Our data support neither explanation. First, all the 9-month-olds could and did crawl and all could turn their heads away from the mirror. Second, the infants under one year of age did not seem to be passively trapped, as they vigorously interacted with the mirror.

Mirror-Directed Behavior

Mirror-directed behavior has been characterized as a sociable response and as other-directed behavior (Amsterdam, 1972; Gallup, 1973). It may also be characterized as exploratory in nature, with infants "testing" the properties of another object in the environment, in this case a mirror. When these behaviors are labeled as sociable or other-directed, they are expected to decrease with age. In the present sample, kissing and hitting did so, while touching the mirror and the image did not. Touching, like smiling, may indicate curiosity about and pleasure in the mirror itself, not merely sociable responses to a playmate or other-directed behavior.

Pointing to the mirror may be considered a social response, an other-directed behavior, or a transitional behavior. The latter seems plausible since pointing often has a "look at me" quality. Remember that pointing would imply a distancing from the mirror, both in space and in time, as pointing occurs before the infant has approached and made contact with the mirror. Anecdotal evidence suggests that pointing was very likely to be coupled with a look to the mother, as if to share or confirm the experience.

Imitation

Imitative behaviors are neither other-directed nor self-directed, since they require the infant to watch himself move but not to touch either the mirror or himself. The nature of the contingent feedback is important here, as the infant is using the feedback provided by the mirror to observe himself. The three types of imitation may be ordered in terms of the complexity of the actions or in terms of the likelihood that the behaviors indicate an awareness of self. The rhythmic movements, which were somewhat more prevalent in the younger infants, might not be indicative of recognition. They would be classified as "watches image" by Amsterdam (1972) or as "Who do dat when I do dat" by Dixon (1957). The mirror contingency elicits both movement and pleasure, as infants who bounced, waved, or clapped also smiled. As Amsterdam's and our data indicate, observing one's own movement is most prevalent from 9 to 12 months of age.

Facial imitations and acting silly or coy seem to indicate a growing awareness of both the properties of reflections and recognition of oneself. In general, acting silly or coy increased with age and did not occur in the first year of life. Other investigators report similar findings. Preyer's (1893) son acted self consciously at approximately 17 months of age; Dixon (1957) observed similar behavior between 12 and 18 months of age; Amsterdam (1972) and Schulman and Kaplowitz (1977) reported self admiration and embarrassment from 14 to 24 months of age. Amsterdam's (1972) age trends correspond rather closely to ours, since coy or silly behaviors were seen only in one of our infants and one of her infants under 15 months of age, but were seen often after 15 months of age. Amsterdam suggests that self admiration is a precursor of self recognition, although our findings suggest that the two appear concurrently: mark-directed behavior and acting silly or coy were first seen at 15 months of age; those infants who touched themselves in the Rouge 1 Condition were more likely to act silly or coy than those who did not (80% versus 45%). Thus, acting silly or coy does not seem to be a precursor of self recognition but rather appears at the same time.

Body-Directed Behavior

Although body-directed behavior is self-directed, it is not clear whether the infants were touching themselves in order to visually and tactually examine themselves and/or to visually examine inaccessible parts of the body, as did Gallup's (1970) apes. Anecdotal evidence suggests that at least some of the infants did so: infants who were wearing shirts with appliqué designs on them often looked in the mirror and then touched their shirts or tried to look at them. Since this was not observed systematically, no statement about age differences can be

made. Interestingly, body-directed behavior has been observed only by
Gallup (1970) and by Dickie and Strader (1974). Dickie and Strader
(1974) reported increased body exploration in the second year of life,
which we also found.

Other Measures of Self Awareness

Self admiration, embarrassment, and fear of the mirror are behaviors that others have thought to be indicative of self awareness and
related to body-directed behavior. As children begin to realize that the
mirror is a reflection of the self, they withdraw or avoid the mirror; such
behaviors Amsterdam (1968) found prevalent in infants over a year and
a half of age and we saw rarely at any age. The negative affect exhibited
to the mirror by Amsterdam's subjects may have been due to fatigue or
boredom; as she states, "only three infants cried in unmistakable fear of
the mirror." Interestingly, although specific fear of the mirror was not
seen in the present study, fear of the rouge was; a few of the oldest
infants reacted quite negatively to the rouge, acting as if they had been
injured, saying, "fix it," "it hurts," "knife," and "boo boo, mommy."

THE EFFECT OF ROUGE APPLICATION ON MIRROR BEHAVIOR AND SELF RECOGNITION

Mark Recognition

The central issue of the study was whether or not the rouge application would affect infants' responses to the mirror and result in mark
recognition. Recognition of the rouge was clearly demonstrated, as 30
infants in the first study touched, wiped, or verbally referred to the
marked nose following the rouge application, and only two infants
touched the nose prior to the mark application. How does this finding
relate to those of others? Amsterdam (1968, 1972) and Bertenthal and
Fischer (1978) also used a mark-on-the-face technique. The percentage
of subjects exhibiting self recognition in our study and in Amsterdam's
(1968) is presented in Figure 2-4. As can be seen, mark-directed behavior
was never exhibited by the 9- to 12-month-olds in either sample and was
more prevalent for the older subjects in the present study than in
Amsterdam's. In addition, Amsterdam first observed mark recognition

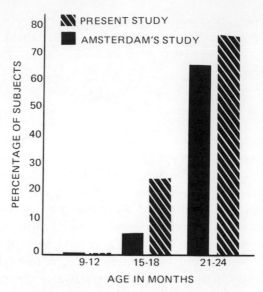

FIGURE 2-4. Percentage of subjects exhibiting mark recognition in the present study and in Amsterdam's (1968) study by age.

in 18-month-olds, whereas the present study observed it in 15-month-olds.

What might account for the earlier and more frequent mark recognition in our sample? There are at least three possible explanations. First, procedural differences may have affected the results. In Amsterdam's study, the infants' clothing was removed before testing, infants were confined to a playpen, the observer was present, a seven and one-half min trial was used, and the rouge was placed on the side of the nose. The first three conditions may have made the Amsterdam setting more stressful than the present one, an explanation that is partially substantiated by the large number of infants who were fussy in that setting. Trial length probably did not affect the incidence of mark-directed behavior, since infants tended to touch their marked noses immediately or not at all. Rouge placement may affect the disparate findings, since rouge on the side of the nose may not be as salient as rouge on the tip of the nose. Second, the social class composition of the two samples was somewhat different, with Amsterdam's being more heterogeneous. However, there were no effects of social class with respect to self recognition within our sample, and Amsterdam (1968) reports no relationship between social class and self recognition. Third, the inclusion of a No Rouge Condition may have affected subsequent mark recognition. Gallup (1968, 1973) reports that prior mirror exposure is necessary for mark-recognition in chimpanzees; such a primer might also be helpful for human infants. However, as we shall see in Chapter 6, mirror experience was not related to mark recognition.

The rouge application also affected the expression of other behaviors. The infants were much more likely to look at themselves, especially for sustained periods of time, to exhibit a concentrate expression, to touch their image, to point to themselves in the mirror, to act silly or coy, and to touch their bodies after the rouge was applied. There were important age differences in the expression of differential responding to the marked and unmarked conditions. The increase in number of looks, sustained looks, concentrate expression, body-directed behavior and touching one's image occurred in all age groups, whereas acting silly or coy and pointing at one's image in the mirror only increased in the older infants.

These age × stimulus condition interactions are important for two reasons. First, differential responding occurred in the youngest infants who were not exhibiting mark-directed behavior. For example, increased body-touching in the rouge condition might indicate self awareness, as the infants were more likely to explore their body without actually touching the rouge. At the same time, the behaviors which are most indicative of self awareness—acting silly or coy and pointing at oneself in the mirror—only increased for the older infants. In fact, there was a tendency (although nonsignificant) for older infants who exhibited mark recognition to act silly or coy, touch their image, point to their image, and smile more than their same-age counterparts who did not notice the rouge.

From which measures are we to infer self awareness? If body-directed behavior is the criterion, then self recognition is common by 9 to 12 months of age. If acting silly or coy, touching the image, and pointing are the criteria, then self recognition is the modal response by 15 to 18 months of age. And if mark-directed behavior is the criterion, then self recognition is not prevalent until 21 to 24 months of age. The problem of measurement is not easily resolved, especially since age-related physical coordination may be affecting the ability to direct behavior visually toward the mark. Pointing and gesturing behaviors imply that the infant must direct his attention to that which is being pointed at, not the pointer itself. Flavell's work with preschool children suggests that this ability follows a developmental course similar to role-taking (Flavell, 1974; Masangkay, McCluskey, McIntyre, Sims-Knight, Vaughn, & Flavell, 1974). It may well be that infants in the first year of life do not have the cognitive capacity to distinguish between the act of pointing and the receiver of the point. Pointing may also have a neurological base, since the failure to point to an object when asked is associated with CNS dysfunction (see for example, Taylor, 1961).

In order to better understand the meaning of the different behaviors from which self recognition is to be inferred, additional data are needed. The data from the videotape and picture studies will provide more information about the measurement of self recognition.

DIFFERENCES IN MARK RECOGNITION

These different experimental factors that may affect or be related to self recognition were explored; these are: (1) the salience of the marked face for different-aged infants, (2) the effect of maternal mark recognition on subsequent self-directed behavior, and (3) the effect of trial length.

The Salience of Marked Faces

Although recognizing a mark on another's face may be qualitatively different from viewing it on oneself, observing it may give us information about the saliency of such a distortion for the infant. Almost one-half of the infants under one year of age noticed the rouge on their mothers, suggesting that the type of distortion used was salient for at least some of the young infants. At the same time, the age differences in maternal mark-directed behavior suggest that age differences in stimulus distortion saliency might also be affecting self-directed behavior. In addition, the act of directing one's own hand to one's own face through the use of a mirror is probably more difficult than directing one's own hand to another's face, making direct comparison between the mother and self conditions impossible.

The Effect of Maternal Mark Recognition on Subsequent Self-Directed Behavior

The primary purpose of the mother condition was to act as a facilitator. It was thought that recognizing the rouge might predispose the infant to look at his own nose in the mirror and to notice the mark. However, there is no evidence of such a facilitating effect. Of the 26 infants in Study I who did not touch their marked noses in the Rouge 1 Condition but did touch their mothers' noses in the Mother Rouge Condition, only one subsequently touched his nose in the Rouge 2 Condition. A similar finding occurred in Condition C of Study II. These findings suggest that the infants did not use the information acquired through the mother condition to examine their own faces more closely. Perhaps the infants were unable to do so because they did not have the necessary cognitive abilities, perhaps the manipulation was not powerful enough to allow for generalization from other to self, or perhaps the infants had been habituated to the mirror condition and, therefore, were less interested in the mirror. In any case, the manipulations used in this series of studies failed to facilitate mark-directed behavior but do suggest saliency did not account for the lack of results.

The Effect of Repeated Mirror Exposure

What effect did repeated exposure to the mirror have on infants' mirror behaviors? As stated earlier, interest waned, fussiness increased, and trial completion decreased over time in Study I. This decrease suggests that (1) some interest- and pleasure-producing objects or persons in the infant's environment may be attended to for relatively short periods of time (mothers report this phenomenon in describing their infants' mirror play), and (2) the high incidence of avoidance and withdrawal from the mirror in Amsterdam's study may have been due to the trial length (7.5 min) and playpen confinement rather than self awareness.

THE DEVELOPMENT OF SELF RECOGNITION: SUMMARY

At least two investigators who have studied infants' responses to mirrors have suggested a stage theory to explain their findings and have offered specific sets of behavior that are thought to be related to these stages (Amsterdam, 1968; Dixon, 1957). For example, social responses to an unfamiliar peer are thought to be characterized by smiling, approaching, and patting the mirror as if it were another; such sociable responses are thought to drop out of the infant's repertoire with age. Our data do not support such a stage theory notion, since few behaviors were seen at only one age and since some behaviors remained constant, while others

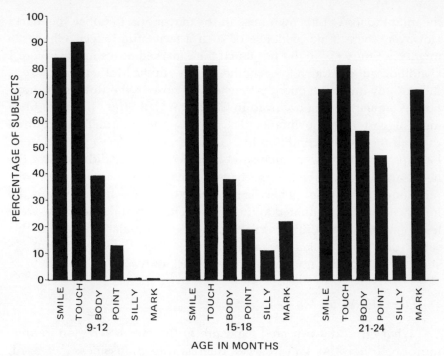

FIGURE 2-5. Percentage of subjects in the Rouge 1 Condition by age who exhibited other- and self-directed behavior.

gradually increased or decreased with age. Figure 2-5, which presents the percentage of infants in three age groups exhibiting six different behaviors in the Rouge 1 Condition, illustrates this point well. Two sociable or mirror-directed (smiling at and touching the mirror), two transitional (acting silly or coy and pointing at the mirror image), and two self-directed behaviors (mark- and body-directed) are represented. As can be seen, some are exhibited by almost all the infants and do not change as a function of age, while others are exhibited by fewer infants and do change as a function of age. Specifically, mirror-directed behaviors remain high across the first two years while self-directed behaviors gradually increase with age. Such data suggest that self recognition may not be a discontinuous phenomenon, and that the transition from other- to self-directed behavior may be a gradual process.

Videotape Representations of Self and Others

Mirrors are unique surfaces since they reflect one's image and provide one-to-one correspondence between one's action and the image. In the last chapter, it was clearly demonstrated that children under two years of age are able to recognize themselves in mirrors. Visual self recognition was defined as self-directed behavior toward a mark on the nose and toward other parts of the body. Although infants did not exhibit mark-directed behavior prior to 15 months of age, they did exhibit body-directed behavior at earlier ages. Moreover, they directed more of it in the marked than in the unmarked condition, thus demonstrating some awareness of the mark as early as 9 months of age, even though mark recognition *per se* did not occur until later.

Mirrors present several features to which the infants who recognized themselves may have been responding. First, the infants could have been responding to the social features that are common to the image and to the self. For example, the infants may have been responding because the image was a small child and because the infants themselves were also small children. Second, the infants could have been responding to the contingency offered by the mirror. Third, the infants could have been responding to the familiarity of the perceptual features in the image, a familiarity due to the knowledge that the image is, in fact, the self.

Until modern technology allowed for pictorial representations of the self, one's own image was only experienced in mirrors and mirror-like reflections, where contingency cues could not be separated from perceptual familiarity cues. The advent of television and videotape provided an opportunity to separate the cues by which we learn to recognize our images. By utilizing videotape feedback systems, it is possible to obtain information on what dimension or dimensions infants use to recognize themselves when confronted with a representation of the self, and at what ages these dimensions are utilized. For example, contingency cues might be used solely for self recognition by younger infants, contingency cues and perceptual features might be used at older ages, and finally, only perceptual features might be used by even older children. Young infants might conclude that only if the image moves as I do (a type of circular reaction) is the image me. Older infants might conclude that only if the image moves and looks like me is the image me, and even older children might conclude that only if the image looks like me is the image me. The use of videotape systems provides an opportunity to explore the dimensions of self recognition and the nature of the use of different cues at different stages of development.

To date, only a few investigators have used videotape systems for such a purpose: Papoušek and Papoušek (1974) explored the saliency of eye-to-eye contact and contingency in 5-month-old infants' responses to videotapes of self and other presented simultaneously; Bigelow (1975) explored the saliency of contingency in 18- to 26-month-old infants' responses to videotapes of self and other presented sequentially; and Amsterdam and Greenberg (1977) examined infants' responses to contingent and noncontingent representations of self. Papoušek and Papoušek (1974) presented a contingent image of self with no eye-to-eye contact and a noncontingent image of self with eye-to-eye contact simultaneously; unfortunately, eye contact and contingency were not systematically varied. Their 5-month-old infants were able to discriminate between the two conditions, preferring noncontingency with eye contact to contingency with no eye contact. However, over repeated presentations, the contingent condition elicited increased attention and movement. The authors suggest that the infants were learning about the contingency during the testing which resulted in increased responding over repeated trials. Using a sequential presentation method to examine older infants' responses to contingent and noncontingent images of self, Bigelow (1975) found no discrimination until about 2 years of age. Amsterdam and Greenberg (1977), using a slightly different method, report results similar to those of Bigelow (1975). However, more detailed analysis of the Papoušek and Papoušek study and our mirror studies suggests that differentiation is possible before the end of the second year.

The purpose of the videotape studies is to vary systematically two dimensions—contingency-noncontingency and self-other—to see whether infants respond to both, one, or neither dimension and to see whether or not these responses are age-related. In Videotape Study 1, three television videotape conditions were used: self contingent feedback, self noncontingent feedback, and other noncontingent feedback. In the self contingent condition, the infant viewed a television monitor that provided immediate feedback of the infant's actions (i.e., in effect a mirror). In the self noncontingent condition, the infant viewed a videotape of self that was made a week earlier and that had no one-to-one correspondence between action and image. In the other noncontingent condition, the infant viewed a videotape of another child who was the same age and sex and was in the same situation as the target infant.

In Videotape Study II, similar conditions were used—self contingent feedback, self noncontingent feedback, and other noncontingent feedback. In each of the above conditions, a stranger approached the infant from behind—an approach which could be seen by the infant on the television monitor. The approach was "live" in the self contingent condition and "taped" in the self noncontingent and other noncontingent conditions. This method allowed for the use of a specific behavior—head turns toward the target or where the target would have been—as a measure of knowledge about self. It was expected that, if the infants distinguished between contingent and noncontingent conditions and between self and other videotapes, head-turning would be differentially exhibited in these conditions.

VIDEOTAPE STUDY I

Experimental Design

Subjects

Ninety-six infants representing six age groups (9, 12, 15, 18, 21, and 24 months of age) were seen. The mean ages and age ranges of the six age groups were 9.17 (8.20–9.73), 12.27 (11.83–12.83), 15.27 (14.53–15.80), 18.33 (17.5–19.0), 21.23 (20.60–22.23), and 24.10 (23.40–25.0). There were eight males and eight females in each age group. One-half of the infants were firstborn, one-half were later-born. Socioeconomic class for the sample was similar to that of the two mirror studies, with infants being distributed among the first three of Hollingshead's (1957) five social classes. All infants were Caucasian, full-term, and healthy.

PROCEDURE

The mothers were given the following instructions to read when they entered the laboratory:

> We are interested in your child's responses to videotape representations of himself and another child. As you remember, we made a videotape of your child during last week's visit. This week we will show your child that tape and a tape of another child the same age and sex. In addition, the TV can reproduce the child's action immediately so that a "mirror-like" condition is possible. These three conditions (mirror-like, tape of your child, tape of another child) will be presented randomly to your child, and approximately 25 different trials will be presented.
>
> Each trial will last at least 25 seconds, and the trial change will not occur unless your child is looking at the TV screen. If your child does not look for a period of time, the experimenter will knock on the outside of the enclosure. Please direct your child's attention to the screen by pointing or saying, "look." When he looks, another condition will appear on the screen. Do not direct your child's attention to the screen at other times, as we want to know which conditions interest him most.
>
> If your child becomes fussy, we will give him a small toy to hold. Please do not give him other toys, bottles, or objects from your purse. If the toy does not soothe him, we will terminate the experiment. If at any time you wish to stop participating please tell the experimenter. Are there any questions?

The infant was then taken to a small enclosure which contained an infant high chair, a table, a television screen, and a chair for the mother. The child was placed in his chair facing the screen, and his mother was seated to the side and behind the child. The screen was approximately one m from the child. One experimenter observed the child through mesh-covered peepholes and another controlled the condition changes from another room.

There were 26 trials representing the three different conditions. Because of the nature of the recording equipment, the noncontingent conditions had to be followed by the self contingent condition. Therefore, equal numbers of contingent and noncontingent trials and equal numbers of self and other trials were presented. Trial length was variable, as the condition was not changed until the infant had looked at least once at the television monitor and at least 25 sec had elapsed; trial length varied from 25 to 45 sec, with the majority lasting between 25 and 35 sec. Trial presentation was counterbalanced using four different presentation orders; one-quarter of the infants received order 1, one-quarter order 2, etc. There were no differences in responding to the four different orders.

Measures

Five categories of behavior were coded—facial expression, vocalizations, movement, attention, and imitative behaviors. The infants' responses were coded live, with the presence or absence of each behavior recorded for each trial (except fixation, which was continuously recorded). These five categories and the behaviors within each are listed in Table 3-1.

Attentional measures include: total fixation/trial length and length of first fixation. Facial expressions included smile, frown, and concentrate. Each was defined by the position of the infant's mouth, a smile being defined as corners of the mouth turned upward, a frown as corners of the mouth turned downward, a concentrate expression as either one or both lips being shaped like a "U," an ellipse, or a square. The infants' vocalizations were coded as either positive (laugh, giggle, coo, babble) or negative (fret, whimper, cry, scream). Movement was coded for both movement

TABLE 3-1
Measures Used in Videotape Study I

Attention
  Total fixation/trial length
  Length of first fixation
Facial expression
  Smile
  Frown
  Concentrate
Vocalization
  Positive (laugh, giggle, coo, babble)
  Negative (cry, scream, whimper, fret)
Movement
  Movement toward videotape image
  Movement away from videotape image
Imitation
  Plays with contingency
  Imitates tape

toward and away from the videotape images. Movement toward the image included pointing at or waving to the screen and any movement of the upper body toward the screen. Movement away was seen so infrequently that it was not included in the data analysis. Imitation included playing contingently and imitating the tape. Playing with the contingent nature of the television image involved repeating actions on the screen. The two most prevalent play behaviors (accounting for 80% of this category) were peek-a-boo (moving one's head, eyes, body, or hand out of the camera's view and, hence, off the screen and then back again) and facial movements (sticking the tongue out, opening the mouth wide and then closing it, and making faces). Imitates tapes was defined as replicating a discrete action portrayed on the tape after it had begun and within two sec of its occurrence. Actions such as waving, sticking the tongue out, putting hands on the head, and pointing at one's body were all coded as imitations. Turning to the mother, a frequently occuring action, was not coded as an imitation. By definition, imitates tape could only occur in the videotape conditions.

INTEROBSERVER RELIABILITY

Interobserver reliability for the discrete behaviors was done by coding videotapes of 12 subjects for each behavior and each trial, using the formula number of agreements/number of agreements and disagreements. The percentages of agreements were quite high, ranging from 80% to 95%, with the exception of the concentrate expression (73%). Interobserver reliability for the continuous fixation measure was done on 10 subjects and Pearson Product Moment Correlations were .94 for first fixation and .91 for proportion of trial spent looking.

DATA ANALYSIS

The discrete behaviors were analyzed using mean proportion data or the proportion of trials for each stimulus condition in which the behavior occurred. Proportions were used since the number of trials differed for each stimulus condition, due to the equipment requirements and differed for each subject, due to the inability of some infants (15%) to complete all trials. Proportion scores were first calculated for individuals and then for groups; thus, equal weighting was given to individuals, not to trials, in keeping with the repeated measures design of the experiment. The discrete behaviors were analyzed by nonparametric statistics; a Friedman two-way analysis of variance was used for the overall comparison among the three stimulus conditions and Wilcoxon matched-pairs signed ranks tests for the specific comparisons. The continuous data (i.e., the fixation data) were analyzed by parametric statistics: mixed model analyses of variance with stimulus condition, age of subject, and sex of subject as factors for overall comparisons, and dependent t tests for specific comparisons. The three specific comparisons were between contingent and noncontingent, noncontingent self and other, and the contingent and noncontingent self conditions.

The stimulus condition differences were analyzed for the total sample, the different age groups, the males and the females, and the age by sex groups. The age of subject analyses were done by collapsing the six age groups into three, the three being 9- to 12-, 15- to 18-, and 21- to 24-month-olds. These are the same age groups that were used in the last chapter.

Results

Trial Effects

Since the infants received such a large number of trials, the infants' responses may have changed over time. Trial effects are common in studies of other phenomena and habituation to a repeated stimulus was first studied as a trial effect (Lewis, 1967). It was expected that, like attention procedures (Lewis, 1969), the repetition of the stimulus condition would result in a decrease in responding over time. To examine possible trial effects, the trials were divided into six blocks of four trials each. The last two trials were often not completed because of fussiness and boredom and are therefore excluded from the following analyses. The mean proportion of subjects who exhibited each behavior in each block of trials was calculated and trend analyses were performed. Figure 3-1 presents the data for the six blocks for a number of behaviors—smile, contingent play, imitates tape, and concentrate. As can be seen, most of these behaviors decreased over time. Smiling exhibited a linear decrease over time [$F(1,63) = 44.68$, $p < .001$], as did the other two positive affective behaviors not exhibited in Figure 3-1 [positive vocalizing:

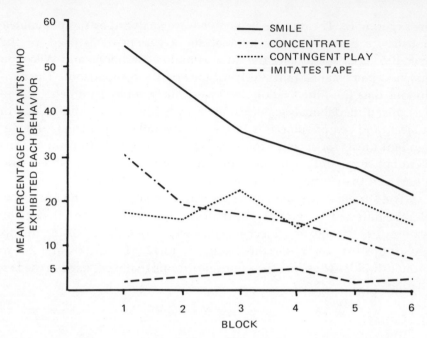

FIGURE 3-1. Mean percentage of subjects who smiled, concentrated, imitated the tapes, and played with the contingencies.

$F(1,64) = 46.60$, $p < .001$; and moving forward: $F(1,63) = 33.92$, $p < .001$]. The concentrate face also exhibited a linear decrease over time [$F(1,63) = 24.28$, $p < .001$]. In contrast, imitation did not decrease linearly over time; contingent play increased in the first 3 blocks, decreased in block 4, increased in block 5, and decreased in block 6, which is reflected in the significant quintic trend [$F(1,63) = 7.43$, $p < .01$]. Imitates tape increased through the first four blocks and then decreased in the last two blocks, which is reflected in the quadratic trend [$F(1,61) = 3.14$, $p < .10$]. Thus, positive affect and attention decreased with time, whereas imitation showed an increase and then a decrease over time.

TRIAL × STIMULUS CONDITION INTERACTIONS

Since trials effects were found, the trial × stimulus condition interaction was examined, although no interaction was expected since presentation order was counterbalanced across subjects and since all three stimulus conditions were dispersed through the 26 trials. As expected, no trial × stimulus condition interactions occurred.

STIMULUS CONDITION EFFECTS

Imitation

   Contingent Play.   Table 3-2 presents the mean proportion of trials
and number of subjects exhibiting contingent play and imitates tape by
stimulus condition for the total sample, the three age groups, and the
two sexes. As can be seen, contingent play was seen primarily in the
contingent condition, although the infants also performed these actions
in the noncontingent conditions. For the total sample, these behaviors
occurred in 27% of the self contingent, 7% of the self noncontingent,
and 4% of the other noncontingent trials [$\chi^2(2) = 58.69$; $p < .001$]. There
was a significant difference between contingent and noncontingent ($T =$
24, $z = 6.79$, $p < .001$), between the self and other noncontingent ($T =$
66, $z = 6.51$, $p < .001$), and between the contingent and noncontingent
self conditions ($T = 23$, $z = 6.80$, $p < .001$).
   Plays with contingency was strongly related to age, as is shown in
Figure 3-2, which presents the mean proportion of trials in which contingent play occurred by stimulus condition and age. The number of
trials in which contingent play was exhibited increased with age, regardless of condition, with the greatest increment occurring between 12 and
15 months of age. However, the greatest increment was between 9 and
12 months of age when we looked at number of subjects exhibiting
contingent play: 7% of the 9-, 53% of the 12-, 71% of the 15-, 93% of the
18-, and 100% of the 21- and 24-month-olds exhibited this behavior at
least once [$\chi^2(5) = 39.18$, $p < .001$].
   Going back to the mean proportion data, we observe that infants
over a year of age, but not under a year of age, differentiated among
conditions [15–18 months: $\chi^2(2) = 22.88$, $p < .001$ and 21–24 months:
$\chi^2(2) = 42.00$, $p < .001$]. In terms of the three comparisons, more contingent play was exhibited in the contingent than the noncontingent condi
tions and in the contingent than the noncontingent self conditions by all
ages (9–12 months: $T = 0$, $p < .01$; 15–18 months: $T = 3$, $p < .01$, and T
= 6.00, $p < .01$; 21–24 months: $T = 7$, $p < .001$, and $T = 3.00$, $p < .001$).
Only the oldest age group exhibited significantly more contingent play
to the self than the other noncontingent conditions (21–24 months: $T =$
12, $p < .01$).
   No sex of subject differences or age of subject × sex of subject
interactions were found. One interesting trend did appear, as the 15- to
18-month-old females were more likely to differentiate between the self

TABLE 3-2

Mean Proportion of Trials and Number of Subjects Exhibiting Contingent Play and Imitates Tape by Stimulus Condition

| | Stimulus condition | | | | | | | |
| | Mean proportions | | | | Number of subjects | | | |
Subjects	Contingent	Non-contingent	Non-contingent self	Non-contingent other	Contingent	Non-contingent	Non-contingent self	Non-contingent other
			Contingent play					
Total	.27	.05	.07	.04	64	27	23	12
9–12[a]	.04	0	0	0	9	0	0	0
15–18[a]	.35	.08	.10	.07	24	13	10	7
21–24[a]	.40	.07	.10	.04	31	14	13	5
Male	.28	.05	.06	.04	33	13	10	8
Female	.25	.05	.07	.03	31	14	13	4
			Imitates tape					
Total	—	.07	.09	.05	—	31	26	13
9–12[a]	—	.02	.01	.02	—	3	1	2
15–18[a]	—	.07	.10	.05	—	12	10	3
21–24[a]	—	.12	.16	.08	—	16	15	8
Male	—	.05	.08	.03	—	14	12	4
Female	—	.08	.10	.07	—	19	14	9

[a] Months.

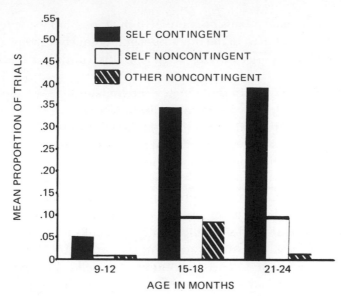

FIGURE 3-2. Contingent play: Mean proportion of trials by stimulus condition and by age.

and other noncontingent conditions than the same-aged males, although not enough subjects exhibited contingent play in these two conditions to test this finding. Specifically, five of the females played contingently only in the self condition, whereas one played in the other condition; the corresponding numbers for the males were five and six.

Imitates Tape. Imitates tape, which by definition could only occur in the noncontingent conditions, occurred in 9% of the self and in 5% of the other trials, as shown in Table 3-2 ($T = 143.5$, $z = 1.83$, $p < .05$). In general, the amount of tape imitation increased with age, as is shown in Figure 3-3, which presents the mean proportion of trials in which infants imitated the tape by stimulus condition and age. The same trend was found for number of subjects: none of the 9-month-olds, 7% of the 12 , 14% of the 15-, 57% of the 18-, 40% of the 21-, and 60% of the 24-month-olds imitated at least one of the noncontingent trials [$\chi^2(5) = 13.19$, $p < .01$]. The age × stimulus condition interaction for the mean data pictured in Figure 3-3 indicates that differentiation of the self and other noncontingent conditions first occurred at 15 months of age and appeared in all groups thereafter. However, none of the differences reached statistical significance because of the small numbers of infants exhibiting this behavior.

Male and female infants both imitated the tapes and exhibited more imitation to the self than to the other noncontingent conditions. As with contingent play, no sex of subject × stimulus condition interactions were found.

Summary.   Plays with contingency and imitates tape were exhibited differentially, the former being more likely to occur in the contingent than in the noncontingent and in the contingent self than in the noncontingent self conditions, and both being more likely to occur in the self than in the other noncontingent conditions. Differentiation increased with age. Figure 3-4 presents the mean difference scores for four comparisons, contingent and noncontingent, self contingent and self noncontingent, and self noncontingent and other noncontingent for the contingent play measure and self-other noncontingent for the imitates tape measure. With regard to the contingent play measure, the difference between contingent and noncontingent and the self contingent and self noncontingent comparison increased with age, with the greatest dif-

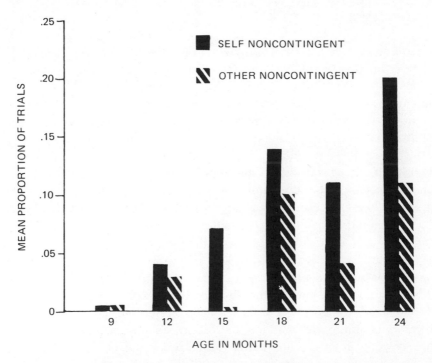

FIGURE 3-3.   Imitates tape: Mean proportion of trials by stimulus condition and by age.

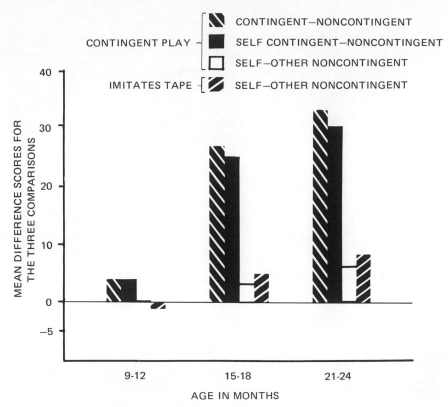

FIGURE 3-4.   Mean difference scores for the three comparisons for contingent play and imitates tape.

ference occurring between 9–12 and 15–18 months of age. Finally, the self–other noncontingent comparisons for both measures exhibited this age effect, with the greatest change occurring between 9–12 and 15–18 months of age, although the mean difference scores are much smaller than for the other comparisons. These data suggest that, even without contingency, the self is recognized by 15 to 18 months of age.

Affect

Three different behaviors that are thought to be indicative of positive affectual responding were coded; these were smiles, positive vocalizations, and moves toward the television image. All three occurred in over one-third of the trials, suggesting that television images of young children elicited delight. Table 3-3 presents the mean proportion of trials in which infants smiled, moved forward, and vocalized positively to the stimulus conditions by age and sex of subject.

Two behaviors indicative of negative affect were coded: frowning and fretting/crying. Both behaviors occurred infrequently (in less than 1% of the trials), strengthening our finding that television images of young children elicit pleasure. Since so few infants exhibited negative affect, no statistical analyses were performed.

Smiles. In terms of smiling, the overall stimulus condition effect was significant [$\chi^2(2) = 15.67$, $p < .001$]; infants smiled at 38% of the

TABLE 3-3

Mean Proportion of Trials in Which the Infants Smiled, Moved toward, and Vocalized Positively to the Stimulus Condition by Age and Sex of Subject

	Stimulus condition			
Subjects	Contingent	Noncontingent	Noncontingent self	Noncontingent other
		Smiles		
Total	.38	.29	.27	.30
9–12[a]	.23	.22	.22	.22
15–18[a]	.38	.27	.26	.29
21–24[a]	.52	.37	.33	.39
Male	.42	.28	.25	.30
Female	.34	.29	.29	.30
		Moves toward		
Total	.42	.37	.36	.39
9–12[a]	.30	.28	.25	.30
15–18[a]	.45	.37	.35	.40
21–24[a]	.50	.45	.44	.47
Male	.39	.35	.35	.34
Female	.45	.39	.36	.44
		Positive vocalization		
Total	.48	.45	.45	.44
9–12[a]	.37	.38	.37	.38
15–18[a]	.46	.41	.41	.37
21–24[a]	.60	.56	.57	.58
Male	.46	.38	.39	.37
Female	.49	.52	.51	.51

[a]Months.

contingent and 29% of the noncontingent trials (T = 769.5, z = 4.42, p < .001), 30% of the other and 27% of the self trials (T = 985, z = 3.44, p < .001), and 38% of the contingent self and 27% of the noncontingent self trials (T = 721, z = 4.64, p < .001). Thus, contingent self received the most smiling, noncontingent other the next, and noncontingent self the least. Smiling was also influenced by the age of the subject, increasing from 9 to 24 months of age. An age × stimulus condition interaction was also found, as the 15- to 18- and 21- to 24-, but not the 9- to 12-month-olds, responded differentially to the stimulus conditions [$\chi^2(2)$ = 6.53, p < .05; $\chi^2(2)$ = 10.66, p < .01]. In terms of the specific comparisons the two older age groups were more likely to smile at the contingent than at the noncontingent conditions (T = 81, z = 2.59, p < .01; T = 52, z = 3.44, p < .001), at the contingent self than at the noncontingent self conditions (T = 59, z = 2.96, p < .01; T = 53.5, z = 3.40, p < .001), but were equally likely to smile at the self and at other noncontingent conditions. The males tended to smile more often to the contingent condition than did the females (42% versus 34%). No other sex differences were found.

   Moves Toward. As can be seen in Table 3-3, moves toward the television image was also exhibited differentially [$\chi^2(2)$ = 9.33, p < .01] with this behavior being more likely to be exhibited in the contingent than in the noncontingent (T = 1292.5, z = 2.90, p < .01), in the contingent self than in the noncontingent self (T = 1149.5, z = 3.49, p < .001), and in the noncontingent other than in the noncontingent self conditions (T = 1306.5, z = 2.85, p < .01). Like smiling, moving toward the image increased with age, although no overall age increase in differentiation appeared. However, in terms of the specific comparisons, contingent-noncontingent differentiation reached significance in the youngest and oldest age groups (9–12: T = 119, z = 2.13, p < .05, and 21–24: T = 140.5, z = 1.89, p < .05); self contingent and self noncontingent in all age groups (9–12: T = 120, z = 2.11, p < .02; 15–18: T = 133, z = 1.83, p < .05; 21–24: T = 142.5, z = 1.85, p < .05); noncontingent other and noncontingent self in the youngest age group (9–12: T = 121.5, z = 2.08, p < .05).

   Positive Vocalization. The infants were less likely to vocalize differentially than to smile differentially, as is illustrated by the nonsignificant overall stimulus effect and is seen in Table 3–3. Vocalizing increased with age, as did smiling, with the 9- to 12-month-olds vocalizing in over one-third of the trials; the 21- to 24-month-olds in over one-half.

There were no overall stimulus condition effects for any of the three age groups or for either the males or the females. In terms of the three comparisons, only the contingent-noncontingent differences reached significance, with the males vocalizing more often to the self contingent, the females to the noncontingent conditions total ($T = 377.5$, $z = 1.78$, $p < .05$; males: $T = 284.5$, $z = 1.78$, $p < .05$; and females: $T = 284.5$, $z = 2.27$, $p < .01$).

Summary.   Positive affect, but not negative affect, was exhibited differentially in the three conditions. Smiling and moving forward were more likely to be exhibited in the contingent than the noncontingent, in the self contingent than in the self noncontingent, and in the other noncontingent than in the self noncontingent conditions. Age trends were apparent, with differentiation increasing with age. Figure 3-5 pre-

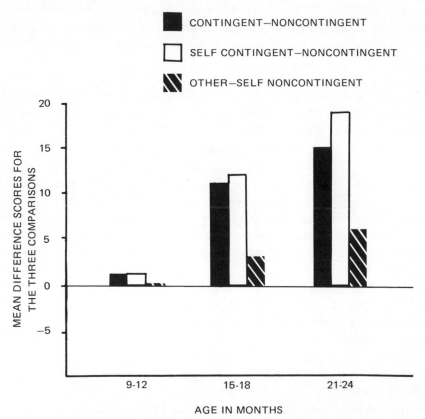

FIGURE 3-5.   Mean difference scores for smiling for the three comparisons.

sents the mean difference scores for smiling in the three comparisons as a function of age.

All three comparisons showed similar age changes. Smiling was not exhibited differentially by the 9- to 12-month-olds. Contingency was the feature that was most likely to produce positive affect in the 15- to 18- and 21- to 24-month-olds. At 21–24 months of age, however, features independent of contingency were effective in eliciting differential affect (self–other noncontingent comparison). Thus, contingency became salient at 15–18 months of age, perceptual features at 21–24 months of age (although a few 15- to 18-month-olds did differentiate self and other noncontingent representations).

Attention

Attention was measured by the incidence of a concentrate face and proportion of trial spent looking (total fixation/trial length). In general, the infants seemed to be very interested in the television images, as they exhibited a concentrate face in approximately 15% of the trials and looked for a total of approximately 44% of each trial. Table 3-4 presents the mean proportion of trial spent looking and mean proportion of trials in which an infant exhibited a concentrate face by stimulus conditions, age, and sex of subject.

Concentrate. As can be seen in Table 3-4, the concentrate expression was used differentially $[\chi^2(2) = 9.62, p < .01]$, and all three comparisons were significant (contingent and noncontingent: $T = 667.5, z = 3.88, p < .001$; self contingent and noncontingent: $T = 901, z = 2.62, p < .01$; and self and other noncontingent: $T = 619.5, z = 4.14, p < .001$). Concentrate expression was exhibited most often to the noncontingent other, next most often to the noncontingent self, and least to the contingent self condition.

Exhibiting a concentrate expression did not increase with age for all conditions, showing an increase only in the noncontingent other condition. In terms of age effects, the 9- to 12-month-olds did not differentiate between conditions, while the 15- to 18- and 21- to 24-month-olds did $[\chi^2(2) = 6.33, p < .05,$ and $\chi^2(2) = 5.24, p < .10]$ (see Tables 3-4 and 3-6). Both older age groups differentiated between contingent and noncontingent ($T = 36, p < .05,$ and $T = 97, z = 1.99, p < .05$) and between self and other noncontingent conditions, although this difference was only significant for the 15- to 18-month-olds ($T = 38, p < .05$). Neither age

Table 3-4

Mean Proportion of Trial Spent Looking, and Mean Proportion of Trial in Which Infants Exhibited a Concentrate Expression to the Stimulus Conditions by Age and Sex of Subject

Subjects	Stimulus condition			
	Contingent	Noncontingent	Noncontingent self	Noncontingent other
	Concentrate expression			
Total	.12	.17	.13	.20
9–12[a]	.11	.14	.13	.15
15–18[a]	.13	.15	.11	.20
21–24[a]	.12	.21	.15	.25
Male	.13	.19	.14	.22
Female	.11	.15	.12	.18
	Proportion of trial spent looking			
Total	.43	.45	.45	.46
9–12[a]	.38	.39	.38	.40
15–18[a]	.43	.46	.46	.47
21–24[a]	.47	.50	.50	.51
Male	.44	.46	.46	.46
Female	.42	.45	.43	.46

[a]Months.

group differentiated between self contingent and noncontingent conditions. Both males and females exhibited these trends.

Fixation. Although nonsignificant, the fixation data present a similar picture to the concentrate face data. Infants looked longer at the noncontingent than at the contingent conditions [proportion of trial attended to: $t(88) = 2.03$, $p < .05$] and somewhat longer at the other than the self noncontingent conditions, as can be seen in Table 3-4. Looking increased with age [$F(2,85) = 3.91$, $p < .02$] although no age and stimulus condition effects were found. No sex differences appeared either.

Summary. Unlike the affect and imitation measures, attention was most likely to be exhibited to the other noncontingent condition than to either of the self conditions. Interestingly, differentiation was greatest when the concentrate, rather than the fixation, measure was considered. Age affected the differential expression of concentration, with the 9- to 12-month-olds not differentiating among conditions, but the 15- to 18- and the 21- to 24-month-olds doing so.

Comparison of Measures

That positive affect was most likely to be exhibited in the contingent self condition, whereas attention was highest in the other noncontingent conditions, suggests that these different measures may be tapping different processes. Attending may have more to do with information seeking, namely, finding out about an unfamiliar stimulus. Therefore, interest is highest in the other child condition which portrays an unfamiliar person and lowest in the self conditions which portray a familiar person. On the other hand, a positive affective response may be related to recognition of a familiar stimulus as well as recognition of contingency. Lewis (1969) reported similar findings in a study of infants' responses to faces. In this study, infants in the first year of life *smiled* more at familiar representations of faces than at distortions of faces (unfamiliar face-like stimuli), whereas they *looked* at distortions more than familiar representations.

Taken together, these results suggest that both contingent and noncontingent self representations are differentiated from other noncontingent representations. More positive affect and more imitation are seen in the contingent, and more attention is seen in the noncontingent representations. In order to explore the contingent-noncontingent and the self–other dimensions further, a second videotape study was performed.

VIDEOTAPE STUDY II

Experimental Design

Subjects

Eighty-seven Caucasian infants representing four age groups were seen. The four age groups, each comprised of approximately 22 infants, were 9–12, 15–18, 21–24, and 30–36 months of age. The number of males and females in each age group were as follows: 9–12 months (12 females, 11 males), 15–18 months (10 females, 11 males), 21–24 months (12 females, 10 males), and 30–36 months (11 females, 10 males). The mean ages and age ranges for each age group in months were 11.47 (9.5–13.5), 16.34 (15.0–19.3), 22.24 (21.2–25.8), and 33.62 (30.0–37.0).

Subjects were recruited through newspaper advertisements and articles in the Princeton area. The subjects generally came from middle and upper-middle class backgrounds and were comparable to the samples collected in the mirror studies and Videotape Study I. Infants were equally likely to be firstborn or later-born, and all were full-term and healthy.

PROCEDURE

The infants and their mothers made two visits to the Infant Laboratory. During the first visit, a videotape of the infant was made. In the second, the experiment itself was run. The following instructions were read by the mothers for each visit:

This is a study on self recognition in infancy. On the first visit your child will be seated in front of a TV screen and will be shown a tape of some children playing with their mothers. You will be seated beside your child. While your child is watching the film, a girl will approach from behind. We are making a tape of this to show the child on the second visit; therefore, we don't want the child to turn around. When you see the girl approach, please direct the child's attention to the screen. It is imperative that the child not see the girl at this time.

During the second visit, you and your child will be seated in the same room as in the first visit. The lights will be dimmed and a tone will be turned on to cover any inadvertent noises. At first your child will see himself/herself live on the TV screen. While he/she is watching, a girl will approach from behind two or three times. It is okay if your child looks at her on this visit. If your child hasn't looked by the third approach, the girl will make some noises to get the child to notice her.

Following this there will be a series of situations on the TV screen of three different kinds: (1) TV videotape of the girl approaching behind another child, (2) the TV videotape of the girl approaching behind your child which we made on the first visit, and (3) a live TV condition in which your child watches himself and the girl will be approaching your child from behind. There will be a total of 12 conditions, presented in a random order.

Please do not talk to your child, except when you hear a knock on the side of the booth. Then you should point to the TV screen and say, "look!" until the child looks at the picture. (We can only change the picture while the child is looking at the screen. Otherwise, it is the child's business whether or not he or she wants to watch the TV.) Again, if you feel your child is upset, let us know so that we can stop the experiment.

The testing was conducted in a small enclosure that surrounded the infant on three sides. Each infant sat in a high chair which was one m from the television monitor. The mother was seated to the left and slightly behind her infant and could not be seen in the television monitor. The stranger entered from the back and to the right of the enclosure. Once the stranger had moved around the enclosure, she only moved her upper body toward the infant, thus minimizing the amount of movement noise associated with the approach. White noise was presented throughout the session in order to "cover up" any inadvertent noise the stranger made while approaching. With the white noise, adults sitting in the enclosure could not hear the stranger approach. Each approach lasted 5 (±1.5) sec so that the stranger's image was on the television monitor for about five sec per approach. Two different female strangers were used during the study, with each infant seeing only one of the strangers (no differences were found between the strangers).

Before the actual testing, a training procedure for turning toward the stranger was conducted. This was done since pretesting indicated that some of the infants would not turn to the stranger until the stranger had been pointed out to them; subsequently, they would turn without prompting. Thus, the infants were given a series of contingent (live) approaches. If, on the first or second training approach, the infant did not look, on the third training approach the stranger would knock on the side of the enclosure when she was in full view on the television monitor and when the infant was looking at the television monitor. Twenty-two percent of the sample spontaneously turned on one of the first two training approaches, with the majority of the sample not turning until the stranger knocked on the enclosure. Differences between these two groups (those who spontaneously turned and those who did not turn until the knock) will be discussed later. In addition, 19% of the sample did not turn toward the target during any of the training trials. Interestingly, no differences between infants who turned and those who did not turn during the training trials were found for the actual test approaches.

After the training procedure, infants received a number of trials representing four conditions: (1) contingent self or live approach, (2) noncontingent self approach (videotape), (3) noncontingent other approach (videotape), and (4) control trials (with no approaches). The noncontingent approaches were identical to the contingent approaches as seen on the television monitor, but, of course, a stranger was actually present in the contingent trials. The noncontingent other was always a same-sex, same-age child who had also been seen as a subject. The noncontingent other was rotated such that not all infants saw the same "other" child. This was done in order to control for differences in the actions of the noncontingent other. The order of presentation of the four conditions was counterbalanced across subjects such that one-quarter of the infants received one order, one-quarter a second order, etc. No presentation order differences were found.

Since the approaches were relatively short (in order to control for spontaneous turning not associated with the approach), infants sometimes "missed" an approach by not looking at the television monitor. This was most likely to occur in the noncontingent trials, as the videotapes of the noncontingent approaches could not be stopped or restarted during a specific trial. If the infant did not see the approach (which was embedded in the videotape of the noncontingent self and other), the next trial was presented. However, when approaches were missed, extra trials were added at the end of the session if the infant was not very fatigued or restless. Our criterion for completing the session was to have "seen" (i.e., looked at the television monitor during the time the approach was visible on the screen) at least two approaches in each of the three approach conditions (contingent self, noncontingent self, and noncontingent other).

MEASURES

A variety of measures were coded in the present study. Five different categories were represented: facial expression, vocalization, contingent play, turning behaviors connected with the stranger approach, and anticipatory turning behaviors. These five categories and the behaviors included in them are presented in Table 3-5.

Facial expressions included smiles and frowns, a smile being coded when the corners of the mouth turned upward and a frown when the corners of the mouth turned downward. Two types of vocalizations were coded: pleasant vocalizations (laugh, squeal, talk, coo, babble) and negative vocalizations (whimper, fret, cry, scream). Contingent play included deliberate facial and body movements that were performed while looking at the television screen. As in Videotape Study I, the two most common behaviors in this category were making faces and playing peek-a-boo games (moving one's face or body back and forth, into and out of the range of the television camera).

Turning behaviors included a wide range of turns, some of which resulted in seeing the stranger and some of which did not. The first was a complete head and body turn around the shoulder that would result in eye contact with the stranger if the stranger were present. The second was a half head turn toward the stranger's side, in which the head does not turn over the shoulder. It is difficult to ascertain whether this type of head turn would result in seeing the stranger, as infants may or may not

Table 3-5
Measures Used in Videtape Study II

Attention
  Looks at approach
  Does not look at approach
Facial expression
  Smile
  Frown
Vocalization
  Positive (laugh, giggle, coo, babble)
  Negative (cry, scream, whimper, fret)
Contingent play
Turning behaviors
  Complete right head turn (toward target)
  Partial right head turn (toward target)
  Right eye turn (toward target)
  Complete left turn (toward mother)
Anticipatory turning behaviors
  Complete right head turn (toward target)
  Partial right head turn (toward target)
  Right eye turn (toward target)
  Complete left turn (toward mother)

see the stranger from this position due to peripheral vision; however, adults taking this position were able to see the stranger through their peripheral vision. The third type of head turn was an eye turn, in which the eyes but not the head or body turn toward the stranger's side. This behavior occurred rarely. Turning to the mother (who was situated on the side opposite the approaching stranger) was also coded. All these turning behaviors were coded *as soon as* (but not before) the infant looked at the television screen after a stranger approach (either contingent or noncontingent) had begun. The infant's behavior was observed from the time the stranger appeared on the television screen, through the entire approach, and for the five sec following the approach. In addition, whether or not the infant looked at the television screen was noted, and only those trials in which the infant looked at the television screen during approach were included for data analysis. Anticipatory turning behavior included the same behaviors coded for turning behavior but were coded *prior to* the stranger approach for each trial (remember that the stranger approaches were embedded in each trial such that the infant experienced the contingent condition prior to the contingent approach, the noncontingent self condition prior to the noncontingent self approach, and so on; these prior sequences lasted from 5 to 10 sec).

INTEROBSERVER RELIABILITIES

Interobserver reliabilities were calculated by the number of agreements/numbr of agreements and disagreements (including omissions as disagreements) for each behavior for 15 subjects' data. Proportion of agreements for the two observers ranged from .75 for frown to .99 for positive vocalization. All the turning behaviors were over .80.

DATA ANALAYSIS

Each approach and the five sec following it were coded for the absence or presence of facial expressions, vocalizations, contingent play behavior, and turning behaviors. Only the trials in which the infants saw the approach on the television monitor were coded. The portion of each trial preceding the approach was coded for anticipatory turning behaviors. The proportion of trials in which each behavior occurred was calculated for each condition, by behavior and by subject. The mean data represent the proportion or percentage of trials in each approach condition in which a behavior occurred using the individual subjects' proportion data.

For each behavior, a mixed model analysis of variance was done with sex and age of subject being the independent variables and with stimulus condition (contingent, noncontingent self, and noncontingent other approaches) being the dependent variable. Dependent t tests were calculated for individual comparisons which were the same as those in Videotape Study I—the contingent and noncontingent, the self contingent and self noncontingent, and the noncontingent self and other comparisons. The results for the total sample, the age groups, and the males and females will be discussed for four different categories of behavior: affect (facial expression and vocalization), turning behavior (turns toward the mother and toward the target), anticipatory turning behavior, and contingent play. Then, the differences between subjects who spontaneously turned and those who turned after being cued during the training trials will be discussed.

RESULTS

HEAD-TURNING BEHAVIOR

Although all head-turning behaviors were examined, behaviors were collapsed for the following analysis. Thus, head turns to the right (toward the target) and to the left (toward the mother) are each presented. By definition, the category "right turns" is comprised of all target turns, including eye movements, partial head turns, and complete head turns. Approximately 90% of the turns were complete turns, 10% were partial turns, and less than 1% were eye movements. Few differences between partial and complete head turns appeared.[1]

Table 3-6 presents the mean proportion of trials in which subjects exhibited right and left turns by age, sex, and stimulus condition.

All Right Turns

As can be seen in Table 3-6, infants turned toward the target (to the right) in one-third to one-half of all the trials. This suggests that the experimental manipulation—the use of live and taped approaches of a stranger—was successful in eliciting turning responses in infants. Right head turns were exhibited differentially to the three stimulus conditions $[F(2, 172) = 12.03, p < .001]$. Infants turned to more of the contingent (live approach) than to the noncontingent (taped approach) conditions $[t(85) = 4.18, p < .001]$, and to the contingent self than the noncontingent self conditions $[t(85) = 4.41, p < .001]$, but were equally likely to turn to the noncontingent self and other conditions.

Although no overall main effect of age on turning toward the target appeared, age trends for specific stimulus conditions did. Turning toward the target increased over the three years for the noncontingent but not for the contingent conditions $[F(3, 85) - 3.35, p < .05]$. As can be seen in Table 3-6 this was true for both the noncontingent other and the

---

[1]However, two interesting differences between partial and target right turns did appear. First, infants were less likely to differentiate among conditions with respect to partial turns than target turns, with the stimulus condition effect being significant for only the latter $[F(2,172) = 16.97, p > .001]$. Second, infants were more likely to make partial turns to the noncontingent than to the contingent approaches [.05 versus .03; $t(85) = 2.32, p > .05$]. In contrast, target turns were more likely to be made in the contingent than in the noncontingent approaches [.46 versus .26; $t(85) = 4.87, p < .001$].

TABLE 3-6

Mean Proportion of Trials in Which Subjects Turned Right and Left by Age, Sex, and Stimulus Condition

Subjects	Stimulus condition			
	Contingent	Noncontingent	Noncontingent self	Noncontingent other
	All right turns (toward target)			
Total	.49	.32	.30	.36
9–12[a]	.54	.25	.19	.35
15–18[a]	.43	.22	.24	.19
21–24[a]	.48	.35	.35	.36
30–36[a]	.51	.46	.42	.52
Male	.46	.26	.24	.26
Female	.50	.38	.35	.40
	All left turns (toward mother)			
Total	.16	.29	.31	.24
9–12[a]	.17	.34	.41	.23
15–18[a]	.19	.34	.34	.33
21–24[a]	.16	.20	.19	.21
30–36[a]	.12	.24	.32	.19
Male	.12	.27	.29	.23
Female	.20	.30	.33	.25
	All anticipatory right turns (toward target)			
Total	.13	.07	.09	.06
9–12[a]	.12	.04	.04	.04
15–18[a]	.11	.03	.06	.01
21–24[a]	.13	.05	.05	.06
30–36[a]	.18	.10	.12	.07
Male	.14	.06	.07	.05
Female	.13	.05	.11	.08

[a]Months.

noncontingent self conditions. The increased turning to the noncontingent but not the contingent approaches resulted in a reduction in stimulus condition differentiation at the older ages. This can be seen in Figure 3-6, which presents the mean proportion difference scores between contingent and noncontingent conditions, between contingent

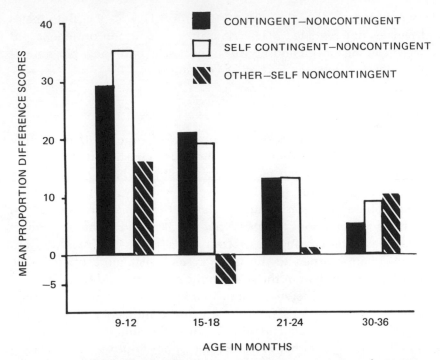

FIGURE 3-6.   Mean proportion difference scores for the three comparisons for target turns by age.

and noncontingent self conditions, and between noncontingent self and noncontingent other conditions for the four age groups.

Although all age groups were more likely to turn to the contingent than the noncontingent conditions and to the contingent self than the noncontingent self conditions, these differences were significant for the 9- to 12-month-olds, approached significance for the 15- to 18-month-olds (p's $< .10$), and were not significant for the two older age groups [9 12: $t(21) = 3.71$, $p < .01$, and $t(21) = 3.80$, $p < .01$]. The third comparison between noncontingent self and other did not yield orderly age changes or significant differences at any age. Thus, the only significant differences were found for the youngest age groups which, along with the fact that turning to the noncontingent conditions increased with age, suggests that only the youngest infants responded solely to the contingency cues.

No significant sex or sex × stimulus condition effects for turning to the target were found. However, the females were somewhat more likely to turn than were the males [$F(2,78) = 3.17$, $p < .05$]. Both males and females differentiated between contingent and noncontingent and between contingent self and noncontingent self conditions, but not between noncontingent self and other conditions.

All Left Turns

Turning toward the mother occurred less frequently than turning toward the target (20% versus 40% of the trials). Like turning toward the target, turning toward the mother was exhibited differentially in the three stimulus conditions [$F(2,172) = 7.54$, $p < .001$]. The infants turned to their mothers significantly more often in the noncontingent than in the contingent conditions [$t(85) = 3.54$, $p < .001$] and in the noncontingent self than in the contingent self conditions [$t(85) = 3.77$, $p < .001$]. In addition, infants turned to the mother somewhat more often in the noncontingent self than in the noncontingent other conditions [$t(85) = 1.84$, $p < .10$]. This difference is important because it suggests the relevance of specific features rather than just contingency cues in differentiating between self and other. Thus, the stimuli ordering of a turning toward the mother is exactly the opposite of that of a turning toward the stranger.

No age or age × stimulus condition interactions were found, as all age groups turned toward the mother equal amounts of time, and all exhibited differential turning. However, there was a nonsignificant tendency for the younger infants to turn toward their mothers more than the older infants. The overall differences between noncontingent and contingent approaches were found for all age groups, although the differences did not reach significance for all of them [9–12: $t(21) = 2.34$, $p < .05$; 15–18: $p < .10$; and 30–36: $t(19) = 2.35$, $p < .05$]. Differences between the contingent and noncontingent self were found for all age groups but only reached significance for the youngest and the oldest age groups [9–12: $t(21) = 2.68$, $p < .05$; 30–36: $t(19) = 3.83$, $p < .01$]. Differentiation of the noncontingent self and other conditions occurred in the youngest and oldest age groups, whereas the 15- to 18- and 21- to 24-month-olds did not exhibit these trends [9–12: $t(21) = 2.12$, $p < .05$; 30–36: $p < .10$].

No sex or sex × stimulus condition effects were found, as both males and females differentiated among the three conditions.

Comparisons of Turning toward Target and Mother

When infants were approached by a stranger in the contingent condition, they were three times as likely to turn toward the stranger as toward their mothers. This was true for all infants, regardless of age or gender. When the infants saw the taped approach in the noncontingent other condition, they were more likely to turn toward the stranger than toward the mother. When infants saw the taped approaches in the self noncontingent condition, the total sample was equally likely to turn toward the mother or the target. However, age differences emerged, such that the 9- to 12- and the 15- to 18-month-old infants were more likely to turn toward their mothers than toward the target, whereas the 21- to 24- and the 30- to 36-month-old infants were more likely to turn toward the target than toward their mothers.

Summary

In terms of eliciting turning to the approach of a stranger, our method proved successful. In terms of salience of dimensions, contingency appeared to be the most powerful elicitor of differential behavior. This was especially true for the 9- to 12- and the 15- to 18-month-olds. In the 21- to 24- and the 30- to 36-month-olds, turning behavior was also affected by the development of specific feature recognition.

Anticipatory Turning Behavior

Anticipatory turning behavior included all turns that occurred prior to the onset of the approach. Anticipatory turning suggests that the infant had an expectation that the stranger would appear on the television screen. The four behaviors that were measured for turning behavior were also measured for anticipatory head-turning behavior; these were left turns, right turns, target turns, and partial turns. Anticipatory partial and target turns, which together make up the right-turn category, each accounted for one-half of the anticipatory right-turn category, with similar results for the two categories. Remember that target turns accounted for 90%, and partial turns for 10% of the approach right turn category. This suggests that anticipatory turns were more often partial turns, reinforcing the idea that infants were expecting the approach to appear at any time, but did not believe that the person was present at that time.

In general, there were far fewer anticipatory turns than approach turns. Anticipatory turns toward the target occurred in 10% of all trials, anticipatory turns toward the mother in 3% of all trials. Not only did anticipatory turning toward the mother occur rarely, but it also was not exhibited differentially, and, therefore, the mean data will not be presented.

Anticipatory right-turn behavior was exhibited differentially, as is reflected in the significant stimulus condition effect [$F(2, 172) = 6.34$, $p < .01$]. These data are presented in Table 3-6. As can be seen in the table, infants were twice as likely to make anticipatory turns toward the target during the contingent as compared to the noncontingent conditions [$t(85) = 2.85$, $p < .01$] and in the contingent self as compared to the noncontingent self condition [$t(85) = 2.16$, $p < .05$]. Infants were somewhat more likely to turn to the noncontingent self than the noncontingent other, although this difference was not significant. No age or age × stimulus effects appeared, as all age groups turned more in the contingent than in the noncontingent and in the contingent self than in the noncontingent self conditions. The 15- to 18- and the 30- to 36-months-olds also turned more often in the noncontingent self than in the noncontingent other trials. Males and females exhibited similar trends for the three comparisons. Thus, the data for anticipatory turns were similar to approach turns.

AFFECTIVE BEHAVIORS

Four measures of affect were taken: smiling, positive vocalization, frowning, and fretting/crying. Table 3-7 presents the mean proportion of trials in which infants smiled, vocalized positively, and played contingently by age, sex, and stimulus condition.

Positive Affect

Infants smiled and vocalized positively in approximately 20% of the trials, suggesting that the approach of the stranger elicited only a moderate amount of positive affect, as can be seen in Table 3-7. This is in direct contrast to the Videotape Study I and Mirror Studies I and II, in

TABLE 3-7
Mean Proportion of Trials in Which Infants Exhibited Positive Affect and Contingent Play by Age, Sex, and Stimulus Condition

| | Stimulus condition | | | |
| | | | Noncontingent | Noncontingent |
Subjects	Contingent	Noncontingent	self	other
		Smile		
Total	.21	.22	.23	.20
9–12[a]	.16	.15	.13	.16
15–18[a]	.25	.16	.17	.13
21–24[a]	.18	.26	.30	.23
30–36[a]	.27	.29	.33	.26
Male	.23	.26	.27	.24
Female	.20	.17	.20	15
		Positive vocalization		
Total	.22	.24	.23	.24
9–12[a]	.13	.10	.07	.12
15–18[a]	.20	.16	.19	.13
21–24[a]	.14	.25	.17	.32
30–36[a]	.42	.47	.54	.40
Male	.22	.23	.23	.23
Female	.22	.25	.25	.25
		Contingent play		
Total	.21	.08	.09	.06
9–12[a]	.08	.05	.06	.04
15–18[a]	.22	.07	.06	.09
21–24[a]	.32	.10	.13	.08
30–36[a]	.24	.07	.11	.04
Male	.24	.06	.07	.05
Female	.19	.09	.11	.08

[a]Months.

which a great deal of positive responding occurred. The relative lack of positive affect may have been due to the presence of the stranger and the strange situation (i.e., a stranger quietly approaching from behind). Not only was there little positive affect, but there was also little differential use of it. For smiling, the overall stimulus effect was not significant, nor were any of the specific comparisons. Although there were no significant age effects, smiling tended to increase with age for the noncontingent self and the other conditions. The 9- to 18-month-olds smiled in approximately 15% of the noncontingent trials, the 21- to 36-month-olds in 27% of these trials. No such age trends were found for the contingent condition. Even with these age trends, no age or sex main effects or interactions effects were found. Similarly, positive vocalization was not exhibited differentially by the total sample. However, vocalization did increase with age [$F(3, 82) = 10.71$, $p < .001$] and did exhibit different response patterns over age [$F(6, 168) = 2.33$, $p < .05$]. The increase in vocalization was seen in all three stimulus conditions [contingent self: $F(3.83) = 4.61$, $p < .01$; noncontingent self: $F(3, 83) = 4.64$, $p < .01$; noncontingent other: $F(3, 83) = 12.68$, $p < .001$]. For the contingent and noncontingent self conditions, the largest age increase was between the 21- to 24- and the 30- to 36-month-olds, for the noncontingent other condition between the 15- to 18- and the 21- to 24-month-olds. The two younger age groups vocalized somewhat more to the contingent condition, the two older age groups somewhat more to the noncontingent conditions. These trends were not significant. No consistent or significant age trends were found for the noncontingent self–other comparison. There were no sex differences in positive vocalization.

Negative Affect

Both frowns and negative vocalizations occurred in approximately 10% of all trials (these data are not presented in tabular form). Thus, this procedure elicited more negative affect than most of our other procedures but did not elicit as much negative as positive affect. The higher incidence of negative affect may be due to the presence of the stranger, the type of approach used, and the novelty of the entire situation. In general, negative affect was not exhibited differentially to the three stimulus conditions. No overall age or age × stimulus interactions were found. However, negative vocalization tended to increase with age for the noncontingent other approach [$F(3, 83) = 3.25$, $p < .05$]. In addition, the 9- to 12-month-olds used negative vocalization differentially, as they were more likely to vocalize negatively during the noncontingent than during the contingent, and during the noncontingent self than in the contingent self approaches [$t(21) = 2.09$, $p < .05$; $t(21) = 2.15$, $p < .05$]. Perhaps the younger infants were more disturbed by the noncontingent approaches or perhaps they expected the stranger to be behind them and were disturbed when the stranger was not there.

Summary

Videotape Study II was less likely to elicit positive responses and more likely to elicit negative ones, in comparison to the mirror studies and to the first videotape study. These differences are probably due to the presence of the stranger in this study.

In general, the affect measures did not yield as consistent differentiation patterns as did the turning measures. There were no significant differences between conditions for the total sample for either positive or negative affect. However, age differences were seen as vocalization, both positive and negative, were more likely to exhibit age trends than facial expression, both smiles and frowns. In general, positive vocalization increased with age, although the younger infants vocalized to more of the contingent approaches, the older infants to the noncontingent approaches. In contrast, negative vocalization decreased with age, with the 9- to 12-month-olds fretting and crying more often to the noncontingent than to the contingent approaches.

CONTINGENT PLAY

One of the two imitation measures observed in the first videotape study was also examined in the present study. This measure was contingent play, which consisted of deliberate body or facial movements performed while looking at the television monitor, the most prevalent movements being making faces, sticking the tongue out, and playing peek-a-boo. Table 3-7 presents the mean proportion of trials in which contingent play (as well as smiles and positive vocalization) was exhibited by age, sex, and stimulus condition.

Contingent play was equally likely to occur in the present study as in the first videotape study, occurring in approximately 15% of the trials (as opposed to 16% in Videotape Study I). Again, contingent play exhibited dramatic stimulus differences [$F(2, 172) = 17.27$, $p < .001$]. The infants were more likely to play contingently in the contingent than in the noncontingent conditions [$t(85) = 5.31$, $p < .001$], and in the contingent self than in the noncontingent self approaches [$t(85) = 4.31$, $p < .001$]. Although the infants were somewhat more likely to play in the noncontingent self than in the other conditions, the trends were not significant. Thus, the ordering of the stimulus conditions was contingent

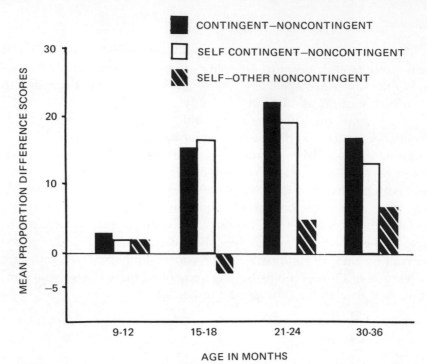

FIGURE 3-7. Mean proportion difference scores for the three comparisons for contingent play by age.

self, noncontingent self, and noncontingent other approach for contingent play.

Although there was no overall significant age effect, the incidence of contingent play changed with age, especially in the contingent condition [$F(3, 83) = 2.66$, $p < .10$]. Interestingly, it increased over the first two years and decreased somewhat in the third year, suggesting that interest in playing with contingency reaches a peak between 15 and 24 months of age. In terms of differentiation, all the infants, even the 9- to 12-month-olds, played more in the contingent than in the noncontingent and in the contingent self than in the noncontingent self conditions. The differences in the first comparison were significant for the three oldest age groups [15–18: $t(19) = 3.18$, $p < .01$; 21–24: $t(20) = 3.19$, $p < .01$; 30–36: $t(19) = 3.18$, $p < .01$], as were the differences for the second comparison [15–18: $t(19) = 2.60$, $p < .05$; 21–24: $t(20) = 2.66$, $p < .01$; 30–36: $t(19) = 2.10$, $p < .05$]. In addition, the four age groups all played more during the noncontingent self than during the noncontingent other approaches, although none of these differences reached significance. To illustrate the overwhelming preference for the contingent condition and the peak differentiation at 15–24 months of age, Figure 3-7 presents the mean proportion difference scores for the three comparisons by age.

No significant sex or sex × stimulus conditions were found, as both the males and females exhibited contingent play differentially to the three stimulus conditions.

TURNING BEHAVIOR DURING THE TRAINING AND TEST TRIALS

As stated previously, the test trials were preceded by a series of training trials. Infants received a number of contingent training approaches; if they did not turn spontaneously during the first two approaches, the stranger knocked on the enclosure. Only 22% of the sample turned spontaneously. We are interested in whether those infants who turned spontaneously differed from those who did not do so, in terms of their behavior during the test trials. Therefore, the infants were divided into two groups—spontaneous and nonspontaneous turners— and the differences between these two groups during the test trials were examined. Table 3-8 presents the mean proportion of turning scores for the test trials for the two groups by stimulus condition. As can be seen, the spontaneous group turned more frequently toward the target during

TABLE 3-8

Mean Proportion of Trials in Which Subjects Turned Right and Left by Stimulus Condition and Turning Group during Training

Subjects	Stimulus condition			
	Contingent	Noncontingent	Noncontingent self	Noncontingent other
	All right turns (toward target)			
Spontaneous	.62	.47	.52	.42
Nonspontaneous	.44	.28	.30	.27
	All left turns (toward mother)			
Spontaneous	.08	.20	.16	.19
Nonspontaneous	.18	.28	.22	.30

the test trials than did the nonspontaneous group, with the former group turning in approximately one-half of the trials, the latter in one-third of the trials. Differences between the two groups for target turning were found for all the stimulus conditions [contingent: $t(68) = 1.95$, $p < .10$; noncontingent: $t(68) = 2.50$, $p < .05$; noncontingent self: $t(68) = 2.40$, $p < .05$; noncontingent other: $t(68) = 1.89$, $p < .10$]. Although more target turning occurred in the spontaneous than in the nonspontaneous group, the differentiation patterns were the same for the two.

As is seen in Table 3-8, turning toward the mother exhibited the opposite pattern: the nonspontaneous group turned twice as often toward the mother as did the spontaneous group. However, the differences between the two groups were not significant, and the two groups exhibited similar differentiation patterns.

No differences with regard to anticipatory turning occurred; consequently these data were not presented in tabular form.

In short, infants who spontaneously turned toward the target during the training trials continued to turn toward the target more often during the test trials. In contrast, infants who did not turn during the training trials turned toward their mothers more often during the test trials. However, both groups exhibited the same response patterns and both differentiated among the stimulus conditions.

DISCUSSION

Videotape Studies I and II examined infants' responses to videotape representations of self and other. Two dimensions thought to be important for the development of self were explored in the videotape studies; these were contingent and noncontingent self representations and self–other noncontingent representations. The results from the two studies indicate that infants are able to differentiate between contingent and noncontingent self representations and between videotapes of themselves and other same-age, same-sex babies in the first two years of life. These differences, however, were affected by both response measure and age.

Age was especially important with regard to the two dimensions. First, infants as young as 9 months were able to respond to the contingency dimension and to differentiate between contingent and noncontingent representations, with the majority of infants doing so by 15 months of age. This finding corresponds nicely with our mirror findings on body- and mark-directed behaviors and with the findings of Papoušek and Papoušek (1974) on the early differentiation of contingent and noncontingent self representations. Second, although dependent on the test procedure, infants were able to differentiate between non-contingent representations of self and other by the middle of the second year, with the majority of the infants doing so by two years of age. Interestingly, we found this differentiation somewhat earlier than Amsterdam and Greenberg (1977), Bigelow (1975), and Zazzo (1948), who report that the ability to recognize a videotape or movie self representation as self does not occur until the end of the second year or the middle of the third year.

The videotape studies address two issues: how do infants respond to videotape representations of themselves and do their responses change with age; and how do infants respond to contingency and features cues and what is the developmental sequence (if any) of their use of these cues?

INFANTS' RESPONSES TO VIDEOTAPE REPRESENTATIONS

Infants' responses to videotape representations of themselves have never been described, just as infants' responses to mirror representations had not been described in great detail prior to this volume. Two issues are of interest in presenting a picture of infants' responses to videotapes. First, what do infants do when seeing their images represented contingently on a screen and, second, how does this differ from what they do when seeing themselves in a mirror? The mirror and contingent videotape conditions were similar in that they provided immediate feedback and reversed images; they were different in that the mirror image was in color, the videotape in black and white; the mirror provided a full-length representation, the videotape only a representation of the head and torso; and the infant could freely move around the room in the mirror setting but was seated in a high chair in the videotape setting.

The behavioral measures used in the two types of studies were somewhat different. Positive affect, interest and attention, and imitation were observed in the mirror and videotape studies. Mirror-directed and self-directed behaviors were coded in the mirror but not in the videotape studies. Interestingly, self-directed behavior was coded in the pretesting of the videotape studies but occurred so rarely that it was dropped as a measure. This finding provides additional support for our belief that touching the body and face in the rouge conditions of the mirror studies was related to the mark on the face, not just to the contingency cues offered by the mirror. In Videotape Study II, the additional behavior measure of turning toward an approaching stranger proved to be valuable. As always, the choice of behavioral measures in infancy is a difficult task because of the immaturity of the infants' response systems and the ambiguity of the meaning of certain responses.

The four primary measures in the Videotape Studies I and II will be discussed with reference to the mirror studies when appropriate. The four measures are affective responses, interest and attention, imitation, and turning responses.

Affective Responses

The overwhelming response to the videotape representations of self was one of pleasure and interest. In Videotape Study I, all infants smiled or vocalized positively at some time and very few cried or frowned. These pleasurable responses were similar to those found in mirror studies which have often been termed other-directed or playmate responses (Amsterdam, 1972; Gallup, 1977). Such responses were thought to represent a stage of development in which the infant perceived the image as another infant and which was thought to drop out of the infant's repertoire with the advent of self awareness. However, pleasureful responses did not decrease with age in the videotape studies and in fact dramatically increased with age in Videotape Study I. For example, 9- to 12-month-olds smiled in 23% of the contingent trials in Videotape Study I, whereas 21- to 24-month-olds smiled in 52% of them. In fact, positive affect increased at the same time that behaviors most indicative of self recognition were also increasing. Thus, the pleasure generated by videotape representations of self was enhanced by the recognition of the representation of self, rather than being replaced by self recognition. In addition, as suggested in Chapter 2, affective responses may be in the service of different motives, motives that change with age.

Although all infants exhibited positive affect sometime during both Videotape Studies I and II, positive affect occurred less frequently in the second than in the first videotape study. For example, smiling occurred in 38% of the contingent trials in Videotape Study I, 21% in Study II. What might account for this difference? First, the time period in which observations were made was longer in the first than in the second study. Remember that the absence or presence of behaviors was coded for the entire trial in Study I and only for the approach segment of the trial in Study II. Second, the use of a stranger approach in Study II may have dampened the positive responses to the videotapes.

Not only was positive affect less likely to be exhibited, but negative affect was also more likely to occur in Study II than in Study I. However, negative responses were infrequent, occurring in less than 10% of the trials and were characterized by frowns and whimpers, not by screams and cry faces. Again, the higher incidence of negative affect in Study II may have been due to the presence of the stranger and the type of approach (silent and from behind). Indeed, given the strangeness of the situation, it is somewhat surprising that more negative responses were not seen. This finding strengthens the premise of those investigators who believe that fear of strangers may not be a universal phenomenon (cf. Lewis & Brooks, 1974; Rheingold & Eckerman, 1973).

Interest and Attention

The infants also found the videotape conditions very interesting, as inferred through looking time and attentive faces. Infants in Study I looked at the television monitor almost 50% of each trial and infants in Study II missed (did not look at) very few approaches, indicating that they were directing a great deal of attention to the television monitor. Interestingly, looking time increased slightly over the first two years (from 39% at 9–12 to 49% at 21–24 months of age in Study I). This is in direct opposition to the mirror studies, in which the youngest infants looked at their mirror images longest. This may be due to the differences in complexity and familiarity of the two representations; seeing one's image in a mirror is a common and thoroughly explored occurrence, whereas seeing contingent and noncontingent video representations is an uncommon and complex experience. Thus, interest in the mirror may decline as knowledge about mirrors increases, but interest in the video may increase as differences between the conditions are perceived. Alternatively, the finding may be related to mobility—the infants were free to move away from the mirror and the older infants were more likely to do so; however, the infants were not free to move away from the video monitor (although they could turn away).

Imitation

Two different types of imitative behaviors were coded—contingent play in Videotape Studies I and II and imitating the videotape in Study I. Contingent play included facial movements and peek-a-boo games and was quite similar to the facial movement category in the mirror studies; imitation of the videotape image involved replicating a discrete action portrayed on the videotape and had no direct analog in the mirror studies. Infants receive quite different feedback from contingent play and imitation. Contingent play is used to observe and test the visual consequences of motoric actions (for example, moving off the television monitor screen); the use of contingent play illustrates the infant's understanding of the nature of contingency. Interestingly, infants did attempt to elicit contingent play responses from the noncontingent representations; they seemed to "test" the noncontingent images by attempting to play peek-a-boo. When the image did not respond, they immediately stopped playing. Imitating the videotape image indicates the infant's understanding of noncontingency; the image is not expected to reciprocate, as there is no one-to-one correspondence with one's own action. This is evident from the fact that, after infants repeated an action seen on the videotape, they did not exhibit any surprise (in the form of a surprise face) when the videotape image did not reciprocate. In the everyday world, other objects and people frequently do not imitate the infant's imitation; therefore, no expectancies for such behavior may exist. Thus, the use of contingent play and imitation indicate a growing awareness of the differences between contingent and noncontingent representations.

In addition, these two behaviors are similar to behaviors reported in the mirror image literature, for example the facial movement response observed in our mirror studies and in silly and self conscious responses observed by Amsterdam (1972) and Preyer (1893). At what age do such behaviors occur? Earlier investigators suggest that these behaviors reach a peak at 15 to 18 months and decrease thereafter. Our videotape studies indicate that such behavior occurs earlier and does not peak until the end of the second year. This was especially true of contingent play in both studies. For example, contingent play was exhibited by approximately 30% of the 9- to 12-month-olds, 60% of the 15- to 18-month-olds, and 90% of the 21- to 24-month-olds in Study I. These findings parallel those of our mirror studies, strengthening our belief that contingent play is not a precursor but rather an indicator of self knowledge and that the nature of contingency is of great interest throughout the first two years of life. This interest seems to decrease somewhat by the third year, as is evidenced in Videotape Study II.

Imitation of videotape images occurs somewhat later and is less prevalent than contingent play. However, infants in the second year of life clearly have the ability to imitate actions portrayed on a videotape, just as they are able to imitate gestures of others (Meltzoff & Moore, 1977; Uzgiris, 1978). For example, none of the 9-month-olds but almost one-quarter of the 12-month-olds imitated the videotape image in Videotape Study I. An increase in the imitation of others' gestures also occurs at the end of the first year of life.

Turning Behavior

Turning behavior was only observed in Videotape Study II and has no direct analogue in any of our other studies. This is true since Study II was designed to take advantage of this response system. However, the situation portrayed in the contingent condition of Study II is not unusual in that infants often see other people's images in the mirror. In fact, mothers will often play with their infants by holding them up in front of a mirror so that they can see both self and mother. Amsterdam's (1972) mirror study can be criticized because infants could see their mothers and the experimenter as well as themselves in the mirror, thus making it difficult to ascertain to whose image the infant was responding. And Bertenthal and Fischer (1978) used turning away from the mirror and toward an object portrayed in the mirror but suspended from the ceiling behind the infant as a measure of one developmental stage of self recognition.

At what age does turning away from the mirror image and toward an object or person occur? In Study II, the youngest infants, the 9- to 12-month-olds, had no difficulty with this task. However, it must be remembered that Study II infants were "primed" for this task by the training trials and that only 22% of the infants spontaneously turned in the training trials. No age differences in spontaneous turning occurred, as all age groups were likely to turn spontaneously. Bertenthal and Fischer (1978) report that turning toward an object suspended behind the infant was exhibited by most infants at approximately 14 to 16 months of age, the age at which mark-directed behavior first occurs in our mirror studies. Taken together, these two findings suggest that infants are able to turn toward objects somewhat earlier than they are able to locate a mark on the face. However, our findings also indicate that infants younger than one year of age are able to turn differentially, turning more in contingent than in noncontingent conditions, but that they need some experience with the procedure in order to do so. The unfamiliarity of the procedures also seemed to affect the older infants in Study II, suggesting that age *per se* was not the sole determinant of turning behavior.

DIMENSIONS OF SELF RECOGNITION

The infant's ability to respond to two dimensions (contingency and noncontingency, and self and other), which were thought to be important to the development of self, was explored through the use of video representations of self and other. Two questions were of interest: first, do children under two years of age respond differently to self representations differing with respect to the dimensions of contingency and noncontingency and self–other, and, second, does this ability differ by age, situation, and responses used to measure this ability?

Contingency-Noncontingency Dimension

The results from both videotape studies suggest that the infants did respond to the contingency-noncontingency dimension. In Videotape Study I, the sample as a whole was more likely to exhibit contingent play and to respond positively to the contingent than to the noncontingent conditions. Several investigators have reported that contingency, as offered by reflective surfaces, elicits positive affect; Rheingold (1971) found that 5-month-old infants responded more positively to a mirror than to a moving picture of a baby; Dixon (1957), Amsterdam (1972), and the infant intelligence test developers report that infants in the first year of life respond very positively to a mirror; and we saw in the last chapter that 9- to 24-month-olds are delighted by their mirror image. This is not surprising, since mirrors reflect back the behavior being exhibited, and many investigators find that a smile from another person elicits a smile from the young child (e.g., Brackbill, 1958; Kreutzer & Charlesworth, 1973; Wolff, 1963). In the present sample, the infants spent a great deal of time exploring the nature of contingency, a finding also reported in the mirror-image stimulation literature (Amsterdam, 1972; Dixon, 1957). However, these behaviors did occur, albeit infrequently, in the noncontingent conditions. It seemed as if the infants were "testing" the television image to see if it would respond; when it did not (as in the noncontingent conditions), the infants would quickly cease their testing. (If the length of time spent in this activity had been measured, it would have been much lower in the noncontingent than in the contingent conditions.)

Unlike contingent play and positive affect, attention was more prevalent in the noncontingent than in the contingent conditions. On the one hand, the infants may have watched the videotapes rather than actively interacted with them. The only related evidence comes from the work on peer relations, as infants often spend a great deal of time watching but not interacting with peers in small group situations (e.g., Lewis & Rosenblum, 1975). On the other hand, this greater attention may reflect the infant's responses to an unfamiliar event, a finding supported by the study of faces by Lewis (1969) in which infants smiled more at normal faced representations but looked more at distorted ones.

The infants also differentiated between the contingent and noncontingent conditions in Videotape Study II. Contingent play was exhibited in 21% of the contingent and 8% of the noncontingent trials, percentages that were almost identical to those in Study I. Infants were more likely to turn toward the target when the target was actually present (contingent condition) and more likely to turn toward the mother when the target was not present (noncontingent condition). These data suggest that infants have learned the meaning of contingency. Interestingly, positive affect was used in equal numbers of contingent and noncontingent conditions. This may have been due to the presence of the stranger, which is reflected in the fact that there were fewer affective responses in Study II than in Study I or in the mirror studies.

Age trends also appeared with respect to the contingency dimension. First, even the youngest age group, the 9- to 12-month-olds, responded differentially. The youngest infants were more likely to play contingently and were more likely to turn in the contingent conditions but were not likely to exhibit positive affect or attention in the contingent conditions. Thus, the youngest infants responded differentially, based on the measures that directly involved using the contingency but not the measures that did not. Interestingly, the 9- to 12-month-olds were more likely to fret in the noncontingent than in the contingent conditions in Study II; this was the only instance of negative affect being used differentially. Perhaps the young infants were more disturbed by the noncontingent approaches or perhaps they expected the stranger to be behind them.

Second, responses to contingency did not reach a peak in the middle of the second year, as some have suggested, but continued to increase over the first two years of life. There was some evidence of a decrease in responding to contingency in the third year, as the 30- to 36-month-olds were less likely to play contingently than the 21- to 24-month-olds in Study II. At the same time, the older infants were equally likely to smile and more likely to vocalize than the younger infants. Of course, the increase in vocalization is because all the 30- to 36-month-olds were quite verbal.

Self–Other Dimension

Were the infants also responding to the self–other dimension? Our results indicate that they were. In Videotape Study I, the infants smiled at, moved toward, and attended to the other more than in the self noncontingent condition, but they imitated and attempted contingent play more in the self- than in the other-noncontingent condition. Thus, affect and attention were directed toward the unfamiliar peer, whereas imitation was directed toward the self. The latter finding may indicate that the infants expected the tape of themselves to respond contingently, since their usual commerce is with mirrors. The affectual and attentional preference for the other tape suggests that the failure to produce contingency responses to the noncontingent self may elicit some avoidance behavior. Alternatively, more affect and attention to the noncontingent other stimulus may reflect the power of stranger infant/child faces to elicit positive affect. Again, the peer literature and the person perception literature suggest that other infants elicit a good deal of positive affect and attention in infants (e.g., Brooks & Lewis, 1976; Lewis & Brooks, 1974; Lewis & Rosenblum, 1975).

The findings from Study II were less clear-cut than those from Study I with regard to the self–other dimension. The sample as a whole was more likely to turn toward the mother and to play contingently in the self condition and to turn toward the target in the other noncontingent condition. Thus, the results with contingent play parallel those of Study I. The turning responses are interesting in that the subjects were more likely to be "fooled" by the other than by the self conditions, as evidenced by more turning to the stranger. Perhaps they understand the properties of contingency for themselves better than for others. At the same time, the infants turned more toward their mother in the self conditions. Perhaps seeing a noncontingent representation of self with a stranger approaching caused some surprise; hence, the turning toward the mother.

The age trends with respect to the self–other dimension suggest that differentiation between the noncontingent self and other representations involved learning the facial features specific to oneself in videotape representations. In Videotape Study I, differentiation of self and other occurred at 15–18 months of age, the same age that mark-directed behavior first appeared in the mirror studies. In Videotape Study II, contingent play was not used differentially until 21–24 months of age, perhaps because of the greater complexity of the procedure.

SUMMARY

As stated in the introduction to this chapter, the use of videotape systems allows us to examine the salience of several dimensions that probably contribute to visual knowledge of the self. We have suggested that three dimensions are central to the acquisition of this knowledge: the contingency cues offered by mirrors, the social categories that are common to the image, and the self and one's own specific perceptual features. In the videotape studies, we have explored the salience of two of these dimensions—contingency and specific perceptual features—while controlling for the third dimension (by using a same-age, same-sex baby as the other). The results of these two studies suggest the following developmental sequence in the use and salience of these two dimensions.

Contingency cues, which are present in the first representation of the self (the mirror), are the cues to which the infant first attends. Indeed, the infant finds contingency pleasurable and interesting from an early age, at least from four months of age on (Papoušek & Papoušek, 1974; Rheingold, 1971). By 9–12 months of age, some infants (over one-quarter in our sample) were exploring the nature of contingency as evidenced by contingent play responses; in addition, these infants were exhibiting only contingent play in contingency conditions. By 15–18 months of age, over three-quarters of the infants played contingently and used this response differentially. And by 21–24 months of age, almost all infants did so. In addition, the older infants used positive affect and attention differentially with regard to the contingency dimension. These infants, as well as the older ones, were also more likely to turn toward a target in contingent than in noncontingent conditions and to the mother in noncontingent than in contingent conditions. Thus, contingency was responded to at a very early age and continued to be important through-out the first two years of life.

Responding to specific perceptual features of the self did not seem to occur as early as responding to contingency. This ability first seemed to occur at 15–18 months of age and was established at 21–24 months of age, as evidenced by differential use of contingent play and imitates tape in Videotape Study I. Interestingly, this ability was seen later in the Study II procedure, a procedure that was relatively more complex. The 15- to 18- and 21- to 24-month-olds did not consistently dif-ferentiate between self and other on any measure, even contingent play. Clear differential responses were not seen until 30–36 months of age, at which time all three turning responses, smiling and vocalizing responses, and contingent play were used differentially.

CHAPTER 4

Pictorial Representations of Self and Others

In our society, the self is experienced visually in pictures as well as in reflective surfaces. Pictorial representations of the self are a medium in which self recognition may be observed and in which stimulus attributes, such as facial expression, size of image projected, amount of person shown (e.g., head versus entire body), and person attributes, such as age and sex, may be systematically varied or controlled. These attributes are very important, since preverbal children's ability to recognize themselves in pictures can be inferred only through their differential responses to pictures of self and of other. The other that is used for comparison purposes should be as similar to the self as possible, since differential responding may be elicited by person perceptions other than self perception. For example, infants respond quite differently to adults and children in live approach sequences (Brooks & Lewis, 1976; Greenberg, Hillman, & Grice, 1973; Lewis & Brooks, 1974) so that differential responses to pictures of self and adults or even to self and older children may not be indicative of self recognition but instead may be indicative of age differentiation. In Picture Studies I and II, infants' responses to pictures of themselves and of other same-aged and same-sex peers were compared in order to see whether, and at what ages, infants differentiate self from other and, by inference, recognize themselves.

As discussed in earlier chapters, we believe it useful to divide the self into two components: the existential and the categorical. Unlike mirrors, pictures offer the opportunity to explore the categorical as well as the existential self, since categories or attributes of the social world can be systematically varied in pictures. We have studied two social categories that seem to be salient from an early age for both self and other; these are gender and age. Infants' responses to pictures of themselves in comparison to peers and to different-aged persons (babies, children and adults, males and females) were examined in Picture Studies I and II. The two studies are very similar, Picture Study II serving as a replication of Picture Study I.

PICTURE STUDY I

EXPERIMENTAL PROCEDURES

SUBJECTS

Fifty-three infants (28 males and 25 females) were seen. Approximately half the infants (14 males, 14 females) were 10 to 12 months of age, the other half (14 males, 11 females) were 16 to 18 months of age. The mean age of the younger group was 11.07 months, the mean age of the older, 17.34 months. These two groups roughly correspond to the first two age groups (9–12 and 15–18 months of age) seen in the mirror and videotape studies.

All the infants were Caucasian, were full-term, and had no congenital defects. The parents of the infants were in their late 20s and early 30s and were well educated. Nineteen percent of the mothers had attended graduate school, 65% had attended college, and 15% had attended high school. Socioeconomic status was also high: 45% of the sample were in Hollingshead's Class I, 28% in Class II, 21% in Class III, and 6% in Class IV. Approximately two-thirds of the sample were firstborn, one-third later-born.

STIMULUS CONDITIONS

Ten 35 mm colored slides of persons were presented to each infant. The 10 social stimuli were (1) the mother of the infant, (2) the infant subject, (3) a female baby the same age as the subject, (4) a male baby the same age as the subject, (5) a female 5-year-old, (6) a male 5-year-old, (7) a female 10-year-old, (8) a male 10-year-old, (9) a female adult, and (10) a male adult. Each age group received different baby pictures (matched for the age of the subject) but received the same child and adult stranger pictures.

Seven to ten days before the experimental session, the slides of the mother and infant were taken in the infant's home. The experimenters set up a white cardboard sheet, which served as the background, and a lighting system that minimized light differences within the homes. Several pictures were taken of each subject. Only the head and upper torso area (neck and shoulders) were photographed. Head length of each stimulus person was constant and was approximately six to seven inches when projected onto a screen in front of the infant. Characteristics such as hair length, hair color, and eye color were not held constant.

Two sets of 10 pictures were shown to each infant. Six different presentation orders for the 10 slides were used so that eight infants received order 1, eight infants received order 2, and so on. No order effects were found. The slides were projected on a screen by rear-screen projection approximately one m in front of the infant. Each slide was projected for 15 sec with a 15-sec intertrial interval between pictures.

PROCEDURE

The following instructions were given to the mothers during the laboratory visit:

You will be sitting a few feet from your infant who will be in a high chair in front of the screen. We would like you to remain quiet during the session unless your infant does not look at a picture. Then, please point to the stimulus and say, "look" once. If he does not look, do *not* insist or repeat the instructions. Do not, under any circumstances, indicate recognition. Do not say, "look, there is mommy," etc. If your baby becomes restless or wants to get out of the chair, you may give him a toy (the mother had a choice of two toys, which were relatively uninteresting). After the first 10 pictures are shown, we will return to the playroom for five minutes. Then we will go back to view the second 10 pictures. Each set of pictures takes approximately five minutes to show, since each picture is projected for 15 seconds and there is a 15-second blank period between pictures. Three observers will be in the room with you. We will be watching your baby through three wire mesh holes. Any questions?

MEASURES

Three types of behavioral measures were coded: visual fixation, positive affect, and spontaneous utterances (the data on verbal labels are presented in Chapter 5). Visual fixation was determined by the position of the infant's eyes and was recorded continuously. Affect was coded as the presence or absence of three different categories of behaviors; these three were facial expression (smile), vocalization (laugh, coo/babble), and movement (points, waves, leans toward stimulus). No negative behaviors (e.g., frown, fret/cry, move away from the screen) were scored.

Scores were assigned to each behavior and were indicative of (1) no positive response, (2) slight positive response, and (3) very positive response. Thus, the behaviors were thought to represent a continuum. The specific behaviors within each category and the scores assigned to each are presented in Table 4-1. The presence or absence of each behavior was assessed twice during each stimulus condition, during the first half and the second half of the trial. The scores for each behavior category range from 2 (no response) to 6 (very positive response). One observer coded fixation, another affect; neither could see or knew which stimulus condition was on the screen.

INTEROBSERVER RELIABILITY

Two observers recorded fixation for eight subjects. Pearson Product Moment Correlations between observers were .97 for total fixation, .94 for first fixation, and .92 for number of looks. All the subjects were rated for affect by two observers; one observed all the subjects "live", one observed videotapes. Interrater reliabilities were calculated as the number of agreements/number of agreements and disagreements and

TABLE 4-1

Behaviors Observed and Scores Assigned to Each Behavior in the Picture Procedure

Behavior	Score
Facial expression	
Broad smile	3
Slight smile	2
No smile	1
Vocalization	
Laugh, squeal	3
Coo, babble, talk	2
No pleasant vocalization	1
Direction of movement	
Points, waves at stimulus	3
Leans forward toward stimulus	2
No forward movement	1

were .95 for facial expression, .94 for vocalization, and .97 for movement. In cases in which the two observers disagreed, consensus ratings were made and used for data analysis.

DATA ANALYSIS

The mean amount of first fixation, length or duration of fixation (total fixation/number of looks), and affect (the sum of the three affect scales scores, the range being 6 to 18) comprise the data. No consistent stimuli differences between the two sets were found, although the infants tended to look longer at the first set than at the second set. In addition, no interactions between set and stimuli appeared. In the light of the similarity of responses across the two sets, the data were averaged across the two sets of pictures for each subject.

Three comparisons were of interest: sex of stranger baby (whether or not infants differentiate between same-aged peers on the basis of gender), age of stranger (whether or not infants differentiate among unfamiliar babies, children, and adults), and self versus other (whether or not infants differentiate between themselves and peers). These comparisons were chosen on an *a priori* basis to reduce the number of comparisons being analyzed.

RESULTS[1]

AGE OF STRANGER COMPARISONS

The age of stranger comparison involved the ability to distinguish between three different classes of unfamiliar persons: babies the same age as the subject, children (5- and 10-year-olds), and adults of parenting age. Differences among the three stranger ages were tested using mixed model analyses of variance, whereas the paired comparisons (baby–child, baby–adult, child–adult) were tested using dependent *t* tests. The mean amount of positive affect, first fixation, and length of fixation are presented by age and sex of subject for the different-aged strangers in Table 4-2.

---

[1]The total fixation data for Picture Study I were reported in Lewis and Brooks (1975) and are not included here.

TABLE 4-2

Mean Amount of Affect and Fixation for the Age of Stranger Comparison

Subjects	Stimulus condition								
	Affect			First fixation			Length of fixation		
	Baby	Child	Adult	Baby	Child	Adult	Baby	Child	Adult
Total sample	7.97	7.56	7.56	4.46	4.20	4.92	3.84	3.39	4.42
Age of subject									
10–12 months	7.21	7.01	7.04	3.74	3.56	4.12	3.15	2.80	3.54
16–18 months	8.84	8.20	8.18	5.31	4.94	5.86	4.65	4.07	5.44
Sex of subject									
Male	8.27	7.88	7.80	4.22	4.01	3.99	3.56	3.14	3.63
Female	7.61	7.19	7.40	4.70	4.42	6.01	4.16	3.67	5.34

Analyses of Variance

Age and Sex of Subject Effects.   There were overall age of subject effects for all three measures such that both looking time and positive affect increased with age. As can be seen in Table 4-2, the 16- to 18-month-olds exhibited more positive affect and longer fixations—first look and length of fixation—than did the 10-to 12-month-olds [$F(1,49) = 10.50$, $p < .01; F(1,49) = 9.23, p < .05$; and $F(1,49) = 11.65, p < .01$].

There were also sex of subject effects such that the females looked at the stranger pictures longer than did the males [first fixation: $F(1,49) = 4.23, p < .05$ and length of fixation: $F(1,49) = 5.03, p < .05$]. There was also a sex of subject × age of subject interaction, as the 16- to 18-month-old females looked at the pictures longer than the same-aged males, whereas the 10- to 12-month-old males and females looked equal amounts of time [first fixation: $F(1,48) = 5.55, p < .05$ and length of fixation: $F(1,48) = 6.11, p < .05$]. The sex of the subject did not affect the expression of affect, although a sex of subject × age of subject interaction paralleled the one found for the fixation data [$F(1,48) = 3.63, p < .06$], that is, the 16- to 18-month-old females exhibited more positive affect than any other group.

Age of Stranger Effects.   The sample as a whole responded differently to the pictures of babies, children, and adults, as is illustrated by the significant age of stranger effects for affect, first fixation, and length of fixation [$F(2,102) = 4.93, p < .01; F(2,102) = 3.68, p < .05$; and $F(2,102) = 8.82, p < .001$, respectively].

There were also interactive effects for fixation measures. The females were more likely to differentiate among the stranger pictures than were the males [age of stranger × sex of subject-first fixation: $F(2,98) = 6.15, p < .01$ and length of fixation: $F(2,98) = 4.10, p < .05$]. In addition, the older females were more likely to exhibit differential looking than were the same-aged males or the younger subjects [age of stranger × age of subject × sex of subject-first fixation: $F(2,90) = 3.26, p < .05$].

Paired Comparisons

Baby-Adult Comparison.   As shown in Table 4-2, the sample as a whole responded differently to the pictures of babies and adults. The infants exhibited more positive affect to the baby pictures than to the adult pictures [$t(50) = 2.32$, $p < .05$], with the older infants being more likely to do so than the younger ones [$t(22) = 2.41$, $p < .05$]. Both males and females exhibited this trend, although the difference was significant for only the males [$t(26) = 2.39$, $p < .05$]. In contrast, infants looked at the adult pictures longer than the baby pictures [length of fixation: $t(50)$ = 2.37, $p < .05$ and first fixation: $p < .10$]. These findings were most pronounced in the older age group [length of fixation: $t(22) = 2.16$, p $< .05$] and for the female subjects [length of fixation: $t(22) = 3.40$, $p < .01$ and first fixation: $t(22) = 3.81$, $p < .001$].

Baby–Child Comparison. The infants also responded differently to the pictures of babies and children. More positive affect was exhibited to the baby than to the child pictures [$t(50) = 2.81$, $p < .01$], with the 16- to 18-month-olds being more likely than the 10- to 12-month-olds to exhibit this difference [$t(22) = 2.90$, $p < .01$]. Both males and females exhibited more positive affect to the babies, although this difference was significant only for the females [$t(22) = 2.22$, $p < .05$]. There was a tendency for the infants to look longer at the baby pictures than at the child pictures, although this trend did not reach significance (p's $< .10$).

Child–Adult Comparison. The infants did not exhibit differential amounts of positive affect to the child and adult pictures, as they had in the two previous comparisons. However, they did look at the adult pictures longer than at the child ones [first fixation: $t(50) = 2.60$, $p < .05$; length of fixation: $t(50) = 4.13$, $p < .001$], this was true for the younger as well as the older, and male as well as female infants (p's $< .10$).

Sex of Peer Comparison

The ability to differentiate between peers on the basis of gender was also explored. Each infant was presented with pictures of male and female same-aged peers (these means are not presented in tabular form). The infants did respond differently to the male and female peer pictures, but only in terms of fixation and only when the sex of the subject was taken into account. Neither the sample as a whole nor the two age groups differentiated between the male and female baby pictures. However, the females looked longer at the female baby pictures than at the male ones [first fixation: $t(22) = 2.42$, $p < .05$ and length of fixation: $t(22) = 2.27$, $p < .05$]. The males, on the other hand, looked somewhat longer at the male baby than at the female baby pictures.

Since these data suggest that there may be a sex of subject × sex of baby picture interaction, infants' responses to same-sex versus opposite-sex baby pictures were analyzed. The mean data for self, same-sex, and opposite-sex baby pictures are presented in Table 4-3 by age and sex of subject. When same-sex and opposite-sex baby picture means are compared, differences appear for looking time. The infants looked longer at pictures of same-sex babies than at opposite-sex ones [first fixation: $t(49)$ = 2.73, $p < .01$ and length of fixation: $t(49) = 2.85$, $p < .01$]. Both age groups exhibited this trend, although the differences did not reach significance for the 10- to 12-month-olds (p's $< .10$) but did so for the 16- to 18-month-olds [first fixation: $p < .10$ and length of fixation: $t(22) = 2.23$, $p < .05$]. These trends were more pronounced in the females than in the males, reaching significance only for the former [first fixation: $t(21) =$ 2.57, $p < .02$ and length of fixation: $t(21) = 2.37$, $p < .05$].

Self–Stranger Peer Comparison

Infants' responses to their own pictures and to those of strangers matched for age and sex were explored to see whether infants would differentiate between self and other. In Table 4-3, the mean data for the pictures of self, same-aged peer, same-sex peer, and opposite-sex peer are presented.

When the self and peer responses are compared, neither the affect nor the fixation behaviors were exhibited differentially to the pictures of self and same-age babies or to self and same-sex peers. However, differential responses were found when self and opposite-sex peers were compared. Infants looked longer at their own than at the opposite-sex peer picture [first fixation: $t(49) = 2.14$, $p < .05$ and length of fixation: $t(49) = 2.12$, $p < .05$]. These differences were exhibited by both age groups, although they did not reach significance for either age group separately. The differences were exhibited by both males and females but only reached significance for the females [first fixation: $t(21) = 2.69$, p $< .02$ and length of fixation: $t(21) = 2.18$, $p < .05$].

PICTURE STUDY II

A 21- to 24-month-old age group was included in Picture Study II to see whether older infants could recognize themselves without the use of any contingent feedback, since infants in the first study only dif-

TABLE 4-3
Mean Amount of Affect and Fixation for the Self–Peer Comparisons

Subjects	Affect				First fixation				Length of fixation			
	Self	Same-age peer	Same-sex peer	Opposite-sex peer	Self	Same-age peer	Same-sex peer	Opposite-sex peer	Self	Same-age peer	Same-sex peer	Opposite-sex peer
Total sample	7.96	7.67	7.78	8.21	4.75	4.46	5.05	3.97	4.05	3.84	4.41	3.32
Age of subject												
10–12 months	7.52	7.21	7.40	7.02	3.93	3.74	4.24	3.35	3.39	3.15	3.50	2.85
16–18 months	8.38	8.84	8.19	9.50	5.71	5.31	5.96	4.66	4.82	4.65	5.43	3.86
Sex of subject												
Male	8.16	8.27	8.02	8.52	4.29	4.22	4.48	3.96	3.71	3.56	3.90	3.23
Female	7.63	7.61	7.43	7.82	5.29	4.75	5.74	3.98	4.45	4.16	5.03	3.44

ferentiated between self and opposite-sex peer, and only in terms of looking time. In a small pilot sample ($N = 10$) of 22-month-olds who were tested using the Picture I procedure, differential responses to self versus same-age peers were found. Specifically, these infants tended to look at and be more positive to the pictures of themselves than to those of their peers (p's < .10 for first fixation, duration of fixation, and positive affect). Therefore, we included an older age group in Picture Study II to confirm our pilot test findings and to have our picture data correspond with our mirror and videotape studies by including the same age range. In addition, we wished to replicate the original findings from Picture Study I.

EXPERIMENTAL PROCEDURE

SUBJECTS

Seventy infants (34 males and 36 females) were seen. Approximately one-third were 9–12 months of age (11 males, 12 females), one-third were 15–18 months (12 males, 12 females), and one-third were 21–24 months (11 males, 12 females). The mean ages and age ranges were as follows: 11.46 months (9.3–13.5), 17.20 months (15.0–19.3), and 23.44 months (21.0–25.3).

All of the infants were Caucasian. As in our other studies, socioeconomic status tended to be high; two-thirds of the families were in Hollingshead's two highest classes. Approximately one-half of the sample was firstborn, one-half later-born.

STIMULUS CONDITIONS

The stimulus conditions were similar to those in Study I with a few exceptions. First, the 10-year-old child strangers were not included. Instead, slides of a very young baby (8 months of age) and of the child's father were included. The social stimuli were: (1) the mother of the infant, (2) the father of the infant, (3) the infant, (4) an 8-month-old strange infant, (5) a strange female peer, (6) a strange male peer, (7) a strange female 5-year-old, (8) a strange male 5-year-old, (9) a strange female adult, and (10) a strange male adult. Thus, the social stimuli included familiar and unfamiliar persons and persons varying in age and gender. As before, the slides were equated on the basis of head size, light intensity, and facial expression. Characteristics such as hair length, hair color, and eye color were not held constant.

The procedures were similar to Picture Study I. Each infant saw two sets of ten pictures. Each set contained different strangers so that there were two representations of each stranger category. Each slide was shown for 15 sec with a 15-sec intertrial interval. The order of slide presentation was counterbalanced using four orders such that one-quarter of the subjects received each order. As in Picture Study I, no order effects or set effects were found. Thus, order was not considered further, and the data for the two sets were averaged for all subsequent data analyses.

MEASURES

Fixation and affect were coded in Picture Study II in the same manner as they had been in the first study. Fixation was recorded continuously, with first fixation and duration of fixation (total fixation/number of looks) being used as measures. Facial expression and vocalization, including both positive and negative behaviors, were also coded. For facial expression, smiles (corners of the mouth turned up) and frowns (corners of the mouth turned down) were coded. Vocalization included positive vocalizations (laugh, talk, coo, babble) and negative ones (whimper, fret, cry). However, negative vocalizations occurred so rarely that analyses were impossible. The absence or presence of each of the affect measures was recorded every five sec, or three times during each 15-sec trial. Thus, for each trial, scores on each affect measure ranged from zero to three.

INTEROBSERVER RELIABILITY

Interobserver reliability for the fixation measures was over .90 (Pearson Product Moment Correlations for ten subjects). The measurement of affect needed extensive training before interobserver reliabilities were satisfactory. Interobserver reliabilities were calculated as the number of agreements/number of agreements and disagreements for each of the behaviors. The reliabilities for ten subjects were .80 for frown, .87 for smile, and .92 for positive vocalization.

DATA ANALYSIS

Four comparisons were of interest: (1) sex of peer (whether or not infants differentiate between same-aged peers on the basis of gender), (2) age of stranger (whether or not infants respond differently to babies, children, and adults), (3) self versus other (whether or not infants respond differently to themselves and same-age peers), and (4) age of baby (whether or not infants respond differently to a young infant and a same-age peer). The first three comparisons were identical to those in Picture Study I. Five measures were examined: first fixation, duration of fixation, smile, frown, and positive vocalization.

RESULTS

AGE OF STRANGER COMPARISON

Table 4-4 presents the mean number of five-sec intervals (range, 0 to 3) in which infants smiled or vocalized and the mean amount of first fixation and total amount of fixation for baby, child, and adult conditions by age and sex of the subject. The data for frowning are not presented in Table 4-4 since the frequency of occurrence was so low (the means for the sample as a whole ranged from .003 to .03).

Analyses of Variance

Age and Sex of Subject Effects. No significant age or sex of subject effects were found for the affect or fixation measures. However, smiling did tend to increase over the three age groups [$F(2,65) = 2.92$, $p < .06$], and males tended to look at the stranger pictures longer than did the females [length of fixation: $F(1,59) = 3.43$, $p < .07$].

Age of Stranger Effects. There was no overall age of stranger effect for the sample as a whole. When differentiation among the three strangers occurred, it tended to be related to age, as is reflected in the nearly significant age of stranger × age of subject interactions for vocalization [$F(4,130) = 2.14$, $p < .08$] and length of fixation [$F(4,118) = 2.05$, $p < .09$].

Paired Comparisons

Baby–Adult Stranger. Infants tended to smile more often at the pictures of strange babies than adults. The two older age groups exhibited

TABLE 4-4
Mean Amount of Positive Affect and Visual Fixation for the Stranger Comparisons

Stimulus condition

Subjects	Smile			Vocalization			Fixed fixation			Length of fixation		
	Baby	Child	Adult	Baby	Child	Adult	Baby	Child	Adult	Baby	Child	Adult
Total sample	.73	.71	.62	.17	.13	.15	5.91	6.31	6.00	5.15	5.49	5.27
Age of subject												
9–12 months	.49	.67	.60	.16	.17	.11	4.98	5.58	5.96	4.31	4.48	5.17
15–18 months	.69	.55	.46	.15	.11	.15	6.61	7.05	5.55	5.46	6.24	4.84
21–24 months	1.01	.92	.80	.20	.11	.17	6.10	6.28	6.51	5.66	5.71	5.81
Sex of subject												
Male	.70	.71	.68	.17	.14	.13	6.42	6.90	6.49	5.48	6.14	5.80
Female	.76	.72	.56	.17	.13	.16	5.42	5.76	5.53	4.84	4.87	4.76

Subjects	Smile		Vocalization		Fixed fixation		Length of fixation	
	Male baby	Female baby	Male baby	Female baby	Male baby	Female baby	Male baby	Female baby
Total sample	.69	.78	.19	.15	6.46	5.53	5.75	4.73
Age of subject								
9–12 months	.54	.45	.15	.17	5.83	4.48	5.35	3.62
15–18 months	.56	.81	.20	.09	7.63	5.54	6.44	4.55
21–24 months	.96	1.07	.22	.18	5.80	6.52	5.38	6.04
Sex of subject								
Male	.71	.71	.20	.14	7.21	5.83	6.32	4.90
Female	.67	.85	.18	.15	5.74	5.26	5.20	4.62

this trend [15- to 18-month-olds: $t(23) = 2.35$, $p < .05$; and 21- to 24-month-olds: $p < .10$], although the 9- to 12-month-olds did not. No other affect measures were used differentially.

There were no differences in fixation for the total sample. However, the 15- to 18-month-olds tended to look at the baby pictures longer than at the adult pictures [first fixation: $t(23) = 2.39$, $p < .05$]. No sex of subject differences were found for any of the measures.

Child–Adult Stranger.   Infants tended to smile more at the child than at the adult stranger pictures, although none of the differences were significant. Conversely, infants were more likely to frown at the adult than at the child strangers (p's $< .10$), although the mean amount of frowning was very low (adult stranger $M, .02$, and child stranger $M, .003$). In terms of positive vocalization, the 9- to 12-month-olds vocalized more to the child, whereas the 15- to 18- and 21- to 24-month-olds vocalized more to the adult (p's $< .10$). This trend may reflect the fact that the older infants, those with language capabilities, were more likely to label the adult than the child strangers, as we shall see in the following chapter.

Although fixation was not used differentially by the sample as a whole, the 15- to 18-month-olds looked at the child longer than at the adult stranger [first fixation: $t(23) = 2.58$, $p < .05$]. The males and females responded to the child and adult stranger pictures similarly. The only exception was that females smiled more often at the child than at the adult ($p < .10$), but the males did not.

Baby–Child Stranger.   The infants smiled and frowned at the baby and child stranger pictures equally often. However, the infants tended to vocalize to the baby pictures more often than to the child pictures ($p < .10$). This was true of the older but not the younger infants ($p < .10$). These age differences were probably because the infants over 15 months of age were more likely to verbally label the baby than the child stranger pictures, as we shall see in Chapter 5.

The fixation measures were not used differentially.

SEX OF PEER COMPARISON

The ability to differentiate between peers on the basis of gender was explored (these data are not presented in tabular form). No consistent trends for smiling or positive vocalization were found. However, male subjects tended to frown more often at the male than at the female baby pictures (M, .06 versus .03), and, conversely, the female subjects tended to frown more to the female than to the male pictures (M, .04 versus .00), although these differences did not reach significance (p's < .10).

In terms of attention, the infants tended to look longer at the male than at the female baby stranger (p's < .10). These trends were exhibited by the 9- to 12-month-olds (p's < .10) and the 15- to 18-month-olds [duration of fixation: $t(23) = 2.08$, $p < .05$ and first fixation: $t(23) = 2.32$, $p < .05$]. This was not true of the 21- to 24-month-olds. Although male and female infants tended to look at the male babies longer than at the female babies, the effect was more pronounced for the males ($p < .10$) than for the females.

Since we found a sex of subject and sex of baby picture interaction in Picture Study I, infants' responses to the same-sex versus opposite-sex baby pictures were analyzed. The mean data for this comparison are presented in Table 4-5. The results from Picture Study I were partially replicated by the findings of Picture Study II. The 15- to 18-month-olds smiled and vocalized more often to but did not look more at the same-sex than at the opposite-sex baby pictures [smile: $t(23) = 2.07$, $p < .05$ and vocalize: $p < .10$].

AGE OF BABY COMPARISON

Unlike Picture Study I, Picture Study II included a picture of an 8-month-old baby, as well as pictures of babies the same age as the infant. Would the infants respond differently to younger babies than to babies the same age as themselves? Few differences were found. Infants vocalized more often to the older than to the younger baby pictures [.17 versus .11, $t(68) = 2.36$, $p < .05$], although they did not smile or frown more often to one or the other. In terms of attention, the female infants, but not the male infants, looked longer at the older than at the younger baby pictures [first fixation: $t(34) = 1.85$, $p < .10$ and length of fixation: $t(34) = 2.14$, $p < .05$].

SELF–STRANGER PEER COMPARISON

The self–other comparison involved the infant's ability to differentiate between pictures of self and other with age held constant. Table 4-5 presents the mean number of 5 sec intervals in which positive affect occurred and the mean amount of fixation for the pictures of self, same-aged peer, same-sex peer, and opposite-sex peer by age and sex of subject.

TABLE 4-5

Mean Amount of Positive Affect and Visual Fixation for the Self–Peer Comparisons

	Smile				Vocalization				First fixation				Length of fixation			
	Self	Same-age peer	Same-sex peer	Opposite-sex peer	Self	Same-age peer	Same-sex peer	Opposite-sex peer	Self	Same-age peer	Same-sex peer	Opposite-sex peer	Self	Same-age peer	Same-sex peer	Opposite-sex peer
Total	.68	.73	.78	.69	.17	.17	.18	.16	6.56	5.91	6.20	5.78	5.64	5.15	5.43	5.05
Age of subject																
9–12[a]	.61	.49	.52	.48	.17	.16	.14	.18	6.50	4.98	4.70	5.60	4.70	4.31	4.46	4.69
15–18[a]	.31	.69	.85	.52	.20	.14	.20	.09	5.92	6.61	7.23	5.96	5.54	5.46	5.80	5.22
21–24[a]	1.13	1.01	.96	1.07	.13	.20	.18	.22	7.28	6.10	6.54	5.77	6.66	5.66	5.98	5.44
Sex of subject																
Male	.64	.70	.71	.71	.20	.17	.20	.14	6.88	6.42	7.21	5.83	6.06	5.48	6.32	4.90
Female	.72	.76	.85	.67	.14	.17	.15	.18	6.24	5.42	5.26	5.74	5.73	4.84	4.62	5.20

[a]Months.

For the self–same-aged peer comparison, the sample as a whole did not use smiling or positive vocalization differentially. Interestingly, an age × stimulus condition interaction for smiling indicated that the youngest and oldest infants tended to smile more often at the self than at the other (p's $< .10$) and the 15- to 18-month-olds more to the other than to the self [$t(23) = 3.24$, $p < .01$]. The 15- to 18-month-olds smiled at themselves very infrequently, as compared to the other age groups (see Table 4-5). In addition to smiling at their own picture more often than at others' pictures, the infants tended to frown more often at the peer than at the self picture ($p < .10$), with this trend being evident in all three age groups.

In terms of attention, the infants tended to look longer at the self than at the peer, although this trend was not significant for the total sample. The 9- to 12- and the 21- to 24-month-olds looked at their own picture longer than at the picture of their peer (first fixation: p's $< .10$). The 15- to 18-month-olds exhibited an opposite, although nonsignificant trend.

Thus, the 9- to 12- and 21- to 24-month-olds were likely to smile and look at their own picture more than at the peer pictures, whereas the 15- to 18-month-olds exhibited the opposite trend. All infants, however, tended to frown more often at the peer than at the self picture.

Like Study I, the infants responded to the self and same-sex baby pictures similarly. Unlike Study I, no overall self–opposite-sex baby picture differences were found except for the 15- to 18-month-olds. As we saw earlier, the 15- to 18-month-olds, but not the other two age groups, responded more to the same-sex than to the opposite-sex baby picture in terms of affect. This age group also vocalized more to self than to opposite-sex baby pictures ($p < .10$). At the same time, the 15- to 18-month-olds smiled more at the same-sex than at the self baby pictures [$t(23) = 3.24$, $p < .01$]. There were no affect differences for the other two age groups.

In terms of attention, no effects were found for self in comparison to same-sex or opposite-sex baby pictures.

Discussion

Picture Studies I and II investigated the ability of infants to distinguish between pictorial representations of people differing with respect to age, sex, and familiarity. In Chapters 2 and 3, we saw that infants as young as one year of age are able to differentiate between different-aged strangers in live approach sequences and to recognize themselves in a mirror. Would infants in the first year of life be able to do so with pictorial representations and, if not, at what age would these abilities develop? Visual self recognition and person differentiation in pictorial representations are demanding tasks, since many "people" cues such as three-dimensionality, height, movement, vocalization, and gestural changes are not available in pictures. In our studies, the pictures were of the face and shoulder area and included facial configuration and facial and hair coloring as possible cues. Not only are fewer cues present, but infants have had less experience with pictures than with reflective surfaces. Many of our mothers reported that their infants see pictures of themselves and other familiar people very infrequently, and many believed that their infants could not recognize themselves in pictures but could recognize themselves in mirror images. Thus, the picture studies may involve the infant's ability to generalize from one situation to another, to represent persons in other forms, to recognize themselves without the aid of contingent feedback, and to use feature recognition rather than contingency cues.

We will discuss four issues: (1) the consistency of results across the two studies, (2) the use of age as a social category, (3) the use of gender as a social category, and (4) the ability to recognize oneself pictorially.

REPLICATION OF RESULTS

The use of two studies allows for a replication of our original findings and for a closer examination of age trends. Remember that an overall affect score (based on facial expression, vocalization, and movement) was used in Study I, but specific facial expressions and vocalizations (smile, frown, positive vocalization) were coded in Study II. First fixation and duration of fixation were the measures of attention in both studies. Common to all three comparisons is the fact that the data using affect and fixation measures were not always identical, nor did the data covary systematically. In some cases, infants may smile and look at one stimulus longer than at the other; in other cases, they may smile longer at one and look longer at another; and in still other cases, they may smile longer at one and look at the two for equal amounts of time.

Age of Stranger Comparisons

The findings from both studies suggest that infants are able to discriminate among different-aged strangers. In both studies, the baby pictures were responded to more positively than the child or adult pictures. The fixation differences were not as strong for the sample as a whole, although, in general, adults were looked at longer than infants. The comparison between pictures of infants and children revealed that babies are smiled and looked at more than children. More positive affect and less negative affect were expressed to pictures of babies than pictures of children and to pictures of children than to pictures of adults. On the other hand, infants looked somewhat longer at adult strangers than at younger strangers. Interestingly, it was the 15- to 18-month-olds in both studies who were most likely to differentiate between baby and other. Differentiation of children and adult strangers was also found in both studies. Specifically, the adults were looked at longer than the children and, in Study II, also were frowned at and vocalized to more.

Sex of Baby Comparisons

The most surprising finding in Picture Study I was that the infants, particularily the 15- to 18-month-olds, looked at the same-sex baby picture longer than at the opposite-sex baby picture. The same trend was found in Picture Study II, as the 15- to 18-month-olds vocalized more often at the same-sex than at the opposite-sex baby pictures. However, it must be remembered that these findings are not consistent across measures. Gender may be a salient feature between the ages of 15 and 18 months, although additional research is necessary.

Self–Stranger Baby Comparison

In the small pilot sample discussed earlier, the 22-month-olds looked more and acted more positively to their own picture than to that of a same-age peer. In Study II, the same age group (21- to 24-month-olds) smiled and looked more at the self than at the matched other. Taken together, these findings suggest that by 21 months of age, self–other differentiation in pictures is clearly established. But what about the younger infants? Although Study I found no differences for the self–

other comparison, the 9- to 12-month-olds smiled more at the picture of self. Interestingly, the 15- to 18-month-olds did just the opposite. To strengthen the finding that infants even under 21 months of age can differentiate between pictures of self and pictures of other is the fact that the Study II infants frowned more often at the other than at the self.

The self–opposite-sex baby picture comparison did not yield consistent results across the two studies nor did the self–same-sex peer comparison.

Summary

In short, the two studies yielded fairly consistent results, indicating that infants can differentiate between different-aged strangers, between self and same-aged peers, and, to a lesser extent, between same- and opposite-sex peers. These findings were heavily influenced by the age of the infant. First, the age trends indicate the 15- to 18-month-olds were most likely to differentiate among conditions. Remember that 15 to 18 months is the time during which self recognition appears in the videotape and mirror procedures. Perhaps the awareness of the self, as having a distinct visual identity sharing social categories with others, brings with it an increased interest in social categories such as age and sex.

Second, the age trends also suggest, at least in the second study, that infants as young as 9–12 months of age appear to show some differentiation between pictures of self and of other. Finally, the age trends suggest that at the time clear self recognition first appears (about 15 to 18 months of age), pictures of self do not elicit a great deal of pleasure. In the second study, the lowest amount of smiling to any baby picture was exhibited by the 15- to 18-month-olds to the picture of self. However, the decrease in smiling was not coupled with an increase in frowning. The low level of smiling may be related to the increase in self consciousness and self awareness of facial features seen at this time in the mirror and videotape studies. This hypothesis is partially substantiated in that the 15- to 18-month-olds in Study II exhibited concentrate expressions more often in the self than in the baby picture conditions [M (range 0 to 3), .77 versus .49, $p < .10$]. Alternatively, the 21- to 24-month-olds, who smiled more at their own pictures, exhibited more concentrate expressions in the baby picture conditions [M, .50 versus .24, $t(22) = 2.49$, $p < .05$].[2]

AGE AS A SOCIAL CATEGORY

The picture studies, in conjunction with other work, present fairly substantial evidence of the importance of age in infants' social categorizations. Research using actual persons rather than representations has shown that infants differentiate between different-aged strangers and prefer young to old strangers (Brooks & Lewis, 1976; Greenberg *et al.*, 1973; Lewis & Brooks, 1974; Lewis *et al.*, 1975). The present studies and that of Fagan (1972) demonstrate similar findings using pictorial representations. In addition, this preference for the young (as inferred through more positive affective and approach responses) is seen by at least the second half of the first year.

Interestingly, the different studies have used different-aged strangers: the live approach studies used preschoolers, not babies as the youngest age point; and the peer/friendship studies and the pictorial representation studies used same-aged peers as the youngest age point. Most studies only used two age groups: young (baby or child) and old (adult). In the present studies, babies, children, and adults were all included as age points. When all three are used, infants respond more positively to babies than to children or adults, and somewhat more positively to children than to adults, whereas they look at adults and babies longer than at children. Children seem to be in an intermediate position, eliciting less interest than the other strangers and less affect than the babies. Perhaps children are more difficult to categorize than babies or adults, since they may share features of both babies and adults.

To what features are infants responding when they differentiate between different-aged strangers? Age encompasses numerous biological and cultural features, including vocalization patterns, syntax, intonations, height, body proportion, movement, facial configuration, facial expression, and hair and dress styles. Infants may be attending to one feature or some combination of them. In addition, the use of these features probably changes over time so that infants are attending to

[2]Concentrate expressions (mouth shaped like "O", a square, or an ellipse) were also coded for the present study. However, since the interobserver reliabilities for the measure were somewhat low (.70) and since the measure did not differentiate among conditions (with the exception of the finding reported here), these data were not presented.

different features at different ages or become more likely to integrate features with increasing age and information-processing ability.

Some information about feature use may be inferred from the literature. First, infants can differentiate between young and old whether or not vocalization or height cues are present. In our stranger approach studies (Brooks & Lewis, 1976; Lewis & Brooks, 1974), the strangers did not vocalize (since the preschoolers could not be trusted to use a standard vocalization sequence), and differentiation still occurred. In the Brooks and Lewis (1976) study, a child and an adult midget (the same height as the child) each approached the infants, and the infants were able to differentiate between the two even without the height differences. Second, in the present studies, infants were able to differentiate between young and old when only the faces of strangers were presented, thereby omitting height and movement cues. These data suggest that facial configurations may be the feature to which infants first respond and that they respond positively to them (Lewis, 1969).

What might account for this preference for young versus old facial configurations? First, Lorenz (1943) and Hess (1970) have suggested that the quality of "babyishness" (e.g., round, protruding cheeks, forehead large in proportion to rest of face, head large in proportion to body; Eibl-Eibesfeldt, 1970, p. 431) may release protective or "mothering" responses in adults. Studies using adult subjects have shown that pictorial representations of the young of many species elicit higher rates of responding (and presumably interest) than do similar representations of older organisms (Hess, 1967). A recent study of this phenomenon suggests that even children exhibit this difference and that the difference may be greatest for girls at the age of puberty (Fullard & Reiling, 1976). Thus, the preference for baby features seems not to be limited to adults and, therefore, may not be related only to protectiveness. Other reasons may play a part in children's responses to peers, for example, the work of Simner (1971) and Sagi and Hoffman (1976) found that 1- to 4-day-old infants respond to the cry of another newborn by crying and are more likely to cry in response to another infant's cry than to a synthetic cry. Hoffman (1975) suggests that this response may be an innate precursor to an empathic distress reaction, whereas Simner (1971) suggests an innate ability to respond to peers. That this response is due to conditioning cannot be ruled out, although this is unlikely (Sameroff, 1971). The cry of the newborn may be a releaser of distress for the infant; perhaps facial configuration of the young is a releaser for pleasure.

Second, the differential responses to age, specifically the positive responses to the baby pictures, also might be explained by a cognitive–motivational theory of self–other evaluation (see Chapter 10 for a full treatment of this issue). The infants may be comparing the strangers to a construct of self; baby pictures, if evaluated as like self or congruent with self, may elicit positive affective responses. In either case, it is clear that facial features are attended to by the infant.

GENDER AS A SOCIAL CATEGORY

The emergence of gender as a social category consistently responded to by the young child is more elusive than that of age. When infants' responses to male and female adults are compared, some studies report differences while others do not. Fagan (1972) and Kagan and Lewis (1965) report that infants differentiate between pictorial representations of male and female adults; Benjamin (1961), Morgan and Ricciuti (1969), and Shaffran and Décarie (1973) report similar findings in live approach sequences. At the same time, Lewis and Brooks (1974) and Greenberg *et al.* (1973) did not find consistent adult gender differentiation.

There is even less work on infants' responses to male and female children and babies. Brooks and Lewis (1976) and Greenberg *et al.* (1973) found no evidence of gender differentiation of preschool strangers in live approach sequences. Infant peer play studies have also reported few differences with respect to sex of peer, although few of these studies have actually looked at sex differences (Bronson, 1975; Brooks-Gunn & Lewis, 1979b; Eckerman, Whatley, & Kutz, 1973). By preschool age, however, sex preferences for playmates seem to be well established (Abel & Sahinkaya, 1962; Langlois, Gottfried, & Seay, 1973). That same-sex peer preferences may exist even before preschool is suggested by Jacklin (1979) who found that 33-month-olds prefer to interact with same-sex peers in terms of both positive and negative behaviors.

Thus, in light of the previous work, the present study's finding that infants differentiate between same- and opposite-sex peers in both studies is at the very least surprising and somewhat puzzling. These findings might be better received in light of the following points. First, most studies have not examined the interaction between sex of the subject and sex of the stimulus; differences might be obscured by this failure. For example, sex of parent differences has been shown to interact with sex of infant (Lamb, 1975; Lewis, Weinraub, & Ban, 1972; Spelke,

Zelazo, Kagan, & Kotelchuck, 1973). Sex of the infant may also be found to interact with sex of preferred playmate in the peer work, as Brooks-Gunn and Lewis (1979b) found that female infants were more likely to interact with other females than with males whereas males interacted equally with males and females. A third example concerns the work on newborns' responses to another's cry (Sagi & Hoffman, 1976; Simner, 1971). In all five studies in the literature, female newborns were somewhat more likely to cry to another's cry than were males [in only one did the difference reach statistical significance (Sagi & Hoffman, 1976) although the probability of all five being in the same direction is less than .03. It should be noted that the newborns heard a female's not a male's cry]. Second, partial replication of the present findings was achieved in our laboratory; some of the Picture Study I infants were retested three months later. The infants who were 16–18 months of age on the first visit (and, therefore, 19–21 months of age on the second visit) also looked more at, but were not more positive toward, the same-sex than at the opposite-sex peer pictures [first fixation: $t(21) = 2.34$, $p < .05$]. Third, the 16- to 18-month-old infants were more likely to make the distinction between same- and opposite-sex baby pictures than were the younger ones. When 18 adults were asked to sort the baby pictures from Study I on the basis of gender, they were more accurate with the 16- to 18- than the 10- to 12-month-old pictures, presumably to an increase in hair and dress style cues. Fourth, this study raises an issue about the type of cues to which the infant might be responding. The most obvious are dress and hair cues; these cues were not always present in our pictures, as evidenced by the fact that adults were not always accurate in classifying. Might there be other cues present in the face? A few studies suggest this might be the case; Tanner (personal communication) found sex differences in the facial muscles and facial shape prior to puberty; Haviland and Lewis (1976) have found sex differences in infants' eye openness when confronted with a stranger. In light of these findings, the results from the present study are provocative, although further work seems warranted.

VISUAL SELF RECOGNITION IN PICTORIAL FORM

With the picture procedure, visual self recognition can only be inferred through the differential responses directed to the pictures of self and others matched for age and sex. In terms of the self versus same-age peer comparison, infants exhibited no differential responding in Study I, but did in Study II, such that the 9- to 12- and 21- to 24-month-olds smiled and looked at the pictures of self longer than at the pictures of same-age babies, whereas the 15- to 18-month-olds did just the opposite. The findings for the older age group replicated the findings from a small pilot sample of infants who were seen at 22 months of age. These findings suggest that pictures of self are responded to as such by 21–24-months of age and are probably responded to even earlier.

EXISTENTIAL AND CATEGORICAL SELF

The present studies speak to the existence of the categorical self more than to the existential self, since the self is inferred through differential responding. Age and sex have been shown to be important determinants of responses to strangers and to the self, suggesting that these two categories are used for both self and other comparisons. The self may be responded to first as "baby." Conversely, the baby stranger may be responded to first as "like me." In either case, age and gender appear to be salient dimensions for children under two years of age.

CHAPTER 5

Verbal Labeling of Self and Others

Spontaneous vocalizations, although seen in most laboratory situations, are often ignored because of their low frequency of occurrence or their lack of consistency across subjects. Much to our surprise, the infants' language production during Picture Study I was neither infrequent nor unsystematic. In this study, one-half of the 16- to 18-month-olds labeled spontaneously at least one of the slides. The first two social labels used were "baby" and "mommy," with the infants' verbal repertoire expanding with age to include proper names, "boy," "girl," "man," and "lady." Many of these labels were applied appropriately in terms of gender, age, and familiarity—suggesting that infants categorize the social world in terms of these dimensions. Since the use of social labels in Picture Study I coincided with the advent of mark recognition in Mirror Study I, it was thought that eliciting verbal labels for self representations might provide an additional and rich source of information about the development of self recognition.

Two studies were conducted to examine the production and comprehension of verbal labels indicative of self recognition. In Labeling Study I, the verbal labels applied to pictures of self and unfamiliar babies, children, and adults were explored for a sample of 15-, 19-, and 22-month-olds. In Labeling Study II, verbal labels used for pictures of self, unfamiliar peers, and younger babies were examined using a larger sample with a wider age range (9 to 36 months of age). Study II infants were asked to point to a specific picture presented in a set of pictures, as is done in the Peabody Picture Vocabulary Test, in order to examine comprehension. Production of social labels was obtained by having the children label a specific picture in the set.

LABELING STUDY I

SUBJECTS

In order to systematically study verbal labeling, 37 infants representing three ages (15, 19, and 22 months of age) were seen. The mean ages and number of subjects in each age group were as follows: 15.47 months (6 males, 8 females), 19.23 months (6 males, 5 females), and 22.11 months (6 males, 6 females). All infants were Caucasian and were full-term and healthy. As in previous studies, infants represented the upper three of the five social class designations of Hollingshead (1957). Approximately one-half of the infants were firstborn, one-half laterborn.

STIMULUS CONDITIONS

The infants were shown three sets of pictures. The first two sets included ten slides each and represented the same stimuli as used in Picture Study I. The third set was composed of six slides representing (1) the infant's mother, (2) the infant, (3) a baby the same age and same sex as the infant, (4) a 9-month-old male infant, (5) an adult female, and (6) an adult male. In the first two sets, each slide was presented for 15 sec with a 15-sec intertrial interval; in the third set, each slide was presented for 15 sec with a short (5-sec) intertrial interval. There were four different presentation orders for the first two sets and three different presentation orders for the third set. No order effects were found. Infants' pictures were taken in their homes approximately two weeks before testing.

PROCEDURE

The mother was given the following instructions for the third set of pictures (the instructions for the first two sets are found in Chapter 4):

We would like to show your infant six slides of familiar and unfamiliar persons. Each slide will be on the screen for 15 seconds and there will only be a 5-second blank period between pictures. When each slide appears, please point to the projected slide and ask your infant, "Who is that?". If your child does not respond verbally, please ask "Who is that?" again. *Do not* correct your child if he gives an incorrect response. We will be observing through the wire mesh holes. Any questions?

MEASURES

The infants' spontaneous vocalizations to the first two sets and their elicited vocalizations to the third set were recorded by an observer. After the testing, the mother was asked what she thought her infant had said to each picture and was asked to whom specific labels referred. For example, one infant referred to the unfamiliar female adult as "Carol." The infant had an aunt named Carol who had hair the same color and length as that of our stranger. If there were any discrepancies (i.e., the observer thought the infant had uttered a proper name and the mother did not, or vice versa), the utterance was not counted. However, the observer and the mother heard the same utterances in the vast majority of cases.

RESULTS

The results section parallels those of Picture Studies I and II. The same three comparisons were of interest—the age of the stranger, the gender of the stranger, and the self–other comparison.

OVERALL FREQUENCY OF VERBAL LABELING

Infants were likely to label at least one picture during the procedures, with 70% doing so. Verbal labeling increased with age, as 29% of the 15-, 91% of the 19-, and 100% of the 22-month-olds labeled at least one of the pictures $[\chi^2(2) = 19.00, p < .001]$. However, labeling was not related to sex of subject. The incidence of labeling and the types of labels used were similar across the two procedures with one interesting exception: boys were more likely to label in the spontaneous than in the elicited condition (90% versus 30% of the verbal boys: $\chi^2 = 4.50$, $p < .05$), whereas the girls were equally likely to do so in the two conditions. Since no differences appeared in types of labels used in each condition, the data were collapsed across the spontaneous and elicited conditions.

AGE OF STRANGER COMPARISON

Age-appropriate labels were used for the pictures of unfamiliar babies (the same age as the infant), children, and adults almost universally. The adult and baby pictures were more likely to be labeled than the child pictures; 18 infants (70% of the verbal infants) labeled at least one of the adult pictures and at least one of the baby pictures, and 11 infants (43%) labeled one of the child pictures [Cochran Q Test: $\chi^2(2) =$ 6.53, $p < .05$]. The infants used the labels in an age-appropriate manner for the adult and baby pictures, with only one of the 18 infants labeling adult pictures using age-inappropriate labels (Binomial Test, $p < .01$), and one of 18 infants labeling baby pictures using age-inappropriate labels (Binomial Test, $p < .01$). They were somewhat more likely to label child pictures age-inappropriately, as 3 of the 11 who labeled child pictures used wrong age labels.

What labels were actually used to represent the different-aged strangers? And what age trends in labeling age were seen? Out of the 34 labels directed to the adult strangers, 71% were "mommy" and "daddy," 24% were "lady" and "man," 6% were names of adult friends, and 3% (one label) were "baby." Age trends were seen such that "lady," "man," and proper names were not used before 22 months of age. At 22 months, "lady," "man," and proper names accounted for one-half of the utterances, "mommy" and "daddy" for the other half.

Of the 37 utterances directed to the peer baby strangers, 54% were variants of "baby," 20% were "boy" or "girl," and 20% were one's own name or proper names. There were age trends such that the labels "boy" and "girl" were only used at 22 months of age, whereas proper names, although used by some 15-month-olds, were not used with any frequency until 22 months. At 22 months, proper names, "boy" or "girl," and "baby" each accounted for one-third of the labels.

The child pictures were only labeled 15 times, with "baby," "boy," or "girl," and "mommy" or "daddy" being used equally. No age trends were found with respect to the labeling of the child pictures.

The frequency data complemented the subject data; in terms of correctness of labels of the 86 used for the pictures of babies, children, and adults, only five were applied incorrectly on the basis of age. In brief, the results from frequency of label usage and the number of subjects using the labels appropriately leads to the same conclusion: infants rarely used age-inappropriate labels.

SEX OF STRANGER COMPARISON

The verbal labels applied to the unfamiliar babies, adults, and children were often gender specific as well as age specific. Within each age category, approximately equal numbers of infants labeled the male and female pictures. Eleven labeled the female adult and 17 the male adult, 9 the child female and 6 the child male, 15 the female baby, and 12 the male baby pictures. Most of the infants used labels that specifically referred to gender for the adult and child pictures but not for the baby pictures. None of the 11 infants who labeled the female adult (Binomial Test, $p < .001$), one of the 17 who labeled the male adult ($p < .001$), two of the 9 who labeled the female child ($p < .10$), and none of the 6 who labeled the male child ($p < .05$) used a label that did not refer to gender. However, less than one-half of the infants used gender referents for the baby pictures (7 for female baby, 4 for male baby picture). Not surprisingly, "baby," a gender neutral label, was the most frequent label for the baby pictures.

Not only did most of the infants use labels that referred to gender, but they also used them correctly: 91% of the subjects who referred to gender used it correctly for the female adult (Binomial Test, $p < .05$), 82% for the male adult ($p < .01$), 100% for the female child ($p < .05$), and 100% for the male child ($p < .05$). In the few cases of gender-specific labels for the baby pictures, 86% were correct for the female baby and 75% for the male baby, although in these instances the trends were not significant because of the small number of infants using such labels.

In terms of the frequency data, what labels were used for the male and female strangers? Of the 13 labels used for the female adult, 62% were "mommy," 24% were "lady," and 16% were proper names (all female). Of the 21 labels uttered in the male adult condition, 67% were "daddy," 19% were "man," and 9% were "mommy." Nine labels were applied to the female children, 33% being "mommy," 22% being "girl," and 22% being proper names of female friends. Six labels were applied to the male children, 50% being "boy" and 16% being proper names of male friends. The baby pictures were labeled without regard to gender (i.e., baby) one-half of the time (9 of 19 labels for female baby, 10 of 16 for male baby); the rest of the labels were equally divided between "boy," "girl," and proper names, with all but one label being correct with respect to gender (interestingly, this subject used both "boy" and "girl" to label a same-sex peer, as if she were not sure which the picture represented). Thus, of the 64 gender-related labels, only 8% were used incorrectly.

SELF, SAME-SEX, AND OPPOSITE-SEX PEER COMPARISON

Table 5-1 presents both the number of subjects and the frequency of labeling by type of label and by age of subject for the pictures of self, same-sex peer, opposite-sex peer, and 9-month-old baby. Infants received self and same-sex peer pictures in both the spontaneous and elicited conditions; the opposite-sex peer pictures in the spontaneous; and the 9-month-old baby picture in the elicited condition. Responses to the picture of self and same-sex peer are most comparable, since both were presented in the spontaneous and elicited conditions and since sex and age of subject and stranger were held constant. Sixteen of the 26 verbal infants labeled the self (which is seen in Table 5-1 in the first row and second to last column), 16 labeled the same-sex, 11 the opposite-sex, and 11 the 9-month-old baby pictures. For the picture of self, all but one of those labeling the picture used an age-appropriate label (Binomial Test, $p < .01$). The data for the same- and opposite-sex peer pictures were very similar. The infants always labeled the 9-month-old baby picture with an age-appropriate label (Binomial Test, $p < .05$), but only three of them used a label that referred to gender (two being used correctly, one incorrectly).

When we turn to the actual labels used for each picture, clear evidence of self recognition and of the age-related nature of this phenomenon is seen. In terms of number of verbal subjects (not presented in Table 5-1), one-half of the verbal subjects labeled their own pictures correctly. Of those who labeled the self pictures (see Table 5-1), 50% of the 15-, 60% of the 19-, and 89% of the 22-month-olds used their own names or personal pronouns, labels that most clearly indicated knowledge of self. Of the total sample, 7% of the 15-, 27% of the 19-, and 67% of the 22-month-olds used these self referents [$\chi^2(2) = 10.64$, $p < .01$]. Interestingly, more girls than boys used their own names (seven females, three males), and more boys than girls used personal pronouns (two males, none of the females). In terms of the 18 labels used, 56% were the subject's own name, 11% were personal pronouns, 6% were "boy" or "girl," and 22% were "baby." None of the infants used another person's name to label their own pictures. In addition, the use of "baby" decreased with age while the use of one's own name and personal pronouns increased with age.

The same-sex peer picture received the same amount of attention in terms of labeling as did the self picture. However, the subjects were less likely to use the self referent labels to same-sex than to self pictures, specifically their own name and personal pronouns (2 versus 12: $\chi^2 = 8.10$, $p < .01$) and more likely to use general labels ("boy," "girl," and "baby") for the stranger than the self pictures (15 versus 5: $\chi^2 = 6.75$, $p < .01$). Of the 20 labels given to the same-sex picture (see Table 5-1), 50% were "baby," 24% were "boy" or "girl," 15% were the names of same-sex friends, and 10% were the subject's own name. Use of "baby" decreased and use of "boy" and "girl" increased with age, which parallels the label use pattern seen in the self condition.

Fewer infants labeled the opposite-sex peer or the 9-month-old baby pictures. This was probably because these two stimulus conditions were not included in both the spontaneous and elicited conditions. Eleven infants each responded to these two conditions, with three-quarters of the infants using "baby," the rest using "boy," "girl," and proper names. Only one subject uttered her own name, labeling both the opposite-sex peer and the younger baby picture with it. Interestingly, all the proper names referred to friends that were approximately the age of the baby picture being represented. In short, the types of labels used for the opposite-sex baby picture were similar to those used in the same-sex peer condition.

SUMMARY

The results of this study clearly point out that infants, when they are capable of producing verbal labels to pictures, are also able to articulate age- and gender-appropriate labels. Moreover, the differential use of proper name and personal pronoun indicates that verbal infants, as young as 15 months, but more commonly by 19 months, have self referent labels and use them only for their own pictures.

In order to explore further infants' verbal labeling behavior, a second study was undertaken. Labeling Study II examined verbal production, using the same procedure as that in Labeling Study I, and verbal comprehension. Since verbal comprehension has been thought to precede production, we expected that infants who had no verbal labels would still distinguish between pictures when an adult used social labels and would possibly show earlier verbal knowledge of self–other differentiation.

TABLE 5-1

Number of Subjects and Frequency with Which Different Labels Are Applied by Baby Picture and by Age of Subject

	Age							
	15 months		19 months		22 months		Total sample	
Stimulus condition	Subjects	Labels	Subjects	Labels	Subjects	Labels	Subjects	Labels
Self picture								
Total number	2	2	5	6	9	10	16	18
(% of labels)[a]								
Baby	50	50	40	33	11	10	25	22
Boy, girl	0	0	0	0	11	10	6	6
Own name	50	50	60	50	67	60	63	56
Personal pronoun	0	0	0	0	22	20	13	11
Other name	0	0	20	17	0	0	6	6
Same-sex peer picture								
Total number	2	3	6	6	8	11	16	20
(% of labels)[a]								
Baby	100	67	83	83	38	27	63	50

Boy, girl	0	0	0	0	50	45	25	25
Own name	50	33	0	0	13	9	13	10
Other name	0	0	17	17	13	18	13	15
Opposite-sex peer picture								
Total number	1	1	3	3	7	11	11	15
(% of labels)[a]								
Baby	100	100	100	100	71	45	81	60
Boy, girl	0	0	0	0	29	18	18	13
Own name	0	0	0	0	14	9	9	7
Other name	0	0	0	0	14	18	9	13
Baby picture								
Total number	1	1	3	3	7	7	11	11
(% of labels)[a]								
Baby	100	100	100	100	57	57	73	73
Boy, girl	0	0	0	0	14	14	9	9
Own name	0	0	0	0	14	14	9	9
Other name	0	0	0	0	14	14	9	9

[a] The percentage of labels used may be more than 100% for number of subjects, since some subjects uttered more than one label.

LABELING STUDY II

EXPERIMENTAL PROCEDURE

SUBJECTS

Ninety-three Caucasian infants, divided among eight age groups, were seen. These groups were 9, 12, 15, 18, 21, 24, 30, and 36 months of age. Approximately 12 infants (6 males and 6 females) were seen at each age, with the exception of the 21-month-old group, which had one less male, and the 30-month-old group, which had one less male and female. The mean ages of each group were 9.85, 12.94, 15.70, 18.70, 21.93, 24.82, 30.60, and 36.83 months of age. Within each age group the age range was 4 to 6 weeks.

All infants were full-term and healthy. Over half of the sample was firstborn. The socioeconomic status of the sample was skewed toward the higher end of the Hollingshead Scale (1957), with one-half of the sample in Social Class I, one-third in Class II, and one-sixth in Class III.

PROCEDURE

VERBAL PRODUCTION

All the subjects were shown pictures of themselves as well as unfamiliar babies, although the procedures varied somewhat for the infants over and under two years of age. The 9- to 24-month-olds were shown 35 mm colored slides of themselves, a female peer, a male peer, and a 6-month-old baby. The infants were photographed in their homes two weeks prior to testing. Only the upper shoulders and head of each person were photographed. Light intensity and background of the pictures were held constant over all slides, but hair length, eye and hair color, and dress cues were not. Facial expressions were all positive, with slight smiles.

Infants were seated by their mothers, approximately one m in front of a screen upon which the slides were projected, each for 15 sec with a 15-sec interval. The mothers were instructed to point to each slide and to ask, "Who is that?" but not to label the pictures themselves or to correct their children. Order of the stimuli was counterbalanced using six different presentation orders such that one-sixth of each age group received order 1, one-sixth order 2, and so on.

The 30- and 36-month-olds were tested using a slightly different procedure. When they arrived at the laboratory, their pictures were taken with a Big Shot Polaroid camera, which produced colored photographs of the head and shoulders. This picture was entered into a large scrapbook that also contained pictures of a same-age female peer, a same-age male peer, and a 6-month-old baby. Each picture was mounted on a separate page. The experimenter and the child sat at a small table, and the experimenter turned the pages asking, "Who is that?" for each picture. Between taking the picture and administering the labeling procedure, each child participated in another task so that at least 15 to 20 min separated the two events.

After each testing session, the mothers were asked about the specific labels their infants had used. When proper names were used, the mothers informed the experimenter as to whom the name referred, the age and gender of the person, and the relationship of the person to the infant. When nicknames were used, their use in place of proper names was verified by the mother.

Verbal Comprehension

Verbal comprehension was examined by creating sets of pictures, with three or four pictures to a set. Table 5-2 presents the nine sets of pictures. Each child was asked by the experimenter to point to one of the three or four pictures in a set. For example, in the set containing the four pictures "baby male," "baby female," "child male," and "child female," the child was asked to point first to the "baby girl," then to the "baby boy," then the "big girl," and finally, the "big boy." The child was required to point to the appropriate picture in order to obtain a correct score. No correction procedure was used.

Pictures of the self were taken in the child's home two weeks prior to the actual testing for the 9- to 24-month-olds and were taken in the laboratory for the 30- and 36-month-olds. Pictures of all the stimuli were taken with a Big Shot Polaroid camera, which produced colored photographs of the head and shoulders. Light intensity and background of the pictures were held constant over all stimuli, and the facial expressions of these stimuli was that of a slight smile.

Table 5-2
Picture Sets for the Verbal Comprehension Task Labeling Study II

Set	Stimulus condition	Set	Stimulus condition
Set 1	Baby male Baby female Child male Child female	Set 6	Baby female Child female Adult female
Set 2	Self Little boy Little girl	Set 7	Daddy Adult male Adult female
Set 3	Baby male Child male Adult male	Set 8	Child male Child female Adult male Adult female
Set 4	Mother Adult female Adult male	Set 9	Daddy Mommy Self
Set 5	Baby male Baby female Little boy Little girl		

The pictures for each set were placed in a book with a transparent plastic cover for each page. The various sets, each on a separate page, were placed in a looseleaf book.

Verbal comprehension was tested after the verbal production task. During the comprehension testing, the infants were seated by their mothers and the experimenter. The experimenter's instructions to the child were as follows:

I'm going to show you a book full of pictures of different people's faces. On each page there are several *different* faces. What I want you to do is to point to the picture of the person I mention. (Experimenter shows child a picture set.) *Show me* the "baby boy." Can you find the "baby boy?" Point to the "baby boy."

Measures

Verbal Production

All utterances made by the infants during the testing session were noted. Utterances that could not be understood by the observer were not coded, even if the mothers stated that they understood the utterance, and phonemes such as "pa," "ba," and "da" were not coded, even though mothers of the younger infants reported that they were variants of social labels.

Verbal Comprehension

A response was considered correct when the child pointed to the correct picture. In the cases of multiple pointing, only the first point was coded.

RESULTS

VERBAL PRODUCTION

Frequency of Labeling

Many infants labeled the pictures and most seemed to enjoy it (as evidenced by smiling and pleasant vocalizing). Over one-half of the sample labeled at least one of the pictures. Social labeling increased with age, as none of the 9- or 12-, only one of the 15-, 42% of the 18-, 64% of the 21-, 83% of the 24-, and all of the 30- and 36-month-olds labeled at least one baby picture [$\chi^2(7) = 59.6$, $p < .001$]. No sex differences appeared.

In terms of labeling the specific pictures, more infants labeled the pictures of self and unfamiliar babies than of the unfamiliar peers. Of the 45 verbal infants, 89% labeled their own pictures, 91% the baby, 80% the male peer, and 73% the female peer [$\chi^2(3) = 6.56$, $p < .10$]. Again, no sex differences were found.

Use of Self Referents

The use of self referents was clearly of interest. Table 5-3 presents the number of subjects who used their own name or the personal pronoun as a label by stimulus condition and age. The 9-, 12- and 15-month-olds were not included since they did not use either their names or personal pronouns. Slightly over one-half (58%) of the verbal

TABLE 5-3
Number of Infants Using Their Own Name and Personal Pronouns

Age	Any baby picture	Self	Female peer	Male peer	Baby
	Stimulus condition				
18 months					
Name	0	0	0	0	0
Personal pronoun	0	0	0	0	0
21 months					
Name	4	4	1	0	2
Personal pronoun	1	1	0	0	0
24 months					
Name	7	7	1	2	0
Personal pronoun	0	0	0	0	0
30 months					
Name	7	7	0	1	0
Personal pronoun	2	2	0	0	0
36 months					
Name	8	8	0	0	0
Personal pronoun	5	5	0	0	0
Total					
Name	26	26	2	3	2
Personal pronoun	8	8	0	0	0

infants used their own name and 18% used a personal pronoun, with the difference between the two being significant ($\chi^2 = 10.32$, $p < .01$). Using one's own name did not increase over the four ages for the verbal infants. Fifty-seven percent of the 21-, 70% of the 24-, 70% of the 30-, and 67% of the 36-month-olds used their own name. Thus, over two-thirds of the verbal infants used their own name. As stated earlier, fewer infants used personal pronouns (18% versus 58%). However, the age changes were quite dramatic: only one verbal infant used a personal pronoun in the first two years of life, whereas 20% of the 30-month-olds and 42% of the 36-month-olds did so.

For which picture were these labels used? In all instances, children who used their own name or a personal pronoun used it for their own picture. In terms of number of infants labeling their own picture with *either label*, 46% of the 21-, 58% of the 24-, 80% of the 30-, and all the

36-month-olds did so, both verbal and nonverbal alike [$\chi^2(3) = 9.72$, $p < .05$]. In terms of the verbal infants only, 70% of the 21-, 70% of the 24-, 90% of the 30-, and all the 36-month-olds correctly labeled their pictures. These findings suggest that correct labeling of one's own picture occurred somewhat earlier than others have suggested (Gesell, 1938; Stutsman, 1931), that verbal labeling of the self is high in the second year, and that by the end of the third year, almost all children have self referents and use them correctly.

In order to see whether self referents were used differentially, a comparison of their usage in the self and other baby conditions was made. As can be seen in Table 5-3, very few instances of self referents in other conditions occurred, as only 13% of the verbal infants did so, with the number of instances declining with age: three 21-month-olds, two 24-month-olds, one 30-month-old, and no 36-month-olds used their own name for another baby. Differences between self and other were significant for each comparison (self–female peer: $\chi^2 = 22.04$, $p < .001$; self–male peer: $\chi^2 = 21.04$, $p < .001$; self–baby: $\chi^2 = 22.04$, $p < .001$).

Infants who incorrectly applied their own names to another baby were equally likely to apply these labels to the three unfamiliar babies (see Table 5-3). Personal pronouns were never incorrectly applied, suggesting that personal pronoun usage is even stronger evidence of self recognition than one's own name.

Use of "Boy" and "Girl"

Gender- and age-appropriate labels were also used, with "boy" and "girl" being the labels that convey both gender- and age-appropriate information. Gender- but not age-appropriate labels, such as "mommy," "daddy," "lady," and "man" were never used for the four baby pictures. Table 5-4 presents the number of subjects using "boy" and "girl" by stimulus condition and age. As in Table 5-3, the 9 to 18-month-olds were not included as they did not use these labels. Slightly more of the verbal infants used "girl" than "boy" (38% versus 29%) although this difference was not significant. There were no sex differences in the use of "boy" and "girl."

As can be seen in Table 5-4, age trends were evident for both labels: 14% of the 21, 30% of the 24-, 50% of the 30-, and 42% of the 36-month-olds, used "boy," whereas 43% of the 21-, none of the 24-, 60% of the

TABLE 5-4
Number of Infants Using "Boy" and "Girl"

| | Stimulus condition | | | | |
Age	Any baby picture	Self	Female peer	Male peer	Baby
21 months					
"Boy"	1	0	0	0	0
"Girl"	3	1	2	1	0
24 months					
"Boy"	2	0	1	1	0
"Girl"	0	0	0	0	0
30 months					
"Boy"	5	1	1	5	0
"Girl"	6	0	6	0	0
36 months					
"Boy"	5	0	0	5	1
"Girl"	8	0	8	0	0
Total					
"Boy"	13	1	2	12	1
"Girl"	17	1	16	1	0

30-, and 67% of the 36-month-olds used "girl." (These percentages are based on the number of verbal infants in each age group so that the 43% figure for the 21-month-olds is only based on three infants. Because of the small number of infants in some cases, chi-squares could not be done.). Thus, both boy and girl labels are first seen, although infrequently, in the second year and are prevalently used by one-half of the children in the third year.

For which pictures were these labels used? In general, they were used for the male and female peer pictures, not the self or the baby pictures. Only three infants labeled their picture or the baby picture "boy" or "girl," whereas 17 and 13 infants used them for the female and male peer, respectively. In addition, "girl" was used for the female and "boy" for the male peer pictures in almost all (over 90%) the cases ("girl" versus "boy" in female peer condition: $\chi^2 = 10.56$, $p < .01$; "girl" versus "boy" in male peer condition: $\chi^2 = 7.69$, $p < .05$). Thus, "boy" and "girl" are gender-appropriate as soon as they appear in the child's repertoire, are used for peers but not the self, and are used for same-age, not younger peers.

VERBAL COMPREHENSION

The verbal comprehension task could not be performed by any infant under 18 months of age. These infants were not able to follow instructions because they either did not understand what was expected of them or were unable to point. The work of Flavell (1974) and Masangkay *et al.* (1974) indicates that pointing is a skill that has a specific developmental course. This fact has important implications for our work on self recognition, since pointing, especially pointing to oneself, has been used in several of the studies reported.

The percentage of subjects who pointed to at least one picture increased over age: 58% of the 18-month-olds, 90% of the 21-month-olds, 83% of the 24-month-olds, and all the 30- and 36-month-olds [$\chi^2(4) = 34.72, p < .001$]. We will present the data for comprehension for the self condition first and then compare the ability to point to the correct picture as a function of age. No sex differences were found for these comparisons.

Self Comprehension

Each infant saw a picture of self, a same-age boy, and a same-age girl. The infants were asked to point to themselves (own name), the "little boy," and the "little girl," respectively. Thus, the infants had to choose between three pictures. Correctly pointing to the self picture when asked to do so exhibited developmental trends similar to the production data. Pointing to the self picture increased with age, with 43% of the 18-, 60% of the 21-, 90% of the 24-, 63% of the 30-, and 90% of the 36-month-olds doing so [$\chi^2(4) = 9.08, p < .05$]. If only the infants who exhibited pointing behavior at some time during the task are included, the age increases in ability to point to self are more linear: 43% of the 18-, 60% of the 21-, 90% of the 24-, 87% of the 30-, and 100% of the 36-month-olds [$\chi^2(4) = 14.32, p < .01$].

Interestingly, infants who did not accurately point to the self picture tended not to point to *any* picture. That is, they did not choose any other picture; when asked to point to self, they chose not to point at all. This was equally true for all age groups: only one subject pointed to another picture, whereas the rest did not point at all. What this means is that the correct pointing of those who pointed to the self picture was consistently high across all the ages (including 18 months). All the 18-, 86% of the 21-, all the 24-, 88% of the 30-, and all the 36-month-olds did so. Thus, infants made very few incorrect choices in the self condition.

Age Comprehension

Table 5-5 presents the percentage of infants who pointed correctly to the pictures by subject age and age of stimulus. Three age groups of stimuli are represented: baby, child, and adult. The specific label used by the experimenter is presented in the left-hand column in Table 5-5. Across all subjects, differential age comprehension was found, with adults receiving the highest percentage of correct responses (83%), and baby and child fewer correct responses (64%) $[\chi^2(2) = 5.60, p < .05]$.

Interestingly and quite surprisingly, this pattern held for all groups except the 18- and 21-month-olds. For the 18-month-olds, comprehen-

TABLE 5-5
*Percentage of Subjects Who Pointed at Least Once
during the Comprehension Task by Stimulus Group*

Stimulus condition	Age in months					
	18	21	24	30	36	Total
Self	100	86	100	88	100	94
Baby boy	67	38	53	59	68	57
Baby girl	80	79	54	67	77	70
Baby	80	64	51	63	72	64
Boy	37	47	60	79	80	65
Girl	71	53	40	58	70	58
Child	62	58	50	68	75	63
Man	47	86	87	91	75	86
Lady	42	69	97	77	92	79
Adult	52	79	97	86	86	83
Male	56	69	63	67	69	65
Female	76	78	61	74	74	71

sion was highest for the baby and lowest for the adult pictures. For 21-month-olds, comprehension was approximately equal for the different-aged strangers, although baby comprehension was somewhat higher than child or adult comprehension. These data indicate an age of subject × age of stimulus interaction with the younger children (18- and 21-month-olds) comprehending the "baby" better than "adult," whereas the reverse is true for the older children (24- to 36-month-olds). This may be due to the age labeling that the children themselves are exposed to. Younger children may not know the labels "man" and "lady." The verbal labeling data suggest this is the case, since "mommy" and "daddy," not "man" and "lady" are used.

Gender Comprehension

When the children are asked to point to a particular picture, their comprehension of gender can be estimated by observing their pointing responses in those cases in which gender discrimination is called for and the set contains stimuli of both genders. Table 5-5 also includes the percentage of subjects who correctly pointed to the male and female strangers. Observation of the data across the age groups indicates several interesting points. The number of subjects giving a correct gender response does not increase with age for both "boy" and "girl" labels. Also, the number of subjects showing correct gender comprehension does not change with age. Thus, gender comprehension occurs in our youngest infants, and correct pointing occurs in two-thirds to three-quarters of the time. By the time infants are able to perform our comprehension task, they are able to use gender labels appropriately.

DISCUSSION

The verbal labeling and comprehension data reflect the infant's ability to recognize self in pictorial representations and to categorize both self and other social objects on the basis of dimensions we have referred to as social categories, these being age and gender.

The results of Labeling Study II, in which both verbal production and comprehension could be observed, reveal a rather interesting and consistent finding vis-à-vis the language development literature. Al-

though none of the 9- to 18-month-old infants in this study could produce verbal labels when asked to in this experimental situation, the
18-month-olds were able to show comprehension of verbal labels when
asked to point to particular pictures. These children certainly demonstrate that verbal comprehension precedes verbal labeling. The language
literature contains a controversy over whether comprehension precedes
production because the context of the situation allows the child to utilize
nonverbal cues for comprehension or whether an actual difference
exists. In our two tasks, the situation was most similar so that nonverbal
cues cannot account for comprehension preceding production.

There is some difference in the ages at which verbal production
occurred across the two studies: in Study I, a few infants produced
verbal labels at 15 months but in Study II, only one child did so. This
small difference is not easily explained and is probably due to sampling
variability. However, the Study I subjects were somewhat more familiar
with our laboratory, as they had participated in other studies. Perhaps
they were more at ease and, therefore, more likely to produce language.
Some support for our belief that ease and familiarity may facilitate language experience comes from mothers who often report that their children use language in general and social labels in particular more often
at home than in our laboratory. This observation coincides with the fact
that many infants and young children become shy and do not perform
well in unfamiliar settings. These findings are important since they
suggest that our results for *both* production and comprehension represent a conservative estimate of the infant's linguistic capacity.

VERBAL PRODUCTION, COMPREHENSION, AND SELF RECOGNITION

Being able to label a picture of oneself appropriately was found to be
an excellent index of self recognition in the two labeling studies. One-
third of the Study I infants exhibited self recognition when it was defined as the correct use of one's own name or a personal pronoun for
one's own (but not another's) picture. This effect was age-related, as 7%
of the 15-, 27% of the 19-, and 67% of the 22-month-olds labeled their
pictures correctly. In Study II, the use of self referents occurred later, as
none of the 15- or 18-month-olds used them (see previous discussion).
However, consistent age trends appeared, as 46% of the 21-, 70% of the
24-, 80% of the 30-, and all the 36-month-olds labeled their pictures

correctly. The comprehension data for Study II parallel these findings nicely, with comprehension occurring earlier and rising more rapidly. Specifically, 43% of the 18-, 60% of the 21-, 90% of the 24-, 87% of the 30-, and 100% of the 36-month-olds correctly pointed to the self picture. That verbal comprehension preceded verbal production lends support to our belief that self recognition has occurred by the middle, not the end, of the second year. Of particular importance in this regard is the finding that, even by 18 months, all infants who pointed to their picture in a set containing a group of pictures did so correctly (see Table 5-5). That is, although the number of subjects who could point to their picture increased with age, there was no increase with age in the *number* of correct responses. By 18 months, children who could understand the task requirement could perform correctly. This finding may mean that infants recognize pictures of themselves even earlier but are unable to indicate this knowledge because of difficulties in understanding the task requirement.

Although the infants' own names were first used at 15 months in Study I and 18 months in Study II, personal pronoun usage did not appear until 21 to 22 months of age in the two studies. Ames (1952) has reported that personal pronouns are not commonplace until the third year of life. The present studies suggest that personal pronouns may be applied correctly, though infrequently, in the second year of life. Others have reported personal pronoun usage in very young children's spontaneous language (e.g., Bloom, Lightbown, & Hood, 1975).

That infants' language may be inhibited in the laboratory, that comprehension precedes production, and that all 18-month-olds who understood the comprehension task pointed to their own pictures suggest that our findings may be conservative estimates of infants' language and self recognition capabilities. Conversations with the mothers tend to confirm this belief, since more of the mothers in the two studies reported that their infants had a specific self label than was actually found in the laboratory testing.

Although verbal self reference seems to be convincing evidence of knowledge of self, a possible limitation needs to be noted. Parents may teach their children to label their own pictures, thus making a verbal self reference no more than an elicited response to a familiar picture. This is unlikely for several reasons. First, an unfamiliar picture of the self, rather than pictures available to the infant in the home, was used in the present study. Second, the children under two years of age had the picture taken two weeks prior to the testing in the home, not in the laboratory. Finally, the comprehension task required the child to reverse the process; that is, the child's name was produced and the child had to locate the picture, a procedure not normally performed.

Another possibility is that infants may learn the features of the person being represented and thus recognize that person in many pictures without knowing that the representation is, in fact, self. An infant may know that the picture represents "Amanda" and that she is also "Amanda," but does she know that the picture "Amanda" is, in fact, herself? Anecdotal evidence suggests that infants who use a self referent to label pictures know that the pictures represent themselves, as they often point to themselves or examine their clothing at the same time. Personal pronoun usage, of course, makes it clear that the infants recognize their pictures.

The ability to recognize oneself visually is also reflected in the differential use of labels for the self and peer pictures and in the reluctance of the infants to label their own picture when an appropriate label was presumably not available. First, the infants labeling the same-sex picture rarely used their own name, using instead the labels "baby," "boy," or "girl," whereas just the opposite was true for the picture of self. In addition, one's own name was almost never used for the opposite-sex peer or the younger baby. Second, few infants who labeled their own picture did not use a clear self referent, suggesting that the infants who did not label themselves may have failed to do so because they did not yet have an appropriate label in their verbal repertoire. This possibility is further substantiated by the fact that several infants were clearly able to use the label "baby" age-appropriately (i.e., for one of the other baby pictures) but did not use it for their own picture.

THE EXISTENTIAL AND CATEGORICAL SELF

The verbal labeling data may be used to illustrate the concept of duality in the self. The existential self or infant's knowledge of self as distinct from other may be inferred through the use of one's own name or a personal pronoun to label an unfamiliar picture of the self and not to others. The categorical self or the categories used by infants to define themselves may be inferred through the social labels that they apply to persons varying on a number of dimensions.

As was suggested earlier, infants may categorize their social world very early by applying certain categories to *both* themselves and others. The use of social labels may reflect the infant's perception of his social world and may provide information about the categories that are salient for the infant, both in terms of self and other. This is not to say that the categorical features do not exist prior to the child's articulation or comprehension of them, but that the articulation and comprehension are a convenient way of examining these categories. In addition, a label or comprehension may be used by infants to represent not just one but several perceptual features so that they may have some categorical distinctions not represented in their verbal repertoire (Clark, 1973). For example, even though infants can differentiate clearly between their parents and other adults, they are inclined to use similar labels for both classes of adults. As soon as the particular concept is available and/or understood, or a specific label for non-parent is acquired, pictures of parents and other adults are labeled differently. In the labeling studies, the younger infants used "mommy" and "daddy" exclusively for the adult stranger pictures, whereas older infants began to use "lady" and "man" or proper names. In addition, the infants did not overgeneralize randomly but assigned specific features to labels: "mommy" was not applied to children but to adults, not to male adults but to female adults; "daddy" was also applied in an age- and sex-appropriate manner. In short, infants' use and comprehension of social labels seems to reflect their social categorization system.

The data from both labeling and comprehension studies indicate that, with the advent of a lexicon, the infant already has knowledge of social dimensions such as self–other, male–female, and age. These data support the results of Chapter 4, in which perceptual differences and affective expression both in terms of gender and age were demonstrated.

These perceptual and affectual differences were demonstrated at ages prior to the onset of language (both production and comprehension), again suggesting that knowledge of self and others exists prior to the ability to express it directly, either through verbal or complex motoric behavior. Taken together, our studies seem to indicate that social knowledge of the self and others is constructed along the dimensions of gender, age, and familiarity; develops quite early; and relates to the general cognitive framework of the developing infant. In terms of the last point, information about self and other may be available early on through differential perceptual cues, based upon discriminable features and unique action–outcome patterns. With the acquisition of a general knowledge of space and permanence, self and others take on different dimensions, finally being verbally expressed and understood with the advent of the lexicon. Whatever the mechanism, it is apparent that the infant labels and comprehends labels of self and other persons appropriately on the basis of gender and age at some time in the beginning of the second year of life.

CHAPTER 6

Individual Differences in the Expression of Self Recognition

In the last four chapters, we have presented several different procedures for measuring one important aspect of the concept of self—visual self recognition. Infants' reactions to seeing themselves in a variety of visual representational forms, including pictures, mirrors, and videotapes, have been explored, with quite striking developmental trends occurring in all three representational forms. Clear trends involve self-directed behavior in mirrors: specifically touching one's nose after the application of rouge, contingent play in contingent self videotape representations, imitative behavior in noncontingent self videotape representations, and verbal labeling and comprehension of pictorial representations. For example, in Mirror Study I, none of the 9- to 12-, one-quarter of the 15- to 18-, and three-quarters of the 21- to 24-month-olds noticed the rouge on their noses. In Videotape Study I, 30% of the 9- to 12-, 82% of the 15- to 18-, and 100% of the 21- to 24-month-olds played contingently in the contingent videotape condition, and 3% of the 9- to 12-, 35% of the 15- to 18-, and 50% of the 21- to 24-month olds imitated a videotape of themselves. These data, in conjunction with our other findings, show that self recognition, regardless of how it is measured, increases dramatically over the first two years of life.

Even so, as can be seen in the examples we have given from preceding chapters, enough individual variance exists within age groups to ask why some infants at a certain age point exhibit evidence of visual self recognition while some do not. Given the experimental procedures and the age categories that have been studied, the individual difference issue becomes of central importance. Not only would the study of individual differences in self recognition be of use for predicting subsequent behavior (i.e., the development of self concepts such as gender identity), but the variables that predict self recognition may explicate the process of self development. This would be especially true for any relationship between self recognition and cognition, since we believe that self knowledge is cognitive in nature and is related to object permanence. By 6 to 8 months of age, infants begin to understand that objects have an existence of their own (Piaget, 1937/1954). If infants know that objects exist, they must also know that they exist, separate from objects. As we have argued earlier, knowledge of others, self, and objects probably develops at the same time. In terms of general cognition, self development may reflect general cognitive activity or may have an active role in other cognitive organization (see Chapters 9 and 10).

Also of interest is the relationship of self recognition and social behavior. Given individual differences in self recognition, are those differences related to the family constellation? Familial measures could include economic and educational variables, as well as specific interaction patterns. Finally, within the familial relationship, such variables as the child's own experiences with reflective surfaces, as well as contact with siblings and other children, may be related to the emerging concept of self and may account for individual differences in self recognition.

Individual differences in cognition and social experience may have important implications for our theory of the origins of the self. To study such relationships, individual differences in self recognition using our mirror and videotape procedures were compared with differences in social and cognitive variables, including social class, parental educational level, birth order, family size, object permanence, and information processing. The role of experience in self recognition was studied by examining the amount of previous exposure to mirrors.

EXPERIMENTAL PROCEDURE

SUBJECTS

Ninety-three Caucasian infants, representing three age groups, were seen. There were 30 9- to 12-month-olds (15 males, 15 females), 31 15- to 18-month-olds (15 males, 16 females), and 32 21- to 24-month-olds (16 males, 16 females). All infants were full-term and healthy and were primarily from upper-middle and middle class families.

Stimulus Conditions

Each infant completed four different tasks: an attentional task, a mirror task, a videotape task and an object permanence task.

Attention Task

Attention distribution has been considered an important measure of perceptual-cognitive ability in the young child, relating to both CNS function and dysfunction (Lewis, 1969, 1971). Attention distribution has been observed by recording the child's responses to redundant information and to changes in the redundancy. Specifically, a single visual event is presented repeatedly to the child for six trials followed by some variation of the stimulus event. Although dependent on such developmental variables as age, stage, and central nervous system integrity, fixation time and autonomic nervous system responses (most often heart rate changes) show response decrement to the redundant stimuli and response recovery to the novel stimuli. The degree of response decrement and recovery are measures of the perceptual-cognitive functioning, with greater decrement and recovery being associated with better functioning (Lewis, 1971, 1975; Lewis, Goldberg, & Campbell, 1969; Lewis, Goldberg, & Rausch, 1967).

In this study, seven colored 35 mm slides were presented by rear-screen projection to each infant. The first six were 20 straight, colored lines and the seventh was 20 curved lines. These stimuli have been used in previous studies on cognitive functioning (Lewis, Goldberg, & Campbell, 1969; Lewis & Scott, 1972). Each trial was 30 sec in length with a 15-sec intertrial interval. The screen was blank during the intertrial interval.

Mirror Task

The mirror apparatus described in Mirror Study I was used. The infant's face was marked with rouge by the mother, and the infant was placed in front of the mirror for approximately 90 sec (± 10 sec). The mother encouraged her infant to look in the mirror at least three times, which all the infants did. As before, the mother could not be seen in the mirror. A TV camera behind the mirror recorded the entire mirror episode.

Videotape Task

The videotape task was the one described in Chapter 3 (Videotape Study I). Briefly, infants received three different videotape conditions: contingent self, noncontingent self, and noncontingent other. The two noncontingent conditions were previously filmed videotapes of the target infant (self) and same-age, same-sex peer (other).

Object Permanence Task

The object permanence test developed by Bell (1970) was used. In this test, infants are required to search for objects which are hidden under screens and which increase in complexity. Infants have to search first for a partially hidden object, then a completely hidden object, then an object hidden within an object. Displacements between screens are first visible and then invisible. Object permanence increases in complexity over the first two years, with infants being able to find a partially hidden object and, finally, being able to find an object hidden after seeing the invisible displacement. Searching for the completely hidden object first occurs at approximately 8 months of age, the age of our youngest subjects.

PROCEDURE

The infants performed the four tasks over two visits. On the first visit, each infant received the attention task and the mirror task; on the second, the videotape task and the object permanence task. The attention and videotape tasks were done in the same setting: a small, uniformly colored room that contained a high chair for the infant, a screen for projecting the slides and the videotape conditions, and a chair for the mother. The mirror task was performed in a second testing room that contained the mirror apparatus, several pieces of furniture, and wall decorations. The object permanence task was given in the waiting room. At the end of the second visit, the mother filled out a background questionnaire, familial information about socioeconomic status, educational level, family size, birth order, and naturally occurring mirror experience.

MEASURES

The Bell Object Permanence Test (1970) was scored according to the stages described by Piaget (1937/1954). The scores ranged from one to seven which correspond to Piaget's stages 3b, 4, 5a, 5b, 6a, 6b, and 6c, respectively. On the average, the 9- to 12-month-olds were in Piaget's Stage 5a (M, 3.19; SD, 1.08); the 15- to 18-month-olds were in Piaget's Stage 6a (M, 4.96; SD, 2.73); and the 21- to 24-month-olds were in Piaget's Stage 6b (M, 6.22; SD, 3.21).

The attention task was scored by observing when the infants' eyes were oriented toward the stimulus. Whenever the projected image was isomorphic with the pupil of the subject's eye, the observer depressed an event recorder switch that marked both the onset and duration of any particular fixation. Duration of fixation (total fixation divided by number of fixations) was calculated, as it incorporates two types of different information—length of looking and number of looks (Cohen, 1972; Lewis, Kagan, Kalafat, & Campbell, 1966).

Two types of attention measures were generated: response habituation, which measures the ability to process redundant information (trials 1–6 being redundant) and response recovery, which measures the ability to detect change (trials 6 and 7 being different). Response habituation and recovery scores were calculated, respectively, by the following formulas:

$$\frac{(trial\,1 - trial\,6)}{trial\,1} \quad and \quad \frac{(trial\,6 - trial\,7)}{trial\,6}$$

In the mirror task, the presence or absence of self-directed behaviors was measured in both conditions. Mark-directed behavior included touching, pointing, or wiping one's own nose, or saying "rouge" or "red". Body-directed behavior included touching the torso or the face, but not specifically the nose. Imitation included clowning or acting silly, or making faces while watching oneself in the mirror.

In the videotape task, the presence or absence of two types of behaviors was coded: contingent play and imitation. Playing with the contingent nature of the television image involved repeating actions and clearly observing these actions on the screen in all three conditions. Imitation was defined as replicating a discrete action portrayed in the noncontingent conditions after it had begun and within two sec of its occurrence. The presence or absence of each behavior for each of the three stimulus conditions was coded.

The background variables included birth order, social class, mother's education, and previous mirror experience. The Hollingshead Two-Factor Index of Social Position (1957) was used to determine socioeconomic status, with Social Class I indicating the highest social class, Social Class V the lowest. The only other background variable which needs explanation is mirror experience. The mothers were asked, "How often does your child look in a mirror (times weekly)?" Their responses were divided into six categories ranging from 1, indicating that the infant looked at himself a minimal amount of time (1 to 4 times a week) to 6, indicating a high amount of mirror exposure (4 or 5 times a day). Not surprisingly, all infants had seen themselves in a mirror before, and only one did not see himself in a mirror at least once every week.

Interobserver Reliability

Two different testers administered the four tasks to ten of the subjects; interobserver reliabilities for these ten subjects were .90 for the Bell Object Permanence Test, .95 for duration of first fixation, and .93 for the number of fixations in the attention task, .93 to .98 for the mirror measures, and .88 to .89 for the two videotape measures.

Data Analysis

Three different questions were of interest. First, what is the relationship between self recognition in the mirror and videotape procedures? Second, what is the relationship between the self recognition measures and the measures of cognition? And third, what is the relationship between self recognition and familial and experiential variables?

Results

Self Recognition across the Mirror and Videotape Procedures

The relationship between measures of self recognition in the mirror and videotape procedures was examined using biserial correlations. Table 6-1 presents the correlations between mark-directed, body-directed, and imitative behaviors in the mirror condition, and contingent play and imitative behaviors in the videotape condition. Self recognition in both conditions was related for some measures but not for others, and the magnitude of the correlations varied across measures. Mark-directed

Table 6-1

Correlations between the Mirror and Videotape Measures of Self Recognition

	Mirror measures		
Videotape measures	Mark-directed	Body-directed	Imitation
Contingent play			
Contingent self	.43[a]	−.04	.21[b]
Noncontingent self	.24[b]	−.17	.21[b]
Noncontingent other	.10	−.15	−.09
Imitates tape			
Noncontingent self	.40[a]	−.16	.20[b]
Noncontingent other	.15	−.11	−.00

[a] $p < .01$.
[b] $p < .05$.

behavior in the mirror condition was significantly related to contingent play and imitation in the videotape condition. The highest correlation was between mark-directed behavior and contingent play in the contingent self condition ($r = .43$, $p < .01$), although mark-directed behavior was also related significantly to contingent play and imitation in the noncontingent self condition (r's $= .24$ and $.40$, respectively). Although significant correlations were found for mark recognition, body-directed behavior was unrelated to the videotape measures. This suggests, along with findings from the mirror tests, that body-directed behavior may only indicate a primitive awareness of self, not self recognition *per se*. Imitation was also measured in the mirror condition and showed moderate and significant correlations with contingent play and imitation of the tape in the self conditions (r's $= .20$ and $.21$, $p < .05$). This lends further support to the notion that imitation, in the form of acting silly and coy, is not a precursor to mark recognition as others have suggested (Amsterdam, 1972) but rather develops at the same time. In addition, these findings suggest that imitation, as measured in the mirror and videotape procedures, is related but not identical.

The final point to be made regarding the relationship between the mirror and videotape measures involves the noncontingent other condition. Infants' responses to the videotape of another child were not related to their responses to themselves in the mirror. This supports our belief that infants' responses to themselves are not determined by specific motoric or cognitive skills but on seeing themselves rather than others: responding to another is separate from and unrelated to responding to the self. In brief, infants who show self recognition in one representational mode are likely to show self recognition in another and to exhibit self recognition in both contingent and noncontingent representations.

SELF RECOGNITION AND COGNITIVE ABILITY

The relationships between the self recognition measures in both the self recognition procedures and the cognition measures—object permanence, response habituation, and response recovery—were examined in three different ways. First, the correlations between the cognitive and self recognition measures were examined for the total sample. Then the relationships for each individual age group were explored. Finally, to test the effect of the cognition variables together with age held constant, multiple regressions were performed.

The correlations between self recognition and cognition for the total sample are presented in Table 6-2. Age of the subject is also included since we found the self-recognition measures to be highly age-related. Besides the self-recognition measures discussed in the preceding section, three additional self-recognition measures were derived and used in subsequent analyses. These measures utilize data from both the mirror and videotape procedures and are rating scales rather than noncontinuous data. Self Recognition I included the mark-directed behavior and the contingent play behavior in the contingent self condition. If infants exhibited both behaviors, they received a score of three; either behavior, a score of two; and neither behavior, a score of one. Self Recognition II included the self mark-directed behavior and the contingent play behavior in the noncontingent self condition; Self Recognition III included the self mark-directed behavior and the imitation behavior in the noncontingent self condition. In this way, self recognition was conceptualized as a continuum rather than just as a dichotomy.

As can be seen in Table 6-2, self recognition and cognitive ability were related, although both were more highly related to age than to each other. When the findings from the mirror procedure were examined, mark-directed behavior was found to be related to object permanence ($r = .45$, $p < .01$) and response recovery ($r = .46$, $p < .01$) but not to response habituation. Imitation in the mirror procedure was related to object permanence ($r = .29$, $p < .01$) but not to habituation or response

TABLE 6-2
Correlations between Self Recognition and Cognitive Measures

Self recognition measures	Cognitive measures			
	Habituation	Recovery	Object permanence	Age
Mirror measures				
Mark-directed	.17	.46^a	.45^a	.64^a
Body-directed	.11	.08	.15	.18
Imitation	.16	.10	.29^a	.35^a
Videotape measures				
Contingent play				
Contingent self	.14	.25^a	.56^a	.59^a
Noncontingent self	.19	.17	.34^a	.39^a
Noncontingent other	.15	.02	.21	.19
Imitates tape				
Noncontingent self	.24^b	.32^a	.51^a	.72^a
Noncontingent other	−.02	.12	.44^a	.63^a
Self recognition combinations				
I (mark and contingent play)	.20	.32^a	.51^a	.72^a
II (mark and contingent play)	.27^a	.36^a	.44^a	.63^a
III (mark and imitates self)	.30	.45^a	.49^a	.69^a
Age	.29^a	.32^a	.78^a	—

$^a p < .01.$
$^b p < .05.$

recovery. Body-directed behavior in the mirror procedure was not related to any of the cognitive measures.

When the findings from the videotape procedure were examined, object permanence was most likely and habituation least likely to be related to the self-recognition measures. Contingent play in the contingent and noncontingent self conditions was related significantly to object permanence and to response recovery (r's range from .25 to .56). Imitates self tape was related to all three measures of cognition, with the highest correlation involving object permanence ($r = .51, p < .01$) and the lowest correlation involving habituation ($r = .24, p < .05$).

The three combinations of self-recognition measures were also related to the cognitive measures. The highest correlations were found for object permanence and self recognition (r's ranged from .44 to .51), the next highest correlations were found for response recovery (r's ranged from .32 to .45), and the lowest correlations for habituation (r's ranged from .20 to .30).

Taken together, these data indicate that self recognition, as measured in mirror and videotape procedures, was related to cognition, as measured by object permanence and information-processing. The strongest relationship was between self recognition and object permanence, as those infants who showed self recognition were also more likely to show higher levels of object permanence. Interestingly, infants who showed self recognition were also likely to show large response recovery, indicating that the ability to respond to changes in the environment is related to self recognition. Infants' responses to redundant information were also positively (but usually nonsignificantly) related to self recognition, with infants who showed greater information-processing ability (i.e., habituation) being somewhat more likely to exhibit self recognition.

In addition, these data indicate that most self recognition measures were highly related to age (r's ranging from .35 to .72), with the exception of body-directed behavior, contingent play and imitation in the noncontingent other conditions. The latter finding is important because responding to self is age-related but responding to other is not. In fact, the *other* measures were much less likely to be related to the cognitive measures than to self measures, and only one out of six correlations reached significance.

As expected, age also affected the cognitive scores, with object permanence exhibiting the strongest age relationship. This is also reflected in the relatively high correlations between object permanence and self recognition (in most cases, the r's were in the .40s and .50s). The correlations between the attention and self recognition measures were lower, which is, in part, accounted for by the less age-related nature of the attention measures.

Because of the age-related nature of both the cognitive and self-recognition tasks and because of our interest in within-age individual differences, correlational analyses identical to those reported in Table 6-2 were performed for each age group separately. Two consistent trends were found. First, imitates tape in the noncontingent self condition was related to cognitive functioning in all three age groups. For the 9- to 12-month-olds, Self Recognition II, which included mark recognition and imitates noncontingent self tape, was positively related to object permanence. For the 15- to 18-month-olds, imitates noncontingent self tape was related to habituation and to object permanence. For the 21- to 24-month-olds, imitates noncontingent self tape and response recovery were positively correlated, as was Self Recognition III (mark recognition and imitates self tape) and response recovery. Thus, in all age groups, imitates noncontingent self tape was the *only* self-recognition measure to be related to cognitive functioning. In addition, mark-directed behavior, in conjunction with imitates self tape, was related to response recovery in two of three age groups.

To isolate the effects of age still further, a series of step-wise multiple regressions were performed with additional variables being entered by the F test criteria. Regressions were performed using each of the self-recognition variables as a dependent measure. Cognitive measures never entered the equation prior to age, further reinforcing the age-related nature of both cognition and self recognition. In three of the eleven regressions, a cognitive measure, when entered, significantly increased the R. Specifically, response recovery increased the R significantly and entered the equations (after age) for imitates noncontingent self tape: [$R = .55$, increase in $R^2 = .03$, $t(88) = 1.97$, $p < .05$], Self Recognition III; [$R = .74$, increase in $R^2 = .06$, $t(89) = 3.52$, $p < .01$], and Self Recognition II; [$R = .65$, increase in $R^2 = .03$, $t(90) = 2.11$, $p < .05$]. These data indicate that the strongest cognitive effect was found for response recovery. When the age dependency of cognition and self recognition was reduced by looking at the within-age group correlations or eliminated by the use of regression techniques, a relationship between self recognition and cognitive performance still emerged, with more advanced cognitive ability being positively related to self recognition.

SELF RECOGNITION, FAMILIAL CHARACTERISTICS, AND EXPERIENTIAL HISTORY

The relationships among self recognition, familial characteristics, and experiential variables are presented in Table 6-3. The familial variables include the social class level of the family, the mother's educational background, the child's birth order, and the number of other siblings in the family. Several of these familial variables have been found to be related to cognitive development and were included here to see if they also relate to self recognition. The child's mirror experience was also investigated to observe whether past experience with their images was related to their self recognition behavior.

With regard to the familial variables, no significant relationships between any of the variables and self recognition appeared. Interest-

TABLE 6-3
Correlations between Self Recognition and Social Measures

	Social measures					
Self-recognition measures	Sex	SES	Mother's education	Birth order	Number of siblings	Mirror experience
Mirror measures						
Mark-directed	−.14	.15	.14	.11	.15	−.18
Body-directed	.01	−.13	−.06	−.06	−.05	−.11
Imitation	−.16	.13	−.01	.04	.05	−.13
Videotape measures						
Contingent play						
Contingent self	−.05	.12	.03	.05	.07	−.05
Noncontingent self	.09	.24	.05	.16	.15	−.11
Noncontingent other	−.12	.00	.06	.01	.01	.06
Imitates tape						
Noncontingent self	.06	.04	.13	.02	.02	−.14
Noncontingent other	.16	.15	.12	.15	.18	−.14

ingly, social class was moderately, although nonsignificantly, related to one self recognition measure (contingent play in the noncontingent self condition). Sex, maternal educational level, birth order, and number of siblings had no relationship to self recognition. In addition, mirror experience and self recognition in the mirror and videotape conditions were unrelated.

PREDICTION OF SELF RECOGNITION FROM COGNITION AND INDIVIDUAL DIFFERENCES

In order to examine the total contribution of both cognitive and familial variables to self recognition, a series of step-wise multiple regressions were performed. Age, the cognitive variables (object permanence, response recovery, decrement, and response recovery), and the three individual variables (sex, social class, and birth order) were the independent variables, and the three self recognition combinations (mark recognition and contingent play in contingent self, mark recognition and contingent play in noncontingent self, and mark recognition and imitates self tape) were the dependent variables. Summaries of the three regressions are presented in Table 6-4.

In all three multiple regressions, age accounted for the bulk of the variance and entered each equation first. Response recovery significantly increased the R for mark recognition play and noncontingent self contingent play (II), and mark recognition and imitates self tape (III) but not for mark recognition play and contingent self contingent play (I). In addition, sex of the subject significantly increased the R for Self Recognition III. This was because girls were somewhat more likely (although not significantly) to imitate a videotape of themselves than were the boys.

Discussion

How are we to explain the individual differences in self recognition that have characterized all our studies thus far? Most obvious are the striking developmental trends found with almost all our measures. Age or developmental status is the single most important determinant of self recognition. This ontogenetic trend may be similar to the phylogenetic trend reported by Gallup (1977). In an ontogenetic sense, self recognition may be absolute (i.e., no infant under 12 months of age will ever exhibit mark recognition, and all children over 2½ years of age, if not cognitively or socially impaired, will exhibit mark recognition). At the same time, individual differences within age groups have also been found. Perhaps age differences may be related to social and cognitive factors, since self recognition is both a social and a cognitive skill. In the social realm, Gallup (1977) has reported that chimpanzees who have

TABLE 6-4
Summary of Multiple Regressions for Self Recognition Combinations

Dependent variable	Independent variable entered	R	t
Self recognition I	Age	.72	9.87[a]
(Mark and contingent play)			
Self recognition II	Age	.63	6.73[a]
(Mark and contingent play)	Recovery	.65	2.11[b]
Self recognition III	Age	.69	8.27[b]
(Mark and imitates self)	Recovery	.74	3.52[a]
	Sex	.75	2.31[b]

[a] $p < .01$.
[b] $p < .05$.

been reared as social isolates do not exhibit mark recognition, even after extensive exposure to mirrors. Perhaps differential social experience also affects the acquisition of self knowledge in man. In the cognitive realm, Mans, Cicchetti, and Sroufe (1978) have reported that a Developmental Quotient of approximately 18 months of age was a necessary but not sufficient condition for the appearance of mark recognition in a sample of Down's Syndrome infants. Whether or not a fine-grained analysis of cognitive functioning and self recognition in a normal population would yield such a relationship is not known. Nonetheless, our study does yield results revelant for some of these issues.

Before turning to the present study, we need to examine current beliefs about cognition. Although cognition or intelligence is often conceptualized as some unitary construct, the infancy literature suggests that early cognition is a loose network of cognitive skills (Lewis, 1976). Thus, we do not expect to find a strong connection between all aspects of cognition but do expect to find different patterns and only some relationships. In the same sense, if self recognition is, in part, a cognitive activity, we would expect only some relationships to appear; specifically, those that involve cognitive skills essential for self development. In the same manner, although certain social skills may be necessary for the evolution of self recognition, little overall connection between these social skills and the ability to recognize the self may be found.

In the present study, individual differences in self recognition were explored: specifically, the relationships of different measures of self recognition, of cognition and self recognition, of self recognition and previous mirror experience, and of social experience and self recognition. Each of these relationships will be discussed in turn.

SELF RECOGNITION IN TWO DIFFERENT REPRESENTATIONS

One purpose of the present study was to examine self recognition in different representational forms—mirrors and videotapes. Positive relationships were found between self recognition measures in the two procedures. Mark-directed behavior was highly related to contingent play in the contingent self condition. This is not surprising, as the contingent self videotape condition is analogous to the mirror self condition, both providing immediate and contingent feedback to the infant. Mark recognition was also related to contingent play and imitates tape in the noncontingent self condition. The fact that measures are related, even though very different, suggests that self recognition can be measured across two quite different forms of representation, both mirrors and videotapes, and contingent and noncontingent representation.

In addition, the infants' responses to the noncontingent other condition were not related to their responses to the mirror. The other condition shares little in common with the mirror, as it is neither contingent nor a representation of the self. Thus, self recognition in the mirror was related to responses to the self but not the other in the videotape.

In brief, a relationship between representations that differ with respect to color, size of infant, type of presentation, and contingent feedback was found. These data support our belief that a notion of self exists in the early years which is not related or restricted to representational forms, although there are some limitations which we shall discuss in Chapter 8.

Cognition and Self Recognition

Cognitive ability and self recognition might be expected to be related since the ability to infer that a mirror or videotape reflection is a representation of the self implies a notion of distancing and representation (Merleau-Ponty, 1964; Sigel & Cocking, 1977). In the present study, two types of cognitive functioning were examined—permanence and attention.

Object permanence has been hypothesized to be related to self recognition in that the self, other people, and objects all have permanence, and infants must learn these permanences simultaneously. How can an infant know that an object exists independently of his or her perception of it without concurrent knowledge of self permanence? If object permanence occurs at the same time or just after self permanence occurs, we would expect to find a relationship between object permanence and self. Our data do suggest that object permanence and self recognition are highly related in both the mirror and videotape procedures. However, these relationships were affected by the age-related nature of both object permanence and self recognition such that most disappeared after age had been controlled. Bertenthal and Fischer (1978), using a procedure in which five mirror-related tasks were scaled in terms of degree of self awareness, also examined the relationship between object permanence and self recognition. Consistent with our results, they report a significant correlation between the two when age was free to vary but not when age was held constant. Our findings and those of Bertenthal and Fischer (1978) are strengthened by the findings from the person perception literature. Object permanence and variables such as maternal separation have not been found to be related (Jackson, Campos, & Fisher, 1978).

Attention, or the ability to process redundant and novel stimuli, was our second measure of cognitive functioning. Attentional distribution, in general response decrement, has been shown to be related to later cognitive functioning in several studies (Lewis, 1969, 1971; Lewis & Baldini, in press). In terms of self recognition, the ability to respond to a change after habituating to redundant stimuli seemed especially important since the mark on the nose and the noncontingent videotape of self each constitutes an alteration of the typical contingent feedback situation an infant experiences (i.e., a mirror). As expected, response recovery was positively related to mirror and videotape measures, *even after* age was taken into account. Specifically, response recovery was related to mark recognition in the mirror procedure and imitates self tape in the videotape procedure. These data suggest that the visual perceptual-cognitive mode, that is, looking at, attending to, and processing information, exhibit consistencies regardless of the specific task. In the mirror and videotape procedures, infants look at, attend to, and respond to self representations; in the attentional task they do so to perceptual-cognitive tasks. Procedures that share similar cognitive functions may be more related to each other than procedures that have a theoretically logical relationship (such as object permanence and self recognition).

Age differences with respect to the relationship of permanence and attention were also found. When the three age groups were examined separately, the most persistent finding involved imitates a videotape of oneself (noncontingent self condition). Imitates the self tape was related to response recovery in the 21- to 24-month-olds and to object permanence in the 9- to 12- and the 15- to 18-month-olds. Imitation, as discussed by Piaget (1937/1954), should be related to object permanence since it requires that the infant be able to separate itself and the object to be imitated. This relationship may have existed only for the two younger age groups, because the 21- to 24-month-olds had achieved most of the skills measured by the object permanence scale, being in Piaget's Stage 6. This constitutes a ceiling effect on the object permanence task. Response recovery, which measures the ability to respond to a novel stimulus, may be related to imitates self since those infants who notice change in inanimate stimuli may be those who also notice that the noncontingent representation of oneself, although oneself, is responding differently (i.e., noncontingently). The older infants are more likely to notice change in both attention and self recognition procedures.

In terms of the two procedures, some measures were correlated with cognition but others were not. In the videotape procedure, contingent play and imitates self tape were both related to cognition, with the relationship between imitates self tape and cognition occurring even after age was held constant. Imitating or playing with a tape of another exhibited no relationship with cognition, strengthening our belief that these results are specific to self development, not social development in general. In the mirror procedure, mark-directed but not body-directed or imitative behaviors were related to cognitive functioning, especially to response recovery. Thus, body-directed behavior, although shown to be a precursor to mark recognition, does not seem to have any strong links to cognitive functioning, at least as measured in the study. Likewise, imitation has few links, although it is somewhat related to object permanence.

THE EFFECT OF MIRROR EXPERIENCE

Individual differences in self recognition may be related to experiential as well as cognitive factors. One logical possibility involves previous mirror experience. Self recognition is related to mirror experience for chimpanzees and nontechnological people. Gallup's (1970) chimpanzees did not exhibit self-directed behavior prior to mirror experience, and Kohler (1927, cited in Amsterdam, 1968) reported that nontechnological persons do not recognize themselves in mirrors. However, our data do not support the notion of mirror exposure as a facilitator of mark recognition. Of course, this finding is limited, since the data are based on mothers' reports and since all infants had some previous mirror experience. Perhaps even a limited amount of mirror experience is sufficient for self recognition. Given the proprioceptive feedback of the facial musculature, a few trials, or even a single trial, may be all that is necessary to associate facial features to this feedback. That chimpanzees acquire facial recognition with so few hours of learning experience supports the belief that a large degree of experience may not be necessary to identify which features go with one's own face. In any case, amount of mirror experience did not differentiate between those who did and those who did not exhibit self recognition in the present study.

THE EFFECT OF SOCIAL EXPERIENCE

Social experience may also affect the expression of self recognition. Following Mead (1934) and Merleau-Ponty (1964), we believe that humans come to know themselves through their interactions with others. Indeed, without others, self knowledge could not exist. Gallup reports supporting evidence, as chimpanzees reared in social isolation were unable to exhibit self-directed behavior in a mirror situation even after extensive exposure (Gallup & McClure, 1971). As a further test of the necessity of social experience, two of the chimpanzees were given three months of group experience, after which time self recognition began to appear (Gallup, McClure, Hill, & Bundy, 1971). Clearly, no analog exists in the human literature, except perhaps in accounts of feral children such as the wild boy of Avignon.

Although the absence or presence of social interaction cannot be studied, as all humans have such experience, individual differences in the type and amount of social interaction may be studied. Gross measures of social experience—birth order, number of siblings, mother's education—have failed to exhibit any relationship with self recognition, either in the present study or that of Amsterdam (1968). This does not negate the potential importance of social experience upon the development of self but only shows that gross measures of social experience are insensitive. Interestingly, the primate literature sheds some light on the issue of social experience. Several investigators have reported that chimpanzees reared by humans may perceive themselves to be like their caregivers. When asked to sort pictures of people and chimpanzees, Viki, a home-reared chimpanzee, put her picture with the human pictures rather than with the chimpanzee pictures (Hayes & Nissen, 1971). And when another chimpanzee, Washoe, first saw other chimpanzees, she referred to them in sign language as "black bugs" (Linden, 1974). One's knowledge of self may be heavily dependent on social experience.

Since the failure to find any evidence for social experience as a mediator of self knowledge in infancy may have to do most with the use of gross measures of social experience, we might ask what measures might be more sensitive. Lewis (Lewis & Freedle, 1973, 1977; Lewis &

Goldberg, 1969) has argued for the importance of the mother–infant interaction (most significantly, response contingency) for perceptual-cognitive development. Early interaction may be equally important for self development (Lewis, 1977). Contingency in early infancy probably provides a framework for the emerging concept of self. Contingency administered by a consistent caregiver may provide the necessary conditions for the self–other distinction. Contingency effects or increases action–outcome pairings, which give rise to increasingly complex and intentional circular reactions. This intentionality allows the development of understanding of means and ends for actions and outcomes. Thus, the intention to try to produce an effect results in agency and intention, aspects of the developing self. These issues are taken up again in more detail in the following chapters. Nevertheless, the relationship of social experience, self recognition, and self concept remains an open question.

CHAPTER 7

Self Recognition and Emotional Development

In the preceding chapter we discussed the relationship between self knowledge and cognition. Briefly stated, we believe that self knowledge is a cognitive act itself which, at the same time, facilitates and accompanies other cognitions. To understand one's world, one must understand the actions in that world as well as the agent of that action, be it self or other. Thus, the consequence of any action is an understanding of the object (the world), the actor or agent (self), and the interaction between the two. The infant's knowledge of self may not be separated from knowledge of the world and of interaction with the world, nor may these three aspects of knowledge be separated from cognition.

In our attempt to understand and measure at least some aspect of that interdependence, we found a relationship between object permanence and self recognition. Moreover, responsivity to environmental changes was also related to self recognition, as both rest on the infant's perceptual-cognitive capacities and skills.

We would also hypothesize that emotional experience and self knowledge have parallel and interdependent developments. In fact, all three—cognition, self knowledge, and emotional experience—seem to be related, a point we will return to in the next chapter. In this chapter, however, we shall examine the relationship between self and affect. To do this, we need to explore first some of the more important features of emotional experience. At least three important features of emotional experience can be demonstrated in children under three years of age. First, children prior to three years of age are capable of understanding at least some questions pertaining to feelings. For example, young children are able to respond appropriately to questions such as, "how do you like this?" Second, young children are capable of verbally responding to emotional questions. Third, children appear to recognize that feelings are located within one's body. For example, if something doesn't taste good, young children will spit it out; if a cut is painful, they will try to take off a bandage to let the hurt out of their bodies. These three features, which are observable in young children, reflect their emotional experience. The use of the word "experience" rather than "expression" is deliberate, because we feel it necessary to distinguish between the expression of an emotion, which may require neither cognition nor self knowledge, and an emotional experience, which requires reflection and, therefore, self knowledge (Lewis & Rosenblum, 1978). For us, emotional experience requires both a conscious feeling and a cognitive evaluation of bodily changes. Both of these features are dependent upon knowing where the bodily change is located and imply an awareness of self, since one must know that the bodily change has a location (the self), and that the change is being experienced or evaluated by the self.

A Definition of Emotion

Our thoughts concerning emotion and emotional development have been influenced primarily by two men: William James and Charles Darwin. Darwin (cf. 1877), and the tradition that followed him, emphasized the surface expression of emotion rather than feeling or emotional state. For Darwin, a particular event—some external situation—elicited both the surface expression and the emotional state. Thus, state and expression are intimately connected; for example, a happy face would be equivalent to a happy feeling. However, a one-to-one correspondence between emotional expression and emotional states has not been demonstrated clearly, even after numerous attempts through the last century. For example, even though the neonate has penile erections and smiles during REM sleep, we would be reluctant to say that the newborn is experiencing a happy state or having a happy dream. Likewise, we might laugh at our boss's joke which we may not find particularly funny, as laughter is not always indicative of a happy or amused state. A close correspondence between expression and state is most likely to occur in the following two conditions. First, as studied by Ekman (1971) and Izard (1971), the primary emotions (fear, anger, etc.) seem to be present in most cultures and to have universal meaning.

Second, in early infancy, an elicitor may produce a synchrony between expression and state in which correspondence is high. However, for emotions considered derived rather than primary (Tomkins, 1962, 1963), and for older children and adults, expression and state are less likely, both theoretically and empirically, to be highly related (cf. Lewis & Rosenblum, 1978).

William James defined emotions as "the bodily changes [that] follow directly the perception of the exciting fact and our feeling of the same changes as they occur is the emotion" (1890/1950 p. 449). For James, in order to experience an emotion, a precipitating event (exciting fact) causes a bodily change. The conscious feeling of that change is the emotional feeling. Thus, emotion is not the precipitating event, nor the bodily change associated with that event, but is the conscious feeling of that bodily change. Although the nature of the bodily change has been questioned [for example, James believed more in the importance of muscular changes, whereas Bard (1934) stressed neurophysiological changes, in particular activation through discharge from the hypothalamus to the cerebral cortex], the James-Lange theory and its derivatives have all maintained that the conscious feeling of bodily change was as central to the concept of emotion as the bodily change itself.

More recently, the conscious feeling of bodily change has been redefined as a cognitive evaluative process by Schacter and Singer (1962), who maintain that the soma changes are not specific for any particular emotional experience but are a more general arousal state (see, for example, Lindsley, 1951). Their conclusion was due, in part, to the fact that sets of physiological responses have not been found to covary with any given emotional experience. Instead, the nature of any specific emotion is thought to be partially determined by the organism's evaluation of its aroused condition, an evaluation that may include contextual cues, past experiences, and individual differences. In brief, the Schacter and Singer and the James–Lange theories are similar in that the elicitor produces a bodily change which is experienced by the organism. The experience of the organism, defined as a "conscious feeling" by James or as a "cognitive evaluative feeling" by Schacter and Singer, is the feeling or emotion.

As we (Lewis, Brooks, & Haviland, 1978) have suggested, these theories are most relevant when studying the ontogenesis of emotions. The infant's experience is determined initially both by the elicitor, which produces a bodily change (including facial expression), and the behavior (both verbal and nonverbal) of the caregiver in response to that bodily change. The synchrony between a facial expression of fear (mouth muscles back and down, eyes wide, body moving backward), and the emotional feeling of fear may be mediated by the caregiver's verbal labeling ("don't be frightened") and the caregiver's responses (holding the child and comforting it). Synchrony would be acquired from the interaction and would be indicative of socialization practices.

Internal and External Stimuli

The ontogenesis of emotion requires locating the feeling within oneself. Location may be discussed vis-à-vis the difference between internal and external stimuli. External stimuli are usually verifiable by others in the sense that others can easily share them, even though experiences may differ. For example, one might say, "look at the snow falling" and have others verify that experience. Internal stimuli are not externally verifiable since they cannot be shared or directly experienced by any other. One would not say, "look at me thinking" or "look at me feeling sad." One would say, "I am thinking" or "I am sad." Thinking and feeling have in common the fact that they are both internal and not easily verified by others. Both can be verified only by asking the person who is experiencing them to introspect, to tell what he or she is thinking and feeling. (Our knowledge of the thoughts and feelings of others, empathy, is explored in Chapter 10.) Infants, of course, cannot tell us what they are thinking and feeling. Indeed, the study of facial and other nonverbal expressions and of the physiological correlates of emotional experiences are attempts to explore these internal states without the use of introspection. Unfortunately, introspection has been discredited as a form of adult inquiry for both the study of thinking and feeling, even though there is no easily demonstrated one-to-one relationship between external and internal events.

The internal-external distinction is also relevant to the concept of self. Internal stimuli have a location inside ourselves, external stimuli outside ourselves. Interestingly, this distinction appears to have an historical development (Jaynes, 1977) and is also likely to have an ontogenetic development. Historically, it appears that people were once reluctant to consider all internal stimuli as emanating from themselves. For example, although a certain stimulus emitted from the stomach region meant that a person was hungry, a set of stimuli emitted from the head (for example, an angry wish) was a god-figure's way of telling a person something. Today, both would be seen as internal. Thus, over a relatively short period of time, a greater set of internal stimuli have been considered as belonging to oneself, a view that was greatly facilitated by Freud's view of the unconscious as part of the self. The distinction between external stimuli and internal stimuli implies both a concept of self and its location within the body.

The ontogenetic development of the internal-external dimension may or may not parallel the historical development. However, the distinction between internal and external stimuli seems to develop ontogenetically and to be related to self awareness. Unfortunately, verification of one's belief in internal stimuli, especially in infancy, is difficult. One possible verification is the use or understanding of empathy. Only by having experienced a feeling is one able to understand or appreciate another's feeling. Without empathy, people's internal experiences would have little connection, a point which will be discussed further in Chapter 10.

Evaluation of Stimuli

Internal stimuli must be evaluated. This evaluation has been conceptualized as a perceptual-cognitive process similar to information-processing of other stimuli, the only difference being that the information to be processed is located within the body. However, whether or not internal and external information is processed similarly is unknown and difficult to determine. In either case, evaluation is related to self awareness. Self awareness, as an information-processing and decision-making process having to do with internal stimuli, would logically require an active organism which can conceptualize itself as an agent or as having agency. Agency refers to that aspect of action that makes reference to the cause of the action, that is, not only who or what is causing this stimulus change, but who is evaluating it. Stimulus change itself should have the effect of both alerting the organism and forcing it to make some type of evaluation.

The evaluation process should have similarities to other cognitive processes for which models have been articulated. For example, the ability of the organism to cause events to occur would seem to require some notion of self. If infants can cause an outcome to occur repeatedly through a behavior, as by secondary circular reactions (Piaget, 1937/ 1954), then they have learned some of the causes and consequences of that behavior. For certain associations between events, the infant has learned the notion of his own agency; e.g., "I" cause something to happen. "I" has a location, although "I" also moves in space, two processes underlying the sense of permanence. This "I," which is different from other, has an internal location, and is permanent across time and space, is the beginning of self. As infants learn to affect their world, they also learn to evaluate themselves.

The evaluation process itself requires an agent of evaluation. A sentence about the evaluation of internal stimuli cannot be constructed without referring to the self. The phrase, "I am experiencing some internal changes" means "I am feeling thus." The source of the stimuli and the agent evaluating the stimuli are the same, with this interface being the self.

The Ontogenesis of Emotional Experience and Self Knowledge

The preceding discussion suggests that, without consciousness and cognitive evaluation, an emotion would not be experienced. Both are dependent upon knowing where the bodily change is located and imply an awareness of self, since one must know that the bodily change has a location (the self) and that the change is being experienced or evaluated by the self. In short, we believe that the organizing principle of self knowledge is necessary for emotional experience.

In order to study the ontogenesis of emotional experience, we also need to explore the development of self. In earlier chapters of the book we have done just that by exploring the ontogenesis of visual self recognition in the opening years of life. Our research suggests that, over the first two years of life, the body begins to be experienced as distinct from others, and the self is realized as being inside rather than outside the body. In addition, the ontogenetic changes in differentiation of videotapes and pictures of self and other suggest that the infant is learning that perceptual features are unique to oneself and that there is a relationship between those features and the self. Such knowledge helps the infant to evaluate his or her own bodily changes (for example, "I am sad"), just as he or she labels self (for example, "I am small" or "I am female"). By constructing the ontogenesis of emotional experience in conjunction with self knowledge and by incorporating the elements of location and evaluation, the expression and development of different emotions may be better understood.

Emotional experience, comprised of evaluation, the conscious feeling, and self awareness, is heavily dependent upon the existence of appropriate cognitive and social facilities. Over the first three years of life, the infant acquires these faculties and with them the ability to experience emotions. Although emotional elicitors may produce specific emotional states and expressions, it is not until the infant has self knowledge that we can speak of the infant as also having emotional experiences. Given this perspective, the newborn or very young infant would not experience emotions. We believe that the newborn or young infant has, but does not experience, a set of stimuli changes. Not until conscious feeling emerges (self awareness and evaluation) can we talk of the child as experiencing emotions. This type of formulation appears, at first, to fly in the face of common sense; a one-week-old, who cries when a loud noise goes off, must be certainly experiencing fright. However, an emotional elicitor, in this case a loud noise, may produce an emotional state but not an emotional experience. The newborn may be in a fearful state but not necessarily experiencing fear.

Not only are there developmental changes in the relationship between experience and state—increased synchrony with increasing age—but some emotional experiences require more conscious feeling and evaluation than others. Thus, we would expect some emotional experiences to emerge earlier than others. For example, fear seems to precede shame since the former requires less evaluative processing than the latter. In order to obtain the sequence of emerging emotional experiences, the child's cognitive abilities, including self knowledge, must be considered. Thus, not until the infant can incorporate the standards of others can we speak of such emotional states as shame or guilt. Even so, as our discussion on the role of self knowledge should make clear, the emergence of self needs to precede the emergence of any emotional experiences. Given the data presented in this volume, emotional experiences should appear in the second half of the first year, as the onset of stranger fear and separation anxiety might well indicate.

The emotional experiences that require less evaluation and therefore appear earliest may then serve to facilitate the development of other emotional experiences through the facilitation of additional self knowledge and the production of structures needed for the subsequent emotional experiences. These early emotional experiences may be those that others have labeled the primary emotions, whereas the latter may be those labeled derived emotions (Tomkins, 1962, 1963). That derived and primary emotions may exist need not imply that one set is any more biologically rooted than another, merely that one set requires less evaluative ability. A model stressing amount of evaluation rather than biological determination should be open to experimental verification, since cognitive evaluation and consciousness, as well as emotional experience, can be measured in the young.

Not only may different emotional experiences have different developmental sequences, but aspects of one emotional experience may progress differently. As an example, let us look at the development of fear or, more specifically, a variety of situations in which fear is reportedly elicited in an infant (Lewis, 1975). A one-year-old infant shows fearful behavior—and presumably experiences fear—either when a loud noise sounds behind him or when his mother, dressing for the evening, puts on a wig. These two examples of "fearful" behavior illustrate two points. First, expressions of fear have different elicitors and different developmental courses; the loud noise would elicit fearful expressions even at one week of age, but the wig would have no effect until much later. Thus, some elicitors need no cognitive structures to produce the fearful expression. These early elicitors may be no more "basic" than the later ones, those resting on cognitive structures, since both may or may not be biologically rooted to produce specific responses (expressions). Second, that emotional expression of fear may occur more readily (or at younger ages) for the loud noise rather than the wig may be because the infant has acquired enough cognitive facility to experience emotions for some elicitors but not enough for others. Thus, early elicitors of fearful expression may be likely to be early elicitors of fearful experiences.

Although emotional experience has been hypothesized to be dependent on self knowledge, a direct comparison between the two is not possible since, without verbal ability and introspection, emotional experiences are difficult to assess. Therefore, in the present study, we made a first approximation, using emotional expression in an emotion-inducing situation as indicative of emotional experience and self recognition in a mirror situation as indicative of self knowledge. It was hypothesized that infants who did not recognize themselves in a mirror would be less likely to exhibit appropriate emotional expression than those who did recognize themselves.

EXPERIMENTAL PROCEDURES[1]

SUBJECTS

Thirty infants representing three age groups were seen. Eleven (five males, six females) were 9 to 12 months of age (*M*, 10.7 months), eleven (five males, six females) were 15 to 18 months of age (*M*, 16.47 months), and eight (four males, four females) were 21 to 24 months of age (*M*, 22.8 months).

All infants were Caucasian, were full-term, and had no congenital abnormalities. Social class was skewed toward the upper end of the Hollingshead Scale (1957), with three-quarters of the fathers being classified as Social Class I or II. Equal numbers of firstborns and later-borns were observed.

PROCEDURE

Each infant received two tasks: a mirror task and a stranger approach sequence.

For the mirror task, infants' responses to seeing themselves in a mirror after their faces were marked with rouge were examined. This procedure was similar to that described in Chapter 2 for Mirror Study I. Infants received two trials: one in which their face was unmarked and one in which their face had been marked. Each trial lasted approximately 90 sec. The entire session was videotaped, and the behaviors used in the original mirror studies were coded.

The situation used to elicit emotional responses from the infant was one that has been commonly used to elicit fear—the approach of a stranger (Morgan & Ricciuti, 1969; Scarr & Salapatek, 1970). However, this situation has been shown recently to elicit a variety of responses other than fear, including wariness, attentiveness, and joy (cf. Brooks & Lewis, 1976; Lewis & Rosenblum, 1975; Rheingold & Eckerman, 1973).

[1]This study was presented in the chapter "Self Knowledge and Emotional Development" by Lewis and Brooks (1978).

These more recent studies suggest that the stranger approach situation is ideal for eliciting a wide range of responses indicative of both positive and negative emotional states.

Infants, accompanied by their mothers, were brought into a room 3 × 4 m in size. The mothers sat to the left of their infants, who were seated in a high chair. On signal, a female stranger appeared at the doorway, smiled at the infant, and said nothing to the child. The stranger remained at the doorway until noticed by the child, and then walked to Position 1 (approximately 1.5 m from the door), which took approximately 3 sec. The stranger paused at Position 1 for approximately one sec and then walked to Position 2 (1.5 m from Position 1), which took another 3 sec. She then walked to Position 3 (1.5 m from Position 2), paused there, and continued to Position 4 (directly in front of the infant). After touching the infant's hand, she turned (Position 5), walked slowly to the door, and exited (E). The entire episode, from entrance to exit, took approximately 25 sec. The mother remained next to the infant during the entire episode. The approach sequence was not begun until the infant was made as comfortable as possible, seemed relaxed, and had a stabilized heart rate.

The total session was videotaped, using a camera mounted on a wall opposite the infant, with the stranger's position marked by an audio signal on the videotape and electrical marker on the polygraph recording.

MEASURES AND INTEROBSERVER RELIABILITIES

The absence or presence of three behaviors was coded from the videotape in the mirror task. These were mark-directed behavior (touching, wiping, or pointing to the marked nose, or saying "nose" or "red"), body-directed behavior (touching the torso, face, or mouth, but not the marked nose), and imitative behavior (acting silly, acting coy, or making faces in the mirror). As in our previous studies, interobserver reliabilities were high (over 85% for eight subjects).

The measurement of facial expression involved the development of a new coding system, which is described in more detail elsewhere (Lewis, Brooks, & Haviland, 1978). The four general categories coded were mouth position, eye direction, eye openness, and eyebrow position. Three major facial patterns were derived from the individual categories. These were: (1) a positive face (corners of the mouth raised, no corners lowered or lips retracted, and eyes directed up and/or ahead); (2) a negative face (corners lowered and eyes averted to the mother's side or diverted downward); and (3) an attentive face (a squared upper or lower lip or relaxed mouth with eyes mainly ahead and up).[2] Each infant was classified in terms of his or her predominant face during the stranger approach sequence. Interobserver reliabilities for these three patterns were over 85%, although this was achieved only after intensive training.

DATA ANALYSIS

Three questions were of interest: (1) What was the incidence of self recognition and three facial patterns? (2) What was the relationship between self recognition and facial expression? and (3) Was this relationship affected by age?

RESULTS AND DISCUSSION

INCIDENCE OF SELF RECOGNITION AND FACIAL EXPRESSION

Table 7-1 presents the percentage of subjects exhibiting self-directed behaviors and the three facial patterns by age. As can be seen, the self recognition data are essentially identical to those reported in Chapter 2. The facial expression data indicate that the modal facial expression was attention, as two-thirds of the infants exhibited an attentive face. One-quarter exhibited a negative expression and only a few exhibited a positive expression. Age differences appeared, as the 21- to 24-month-olds were more likely to exhibit attentive expressions, whereas the 15- to 18-month-olds were as likely to exhibit negative expressions.

Others have reported more negative responding in infants over one year of age than under one year of age (e.g., Lewis & Brooks, 1974; Morgan & Ricciuti, 1969; Scarr & Salapatek, 1970; Schaeffer, 1966). A high incidence of the attentive face has also been reported by others,

---

[2]A fourth facial pattern—attentive-negative face (retracted lips with eyes and forehead related)—is discussed in the Lewis *et al.* (1978) study. Interestingly, this pattern was not seen in any of the present sample, partly because in the Lewis *et al.* study, most of the instances of attentive-negative face were seen in the 6- to 8-month-olds, an age group not represented in the present study.

TABLE 7-1
Percentage of Subjects Exhibiting Self-Directed
Behaviors and Facial Expressions

	Age in months			
	9–12	15–18	21–24	Total
Self-directed behaviors				
Mark-directed	0	45	75	37
Body-directed	27	45	38	36
Imitation	9	27	50	27
Facial expressions				
Positive	18	0	0	7
Negative	18	45	13	27
Attention	55	55	88	63

although the frequency of occurrence of this facial expression has been systematically examined only recently (e.g., Brooks & Lewis, 1976; Emde, Kligman, Reich, & Wade, 1978; Sroufe, Waters, & Matas, 1974). In the past, attentive expressions were considered evidence of wariness, a practice that may have artificially raised the incidence of negative responding in many studies. However, our data seem to be in accordance with more recent reports of infants' responses to stranger's approaches.

RELATIONSHIP BETWEEN SELF RECOGNITION AND FACIAL EXPRESSION

The relationship between the three measures of self recognition and the three facial patterns was tested, using chi-square statistics and the chi-square data are presented in Table 7-2. The total sample is included in only one analysis, since the 9- to 12-month-olds exhibited body-directed, but not mark-directed or imitative behaviors. As can be seen for the total sample, the presence of body-directed behavior was likely to be related to negative facial expressions, the absence of body-directed behavior to be related to attentive facial expressions [$\chi^2(2) = 6.99, p < .05$].

The relationship between self recognition and facial expression was examined for all three mirror measures for the older infants. Positive facial expression is not included in Table 7-2 for the older infants or in the analysis, as it was exhibited only by the 9- to 12-month-olds. For the 15- to 24-month-olds, body-directed behavior was found to be related to

TABLE 7-2
*Relationship between Self Recognition and
Facial Expressions (Number of Subjects)*

Facial expression	Self recognition		
	Total sample		
	Yes	No	Total
	Body-directed behavior		
Positive	0	2	2
Negative	6	2	8
Attentive	5	14	19
Total	11	18	29
	15- to 24-month-olds		
	Mark-directed behavior		
Negative	5	1	6
Attentive	6	7	13
Total	11	8	19
	Imitative behavior		
Negative	3	3	6
Attentive	4	9	13
Total	7	12	19
	Body-directed behavior		
Negative	5	1	6
Attentive	3	10	13
Total	8	11	19

negative facial expression ($\chi^2 = 3.89$, $p < .05$) as it had been for the total sample. Overall, mark-directed and imitative behaviors were not related to facial expression. However, individual cell analyses indicate that the *absence* of mark-directed behavior was related to an attentive face (88% of those not noticing the rouge exhibited an attentive face, 13% exhibited a negative face, Binomial Test, $p < .05$), but the presence of mark-directed behavior was not related to facial expression.

In short, the results of this study tend to support our hypothesis that self awareness and emotional experience are related when self awareness is inferred through visual self recognition and when emotion is inferred through facial expressions exhibited during an emotion-inducing situation. Interestingly, not all self recognition measures were related to facial expression. Only those that involved directing body movement toward the self, measures that may be most indicative of self location, were related. These results also speak to the existence of emotional experiences. If we are correct in assuming that emotional experiences are dependent on self knowledge, then the presence of self recognition and facial expression may be used to infer the presence of emotion as we have defined it.

These findings have implications for knowledge of others as it relates to emotional experience, as well as implications for self knowledge. We have argued that the child's knowledge of others cannot occur without some knowledge of self, and knowledge of others is developed through one's interaction with these others. Without interaction with the social world, little knowledge would exist. In acquiring knowledge about others, infants learn about themselves. As an example, the well-known phenomenon of stranger fear that occurs in many, if not all, cultures around eight months of age (Kagan, 1977) must be related to the developing knowledge of the self. That is, as infants differentiate between familiar and unfamiliar objects and people and learn about the permanence of these objects and people, they are also learning about themselves. As infants learn that their mothers and fathers are different people, they also learn that they are neither mother nor father but unique persons.

An alternative to making this emotional experience dependent upon self knowledge and cognition would be to assume that stranger fear is elicited by a set of stimuli, through some unlearned association between an elicitor and an emotional expression. Although this is probably true for a limited set of events (e.g., a loud noise), our findings suggest that negative emotional expression in a fear-producing situation is related to self awareness, and the fear literature (cf. Lewis & Rosenblum, 1974) suggests that so-called fearful behaviors are related to cognitive factors including object permanence and information processing (Weinraub & Lewis, 1977). Cognition, self knowledge, and emotional expression seem to be linked, as the infant must have a concept of "I" in order to experience a feeling ("I am happy"). Without the "I" in "I am fearful," the emotional experiences implied by the phrase have little meaning for the Western mind.

Chapter 8

The Development of Self Recognition

In the preceding chapters we have outlined the course of visual self recognition over the first few years of life. Using a variety of procedures, measures, and representational forms, we have seen that self recognition does occur in the first two years of life, prior to the onset of language. However, a number of issues still need to be considered, including the differences between representational forms, the differences between measures of self recognition, the criteria for self recognition, and individual differences in self recognition. The present chapter addresses all these issues.

The major focus of our work has been on the acquisition of self recognition, but our interest is in understanding how the young child constructs a concept of self. Although the self is an explanation of a series of internal and external events, we do not consider its construction a meta-theory, even though that, too, is possible to study: children's growing knowledge of knowledge about themselves. Rather, we are concerned with the development of self, that is, the development of the knowledge, whether known to the subject or not, that the self is different than others (people as well as things), and that the self has attributes. It is our belief that children acquire such knowledge long before they are able to reflect upon it, just as a cat knows how to walk around an obstacle rather than through it. Without reflection, infants may know that they are different from others without having knowledge of that knowledge.

The present chapter serves to integrate our studies and others, as well as to develop our notion of how the child's knowledge of self (inferred from self recognition) evolves.

REPRESENTATIONAL FORMS OF THE SELF

In choosing to investigate visual self recognition as a method for exploring the development of self, three different procedures using three different types of self image were studied, each related to naturally occurring situations. We observed infants' response to mirrors, video-tapes, and pictorial representations of the self, since all three sources present the child with different types of information and with different tasks. Let us look at the information provided by each of these forms.

Recognition of pictorial representations of one's face requires prior experience with the face itself in a reflective surface or prior labeling of the face, as seen in a mirror or picture by another. However, an infant could conceivably learn to differentiate some features of self and other without specific visual experiences. If, for instance, an infant learns that age is an important and discriminable feature of the social world and learns that he is a baby (young), not an adult (old), then, conceivably, he could differentiate between self and other. Since infants are able to respond differently to and correctly label pictures of babies and adults, self–adult differentiation without knowledge of one's own perceptual features would be possible. That is, given two pictures, one of self and one of an adult, infants are able not only to differentiate between the two pictures but also prefer to look at their own. The picture of self represents a category (baby) to which infants may know they belong, whereas the adult picture does not represent such a category. This suggests that the infant has some attributes of self knowledge ("I am a baby") but not others ("the specific facial features of the person in that picture are mine"). The same argument can be made for gender differentiation: if an infant differentiates among others on the basis of gender and knows his or her own gender, then differentiation of the self and an opposite-sex person should be possible without explicit knowledge of one's own facial features. However, in order to differentiate between pictures of oneself and a same-age, same-sex person, the specific facial features which are unique to oneself must be learned. Thus, some prior experience with self representations (i.e., pictures or mirrors) is necessary. In addition, the fact that attributes of the self that are common social attributes (i.e., age and gender) can be known with specific visual experience suggests that we should be careful in selecting the "other" with which to compare oneself and cautious in interpreting self–other differentiation when the gender and age of the comparison person are different from those of the self.

The knowledge that a reflection in the mirror is oneself and not another seems an easier task than picture recognition. Mirrors possess special and unique properties as they are three-dimensional, relatively distortion-free, and reproduce one's actions simultaneously. The one-to-one correspondence of one's actions and the reflection of those actions is naturally present in light-reflecting surfaces. Such contingencies give valuable feedback, as infants learn that other people do not produce behavior sequences identical to theirs and that only a reflective image of themselves does so. An infant must discover the contingent nature of mirrors, making the inference that a reflection is not another, but is the self. With this knowledge, the special features unique to oneself may be learned.

Videotape representations have features of both pictorial and mirror representations. Like mirrors, videotapes can present immediate, direct, and contingent self representations, although these representations differ from mirrors in several important ways. First, most videotape systems utilize black and white rather than color representations. Even those using color cannot match naturally occurring colors. Second, videotapes are usually presented on a television monitor which is clearly discriminable from a mirror. Although in our procedures the television aspect of the monitor was hidden, differences might still exist. Finally, videotape resolution, no matter how good, is more distorted than a mirror image. Videotape images also are different since they present the face without the left-right reversal of mirrors. To correct for this, we arranged for the videotaped image to have the same left-right reversal as do mirrors. Considering all these factors, simultaneous videotape representators are nevertheless similar to mirror images in terms of direct, contingent feedback and feature likeness. Videotapes also may be presented "after the fact" rather than simultaneously, with the videotapes being similar to home movies and having feature similarity but not contingency cues. Like pictures, they maintain feature similarity, but, unlike pictures, they present them in motion. Moving pictures differ from still pictures as they contain more information; understanding one's own movement is probably a unique feature of people, although we would suggest that it is a rather limited feature of self recognition, since we do not often see ourselves moving.

In sum, pictorial, mirror, and videotape (both contingent and noncontingent) representations present different information about the self and allow us three uniquely different ways of representing the self. In the following discussion, we shall examine each representation with emphasis placed on mirror representations, as they have been studied extensively and are likely to be experienced in the child's natural environment.

Pictorial Representations

The pictorial representations we used were always of the face, reflecting our belief that the face is the most "recognizable" feature of the body. Although there is almost no work on infants' responses to representations of their entire bodies, the work of Woodworth and Schlosberg (1938/1954) has shown that adult subjects have considerable difficulty recognizing their own features other than the face (for example, recognizing one's own hands or shoulders). In the present work, recognition of faces was investigated rather than recognition of the total body. The effects on self recognition of showing the infants both face and body are not clear, but Lewis, Wilson, and Baumel (1971) have shown that two-year-olds attend to the head rather than to the body when shown distortions of each.

Preverbal children's ability to recognize their faces in pictures is best inferred through differential responses to pictures of self and other. The "other" that is used for comparison purposes should be as similar to the self as possible, since differential responding may be elicited by person perceptions other than self perception. For example, infants respond quite differently to adults and children in live approach sequences (Brooks & Lewis, 1976; Greenberg et al., 1973; Lewis & Brooks, 1974), so that differential responses to pictures of self and adults or even to self and older children may not be indicative of self recognition but may be indicative of age differentiation.

Two methods of observing self recognition were used, one of which involved studying the children's perceptual and affective responses to the pictures and one which involved the children's verbal responses. Since personal pronouns appear late in the first three years, anywhere from 24 to 30 months, a variety of other verbal responses had to be observed in order to find some that distinguished between self and other, with one's own name being most important at earlier ages. Using one's own name when observing one's own picture may mean that the child knows that the picture is "self." However, this may not always be true, as the child may know that the child in the picture is "Amanda" and that she is "Amanda," but may not know that the two "Amanda's" are the same person. Even so, the ability to label one's own picture with one's own name and not labeling a same-age, same-sex peer picture with that appellation suggests that children have learned that a name (their own name) is coupled with a set of facial features. Such data, in conjunction with other self recognition observations, provide a more complete picture of the child's unfolding skill. The use of verbal self referents in mirror studies has been used as a measure of self recognition in many other studies (cf. Bertenthal & Fischer, 1978; Bigelow, 1975; Gesell, 1928; Zazzo, 1948).

Looking at our studies of pictorial self recognition, we find that children under two years, and in some cases under one year, respond differentially to pictorial representations of self and other in terms of smiling, frowning, and fixation time differences. Infants respond differentially to pictorial representations having to do with gender and age—important dimensions of the social world. Several of our findings suggest that early self–other differentiation may require additional perceptual-cognitive support structures. For example, some of our young infants differentiated between self and opposite-sex baby pictures but not between self and same-sex baby pictures. The ability to differentiate early self from other may require featural differences that have categorical qualities, such as age or gender. The presentation of strangers varying in age and gender attributes was an attempt to see whether this was the case. The data, at least in part, support our belief that self–other differentiation in the first year of life is dependent on additional perceptional cues and that not until the middle of the second year are children capable of recognizing their own pictures using only perceptual feature differences. In our first study, the younger infants (10- to 18-month-olds) did not respond differently to pictures of themselves or other infants. However, a small pilot sample of 22-month-olds did, smiling and looking more at their own picture than at pictures of same-aged babies. In the second study, the 9- to 12- and 21- to 24-month-olds smiled more at the self than at the same-aged baby, whereas the 15- to 18-month-olds did just the opposite. In addition, the infants in the second study tended to frown more often at the peer than at the self picture. These trends suggest that infants as young as 9 to 12 months of age are capable of some differentiation between pictorial representations of self and other, although the evidence for differentiation becomes stronger in the second year. It is interesting that a relatively low amount of smiling was exhibited to the picture of self by the 15- to 18-month-olds. Since this decrease in smiling was not coupled with an increase in frowning or avoidance, it may be related to the increase in self consciousness and/or in self knowledge of facial features seen at this time in the mirror and videotape studies.

The childrens' verbal responses to pictorial representations also were studied, using verbal comprehension and production; both elicited and spontaneous verbalizations were used. In the verbal comprehension task, infants were given a set of pictures, including their own, and asked to point to their pictures. In the verbal production task, infants were shown pictures of themselves and others and asked to label the pictures. As many language studies have shown, comprehension precedes verbal production. This was true for the task of self recognition. Comprehension, as measured by the infants' correctly pointing to their own picture as opposed to another, was observed as early as 18 months of age, although correct labeling of the self picture did not occur until somewhat later in the second year. Personal pronouns did not appear until 21 to 24 months and were used frequently thereafter. Ames (1952) and Gesell (1928) also report that personal pronouns were not commonplace until the third year of life. Use of one's own name for one's own picture but not for the picture of another baby appeared prior to personal pronouns, and in one case, in a child of 16 months. In the first study, one-quarter of the 18-month-olds and two-thirds of the 22-month-olds labeled their pictures correctly. These data parallel the age increases seen for mark-directed behavior and illustrate the occurrence of correct picture labeling before the end of the second year, not in the middle of the third year, as others have assumed.

Picture representations of the self provide information about children's acquisition of self recognition in the first three years of life. Although perceptual-affective responses give us some information, verbal responses, either verbal production or comprehension, are more indicative of self recognition. Given that verbal behavior is a late-emerging skill during infancy, the need to explore earlier knowledge requires that we use perceptual-affective responses prior to language.

Mirror-Image Representations

Mirror-image representation has received the most attention. Given its natural occurrence in human experience, both from reflecting surfaces found in nature as well as the long history of technology—the use of bronze mirrors dates back to humans' earliest records—its ecological validity is most relevant. The use of mirrors to study self recognition dates back to Darwin (1877) and Preyer (1893).

Infants' responses to mirrors have been observed in several experimental situations. The most commonly used situation was developed by Amsterdam (1968) for infants and by Gallup (1970) for chimpanzees. In the Amsterdam procedure, the infant's face is marked either by rouge or tape, and the infant's response to seeing the marked face in a mirror is observed. The operational definition of self recognition is directing behavior toward the mark, since the infant must recognize that the image in the mirror is, in fact, itself and that the mark resides not on the image's face, but on its own. Several investigators besides ourselves have used variants of this procedure (Amsterdam, 1968, 1972; Dickie & Strader, 1974; Bertenthal & Fischer, 1978). Two other methods have been designed, one in which infants' responses to self and to peers are compared and one in which infants' responses to distorted and flat mirrors are compared (Dixon, 1957; Schulman & Kaplowitz, 1977, respectively). The results of these as well as our own studies of mirror representations have generated a body of information pertaining to children's self recognition and mirror behavior.

Mirrors elicit a great deal of attention. People of all ages like to, and do, look at their reflections. In fact, in our culture, social prohibitions exist against looking at oneself in a mirror for too long. Adults in our society would be reluctant to admit spending much time looking at themselves; it is considered vain. Nevertheless, looking at one's reflected image does elicit attention even at very young ages. Boulanger-Balleyguier (1964) observed interest in mirrors at one month of age. When interest in the mother, a female stranger, and one's own mirror image were compared, infants preferred to look longer at their own image than at the unfamiliar person but less than at the familiar person. Other investigators have reported interest in mirrors occurring around 3 to 4 months of age (Amsterdam, 1972; Dixon, 1957), and the infant intelligence tests place this item at 5 to 8 months of age. Thus, interest in reflected surfaces occurs very early in life. Interest in mirrors is sustained throughout the first and second years of life, although, with increasing age, prolonged attention decreases. Infants typically observe themselves for relatively short but frequent bursts of time, unlike the long bouts of looking reported for other social objects—infants look at their mother or their peers for much longer periods of time.

Affective responses point to the mirror representation as being extremely pleasurable. The overwhelming response to a mirror is one of smiling, vocalizing, and touching. Pleasurable responses have been thought to be most prevalent in the second half of the first year of life, dropping out as self recognition develops (Amsterdam, 1968; Dixon, 1957). This appears not to be the case, since sociable and pleasurable responses are seen in infants from 1 to 24 months of age. Boulanger-Balleyguier (1964) reported smiling to mirrors in advanced one-month-olds. Amsterdam (1972), Schulman and Kaplowitz (1977), and Dickie and Strader (1974) reported smiling in 6- to 24-month-olds. In terms of pleasurable responses, Amsterdam (1972) finds the most sociable behavior in infants 5 to 14 months of age; Dixon (1957) from 5 to 12 months of age, Schulman and Kaplowitz (1977) from 7 to 18 months of age, and Dickie and Strader (1974) at 12 months of age. In our studies, we find no age differences in social responses. Instead of age differences, pleasurable responses were coupled with different behaviors at different ages: with sustained looking, kissing, and hitting at 9 to 12 months; and touching the body, touching the mark, and acting silly at 21 to 24 months. This coupling suggests to us that there may be a pleasure component that is independent of other systems, or that affect may be in the service of different motives—pleasure or excitement as well as self recognition. Taken together, the attention and affect data suggest that infants are interested in and derive pleasure from looking at their reflection in the mirror. This appears to be true of almost all infants in the first two years of life.

Some of our children exhibited a set of behaviors that are reminiscent of coyness, embarrassment, shyness or, as Amsterdam (1972) has used the term, self conscious behaviors. Amsterdam (1972) and Schulman and Kaplowitz (1977) report self admiration and embarrassment from 15 to 24 months, whereas Dixon (1957) and Preyer (1893) observed similar behavior in infants 12 and 18 months of age. In our studies, silly or coy behaviors were seen in very few infants under 15 months of age and were not the modal response until 18 months. Amsterdam suggests that self conscious behavior is a precursor of mark recognition, yet our findings and those of Schulman and Kaplowitz (1977) suggest that, in general, the two appear concurrently. In our first study, for example, 80% of those who noticed the mark acted silly or coy, but only 45% of those who did not notice the mark acted silly or coy. The occurrence of silly, coy, or embarrassed behavior is rather interesting, for it may be related to self awareness in a variety of ways. Self regard behavior may have been negatively reinforced because of the social prohibition against looking too long in the mirror. The release of social inhibitions—being allowed to look at oneself—may result in silliness or embarrassment. Alternatively, the silliness may be directly related to the action of looking at oneself. Looking at oneself acting may be considered a circular reaction, which, unless broken, tends to maintain itself. Thus, watching oneself in action has a kind of "locking in" process—a type of inhibitory mechanism which, once entered into, is not easily broken. For example, Tolman (1965) reported that when chickens are held tightly and then released, they tend, for a short period, not to move. When studying further the external factors which prolong this inhibitory response and help release it, Tolman found that placing a chicken in front of a mirror where it could watch itself tended to prolong the inhibitory movement state, but placing it in front of other moving chickens tended to result in faster release. If Tolman's finding has any relevance for infant's mirror behavior, it may indicate that looking in the mirror has a type of captivating effect that needs to be broken. To offset the intense attention and positive affect elicited by the mirror, the infant may act silly or embarrassed. Perhaps, then, these behaviors act as releasers much in the same way as the social prohibition against being vain and looking in the mirror acts as an inhibitor.

A final social response seen in children when they observe their mirror reflections is mirror-directed behavior. For some, mirror-directed behavior appears to resemble behavior directed toward another social object, as in the case in which chimpanzees and children look behind a mirror, presumably to see where the other child went (Amsterdam, 1972; Gallup, 1973). Mirror behavior was thought to occur prior to the development of self recognition and to disappear with its onset. Most studies, ours included, report decreases throughout the second year for behaviors such as kissing, hitting, and touching the mirror (Amsterdam, 1972; Dickie & Strader, 1974; Schulman & Kaplowitz, 1977). Interestingly, one mirror-directed behavior—pointing—may indicate some awareness of the mirror image as a reflection of oneself, since a point often has a "look at me" quality. Pointing may imply a distancing from the mirror, in both time and space. In the present studies and especially Study I, pointing was most prevalent in the 21-month-olds (56% of this age group pointed, as compared to 25% of the other age groups), the age at which mark-directed behavior is first seen in almost all infants.

Self-directed behaviors, as seen in mirrors, are one of the most direct measures for inferring self recognition. Imitation has some of the properties of self-directed behavior in that the behavior taking place at one point in space (in the mirror) is replicated at another point in space. It is possible to imitate another, which may limit the value of imitation for self recognition. However, imitation is more likely to occur to one's own image than to another's image, which suggests that it is part of the self recognition process.

We have observed two types of imitation, with the first being less related to self recognition than the second. The first type includes rhythmic movements, such as bouncing, waving, and clapping, which are most prevalent in infants between 9 and 12 months of age. The second type, imitation proper, involves facial movements (i.e., making faces, sticking the tongue out) or playing with the contingency of the mirror (i.e., watching oneself disappear and reapppear at the side of the mirror). These behaviors seem to indicate a growing awareness of the properties of reflections and, perhaps, are related to self recogniton. To our knowledge, these latter behaviors have been observed only in our studies, where they first occurred at 15 to 18 months of age, becoming prevalent at 21 to 24 months of age. These behaviors appear at the same time as mark-directed self recognition behavior, not earlier as some have proposed, suggesting that at least some forms of imitation are related to self recognition.

The two types of behaviors typically studied and usually thought to imply self recognition are body-directed and mark directed behaviors. In general, mark-directed rather than body-directed behavior has been studied, with the exception of Gallup's (1973) work with chimpanzees. In our studies, we have consistently found that one-quarter of the infants from 9 to 24 months of age touch their bodies or faces when placed in front of a mirror without their faces being marked. Moreover, the number of subjects who do this increases with age. Body-directed behavior increases after being marked with rouge, even in infants who did not specifically touch the rouge and even in our youngest infants. The increase in body-directed behavior after being marked is seen in all our age groups and may be similar to chimpanzees' use of the mirror to locate and touch visually inaccessible parts of the body (Gallup, 1973).

Mark-directed behavior in infants has been examined in at least four studies. All the studies report surprisingly consistent results: mark-directed behavior was never exhibited by infants younger than 15 months of age, while 15 to 18 months marked the beginning of self recognition. One-quarter of our sample, 5% of Amsterdam's (1972), and none of Schulman and Kaplowitz's (1977) 15- to 18-month-olds exhibited mark-directed behavior. However, between 18 and 20 months, a dramatic increase occurs, with approximately three-quarters of the 18- to 24-month-olds in all three studies exhibiting mark recognition. Before leaving the issue of mark-directed behavior, it is necessary to consider explanations other than self recognition to account for its occurrence. First, the act of applying the mark may sensitize the child and cause more touching. However, touching the nose without applying rouge did not result in increased nose-directed behavior, invalidating this explanation. Second, time spent in front of the mirror may increase the likelihood of mark-directed behavior, as infants may spontaneously touch their noses given long enough time. Alteration of the duration of time spent in front of the mirror and the temporal order of trials did not alter our results (see Chapter 2). In addition, infants tended to touch the mark immediately or not at all. Finally, Gallup (1977) has suggested that olfactory and visual cues (parts of the nose can be seen by looking cross-eyed) may account for the results. The visual cues of the rouge on the nose do not appear relevant, as adults marked with rouge are unable to see the mark. Moreover, no observer reported cross-eyed behavior in our infant studies. Mark-directed behavior in front of the mirror appears to be best explained by the infants having seen the marked nose by checking the mirror. Mark-directed behavior is clearly the strongest measure of self recognition available in mirror studies. Nonetheless, the age trends associated with the motoric ability to point (Masangkay *et al.*, 1974) and the neuromuscular development of this skill suggest that pointing has a developmental course of its own and may not be a response available to the infant prior to 15 months of age. This being the case, the use of this response alone to infer self recognition must be interpreted with care.

Videotape Representations

It is quite clear from the literature reviewed thus far that young children are able to recognize themselves in mirrors and in still-picture representations. However, it is not clear what dimensions of self representation are salient for the young infant and whether these change with age. As we have noted, infants could be responding to the social features that are common to the image and to the self (i.e., same-age, same-sex peer), to the contingent feedback offered by the mirror, to the familiarity of the perceptual features in the mirror (i.e., specific facial features common to self and image), or to some combination of these. By utilizing videotape feedback systems, it is possible to obtain information on the salience of various dimensions for self recognition as well as age changes in their use.

To date, only a few investigators have utilized videotape systems: Papoušek and Papoušek (1974) explored the saliency of eye-to-eye contact and contingency in 5-month-old infants' responses to videotapes of self and other presented simultaneously; Bigelow (1975) studied the salience of contingency in 18- to 26-month-olds' responses to videotape and stimultaneous representations of self; Amsterdam and Greenberg (1977) observed 10-, 15-, and 20-month-olds' responses to simultaneous self images, past self images (videotape), and a control child in the same situation (videotape); and in our studies (Chapter 3), we have explored 9- to 36-month-olds' responses to contingent self (simultaneous feedback analogous to a mirror) and noncontingent self and noncontingent other (both analogous to the pictorial representations). Three issues are raised by these videotape studies: (1) the similarity between contingent videotape representations and mirror images, (2) the similarity between pictures and noncontingent videotape representations, and (3) the similarity of infants' responses to contingent and noncontingent representations of themselves.

Attention and positive affect were exhibited to the contingent videotape representations and, in this regard, were similar to the mirror condition. In both our studies and that of Amsterdam and Greenberg (1977), almost all infants smiled or vocalized positively and very few infants cried or frowned to the representations. However, unlike some of the mirror studies that reported decreases in sociable behavior during the second year of life, the videotape studies report either no change, as in the Amsterdam and Greenberg (1977) study, or an increase in sociability over the first two years, as in our studies. Thus, the pleasure generated by videotape representations, like the pleasure generated by the mirror representations, was enhanced by the recognition of the representation as oneself rather than being replaced by self recognition. Self conscious behavior also seems to have parallels in both the mirror and videotape representations. For example, Amsterdam found the modal response of self conscious behavior occurred at 20 months in her mirror and videotape studies (1972; Amsterdam & Greenberg, 1977).

Turning behavior, in order to locate a person seen on the videotape, was observed in Videotape Study II and was most similar to mark-directed behavior in that both required a body orientation to mark the physical position of the self in relationship to the representation. Bertenthal and Fischer (1978) used turning away from the mirror and toward any object portrayed in the mirror (suspended from the ceiling and behind the infant) as a measure of the development of self recognition and found the ability occurring in the beginning of the first year. Our youngest infants, the 9- to 12-month-olds, had no difficulty turning toward an object or person in our contingent videotape condition. Taken together, these findings suggest that infants are able to turn toward objects at an earlier age than they are able to locate a mark on the face. In addition, our findings indicate that infants younger than one year are able to turn toward objects presented in simultaneous and contingent conditions.

The videotape studies were also used to compare self and other. In the picture studies of self and other, both perceptual-affective and verbal behaviors were used as measures, whereas in the videotape studies the self–other comparison used only perceptual-affective measures. In our first videotape study, infants exhibited more positive affect and attention to the other than to the self, whereas they exhibited more imitation and contingent play to the self than to the other noncontingent conditions. Thus, affect and attention were more likely to be directed toward the unfamiliar peer, and imitation toward the self. In our second study, infants were more likely to turn toward the target in the other than in the self noncontingent condition.

Differentiation of self and other occurred between 15 and 18 months of age in our first study and between 21 and 24 months of age in our second study. Other studies report that this discrimination does not occur until about two years of age, at the same time that verbal self referents begin to appear (Bigelow, 1975) or not at all (Amsterdam & Greenberg, 1977). Our data from both pictures and videotape studies suggest an earlier and similar course of self–other differentiation (our infants began to use their proper names only for their pictures and no peers as early as 16 months).

The final question pertains to the relationship between contingent and noncontingent representations and the effect of this dimension on the child's self recognition. How important is contingency for recognition? The results from several studies indicate that infants respond differently to contingent and noncontingent representations and do so very early. Papoušek and Papoušek (1974) report that 5-month-olds discriminated between noncontingent eye contact and contingent no-eye contact representations of self, first preferring the latter. However, over repeated presentations, the contingent condition elicited increased attention and movement. The authors hypothesize that the infants were learning about the contingency during the testing, which might account for the increase in responding over repeated trials. Rheingold (1971) found that 5-month-old infants responded more positively to a mirror than to a moving picture of an unfamiliar baby. Given these findings with young infants, it is not surprising that we found differentiation between contingent and noncontingent representations in both our studies. In the first study, infants were much more likely to exhibit contingent play and to respond positively to the contingent than to the noncontingent conditions, but were more likely to watch the noncontingent than the contingent conditions. The infants seemed to sit back and watch the noncontingent videotape but to interact actively with the contingent condition. In the second study, infants were more likely to turn toward the target when the target was actually present (contingent condition) and more likely to turn toward the mother when the target was not present (noncontingent condition). Given these findings, Amsterdam and Greenberg's (1977) failure to find differences between contingent and noncontingent representation is surprising.

Although age trends were found in our studies, even the youngest infants (those 9 to 12 months of age) responded differentially, supporting our belief that contingency is learned early. Given the role of contingency in the young child's development of action in the world—specifically, the development of means and ends relationships within the circular reactions—it is not surprising to find that children acquire this skill quite early and utilize it in recognizing themselves (Lewis,

1977). It would appear that the contingent-noncontingent dimensions differentiate earlier than the self–other or feature dimensions. Early self recognition is facilitated by contingency, and not until later are representations of the self, utilizing perceptual features, recognized.

CRITERIA FOR SELF RECOGNITION

The studies we have reviewed make clear the importance of the criteria used for self recognition. A variety of behaviors in the infant's repertoire have been observed, some that may be indicative of self recognition, some that may not.

How do we know that one recognizes oneself? With adults, one simply asks them whether or not a specific picture or reflection represents them or another. Adults usually make the verbal distinction, "That is me" or "That is not me." By 3 years of age, most children are able to use personal pronouns correctly (Ames, 1952; Gesell & Thompson, 1938). But what about the 2-year-old who rarely uses the personal pronoun and the 9-month-old who has no verbal labels at all? At least four types of behavior have been used that may be indicative of self recognition: self-directed behavior, verbal production, comprehension, and differential responding to different stimulus conditions.

The occurrence of self-directed behavior implies that the child is making a distinction between the self and the representation and that the behavior is being directed to the self in a purposeful manner. Mark recognition is the most compelling example of self-directed behavior. A less obvious example is body-directed behavior. Infants may attempt to explore their bodies, to inspect visually inaccessible parts of their bodies, or to look at their clothing. Such behaviors occur fairly frequently in mirror procedures but rarely in picture or videotape procedures. Self conscious and some imitative behaviors might also be labeled self-directed, even though the self as the referent is not indicated by a movement toward the self (Amsterdam, 1972).

Like self-directed behavior, verbal labeling and comprehension indicate an awareness of self that is relatively clear-cut. Infants may refer to their image or their picture by name or by personal pronoun or may point to that picture when given the referent. Such behavior was more prevalent in picture procedures than in mirror and videotape procedures. Self awareness may also be reflected by verbal references to the specific procedures. For example, some of our 21- to 24-month-olds verbally referred to the rouge on the nose, sometimes regarding it as an injury ("boo boo," "it hurts"), yet others referred to their clothing as seen in their picture ("That's my dress"). Such utterances seem to indicate an awareness that the picture represents the self. This awareness may be mediated by a learning function; for example, parents may teach their children to label pictures. A child may know that the picture is "Amanda" and that she is "Amanda," but does she know that the two "Amandas" represent the same person? However, the differential use of proper names, the ability to point differentially, and the use of the personal pronoun seem to make this explanation implausible.

The amount of fixation and affect directed to pictures of self and same-age babies, the verbal labels applied to pictures of self and other, the response patterns in the unmarked and marked mirror conditions, and the self and other videotapes have also been observed. These methods utilize differential responses and are, therefore, inferential, telling us only that the two conditions are perceived as different. However, differential responding may be of a specific nature and may be most likely to occur if self recognition exists. That is, we believe that familiar social objects will be preferred to unfamiliar objects, the former being more likely to elicit positive affect and self-directed behaviors than the latter. Almost all the studies support this prediction: (1) infants not only labeled the pictures of self and of same-age, same-sex baby differently but were also more likely to use their own name in the self condition; (2) infants, especially the 21- to 24-month-olds, smiled at the pictures of self and same-age baby different amounts of time but smiled longer at their own than at the other pictures; (3) infants not only exhibited differential behavior in unmarked and marked mirror conditions but were also more likely to explore their bodies, to touch their noses, and to exhibit silly and coy behavior in the marked than in the unmarked condition; (4) infants not only exhibited differential behavior in contingent and noncontingent representations but also exhibited more contingent play, affect, self-conscious, and turning behaviors to videotape representations of self and other, but imitated and played contingently more often in the former than in the latter.

In short, all four types of behavior tell us something about the development of self recognition, even though some present more compelling evidence than others. The infant who says, "That's me" or "That's David" when seeing his picture and who touches himself when seeing his marked face in a mirror certainly recognizes himself. How-

ever, when David touches his body in the marked but not in the unmarked condition, looks longer at or is more positive to a picture of
himself than to a picture of another, and imitates videotapes of himself
more than a videotape of another, he may also be said to have an awareness of self.

THE ONTOGENY OF SELF RECOGNITION

Our studies, taken together with those of previous investigators,
allow for several general statements about the ontogenesis of self recognition. However, the picture of the development of self recognition is
dependent on the situations used to observe it, the behaviors used to
measure it, and the representational forms available to study it. In the
following discussion the ontogeny of self recognition, based on the data
we have presented, is constructed.

Within the last quarter of the first year of life, the infant appears to
possess some notion, albeit somewhat primitive, of visual self recognition. The 9- to 12-month-old is able to differentiate easily between contingent and noncontingent representations of self, which is not surprising given the salience of contingency for cognitive development, such as
means and ends abilities and circular reactions. We know that infants
even younger than 9 months are able to use contingency appropriately.
Papoušek and Papoušek (1974) and Rheingold (1971) demonstrated this
in 5-month-olds. In addition, 9- to 12-month-olds are able to differentiate between unmarked and marked mirror conditions, even
though they are not able to touch directly the rouge mark on their noses
and are able to use the mirror to turn toward an approaching stranger.
When noncontingent representational modes are involved, the data for
the 9- to 12-month-olds are equivocal. Using certain procedures, they are
able to distinguish self from other but fail to do so in other procedures.
For example, in Videotape Study II, this age group did not differentiate
between the approach of a stranger in the self and other conditions; in
Picture Study II, this age group did differentiate between pictures of self
and other, although in Picture Study I, they did not. Given the differences across procedures, it would seem that, for this age, contingency
is a necessary condition for the demonstration of self recognition.

Between 15 to 18 months of age, new behavioral indications of self
recognition emerge as self recognition becomes more organized and less

dependent upon contingency. Infants of this age differentiate easily between contingent and noncontingent representations. They exhibit not
only body-directed behavior but also mark-directed behavior to some
extent, contingent play, and self conscious behavior in contingent representations. In noncontingent representations, they exhibit differential
attention, imitation, and affect between representations of self and
other. Finally, they are able to label and point to pictures of themselves.
At this point, contingency is no longer needed to recognize oneself. A
more detailed breakdown by age within this period suggests a shift
toward greater self recognition between 14 to 15 months and 18 to 19
months of age.

Between 18 and 21 months of age, a large increase in the number of
infants demonstrating self recognition abilities is seen across a wide
range of representative modes. All infants now play with contingency in
contingent representations, whereas over three-quarters notice the
rouge and show self conscious behavior. In noncontingent modes,
self–other differentiation is apparent, with one-half of the infants imitating their own videotape. In pictorial representations, two-thirds point to
their own picture and use self labels to distinguish self from other. At
the same time, personal pronouns begin to be used. Clearly, self recognition is well established by 21 months of age, and from this age on-
ward, self recognition increases across all representations.

In brief, there is a gradual increase in children's ability to recognize
themselves across the first two years of life. Self recognition is at first
highly dependent on both feature recognition and contingency. Around
15 months, and certainly by 21 months of age, featural recognition, independent of contingency, accounts for self recognition.

Although there is relatively little work on the ontogeny of self recognition utilizing as wide a set of representational forms as we have
used, there is some data bearing on this developmental question.
Amsterdam (1972) and Dixon (1957) have postulated several stages of
self recognition development, but both these studies have considered
only mirror representations. As we have seen, mirror representations,
which include contingency as well as feature recognition, allow for earlier self recognition than the videotape and pictorial representations.
These studies will be compared to our work with mirrors, keeping in
mind that mirror representations do not tell the whole story. Dixon
(1957) outlines an ontogenetic sequence of four stages: (1) "Mother," (2)
"Playmate," (3) "Who do dat when I do dat?," and (4) "Coy." In the

"Mother" stage (4 or 5 months of age), the infant enjoys observing mother's movement in the mirror; in the "Playmate" stage (5 to 6 months of age), the infant responds playfully to his own image as if it were a peer; in the "Who do dat when I do I do dat?" stage (6 to 12 months), the infant is interested in observing the actions performed by himself; and in the "Coy" stage (12 to 18 months), the infant acts coy, shy, or fearful in front of the mirror. Dixon believes the "Coy" stage to be indicative of self recognition.

This sequence and its age-related activities dovetail nicely into our findings, although there are some important differences. The first two stages are not supported by our data; however, we have not studied children in the first months of life. Nevertheless, enjoying another's and one's own movements in the mirror have never been separated adequately, providing little evidence for the "Mother" stage. The "Playmate" stage does not seem unique, as infants of all ages in our studies responded playfully to the mirror image. The third stage, "Who do dat when I do dat"? corresponds with our findings that infants first respond to contingency in the mirror and videotape studies at 9 to 12 months of age. Dixon's "Coy" stage is somewhat akin to our findings on self-conscious behaviors; however, mark-directed behavior occurred later, and body-directed behavior occurred earlier than self-conscious behavior. Dixon believes that self recognition emerges in a stage-like fashion, an all-or-none phenomenon, whereas our results suggest a gradual emergence of self recognition which first requires contingency as well as featural recognition.

Amsterdam (1972) also employs a stage theory with three stages of self recognitory responses. The first involves social responding to the mirror, the second is indicative of self awareness, and the third is self recognition. The social stage is prevalent from 6 to 12 months of age, the transitional stage is from 12 to 18 months of age, and the self recognition stage is from 20 to 24 months of age. Like Dixon, Amsterdam reports little overlap between stages. Again, our data show some lines of convergence with Amsterdam's data, although not enough to postulate the existence of three separate stages. First, in our samples, social responses did not drop out after the first year of life, but actually increased in some instances. Second, the behaviors that Amsterdam termed transitional co-occurred with behaviors termed self recognitory in our sample. Finally, in Amsterdam's study, the infants could see their mothers and the observer as well as themselves, making inferences about responses to their own reflections difficult.

Perhaps the most careful study of the sequence of self recognition has been performed by Bertenthal and Fischer (1978) who, like us, find a slowly emerging ability to recognize one's self. They developed five self recognition tasks that corresponded to five stages, employing the coordination of actions under the infant's control. These five were: (1) tactual exploration—use of the mirror to explore the image; (2) hat task—use of the mirror to discover a hat that was above the infant's head and was attached to the infant; (3) toy task—use of the mirror to discover a toy behind the infant but not attached to the infant; (4) rouge task—use of the mirror to discover rouge on the nose; and (5) name task—use of the mirror to name oneself.

For the most part, we find our infants showing these behaviors somewhat earlier than Bertenthal and Fischer report. For example, mark-directed behavior first occurred at 15 months of age in our sample, but they report it at 20 months for their sample. Likewise, verbal labeling of self appears earlier in our picture sample—as early as 16 months— whereas they find verbal ability to occur at 24 months of age. By that age, between 70 and 90% of our verbal infants label their picture (a more difficult representational mode), and 90% can point to their picture when asked. More examples of the age discrepancy are possible. For example, the approach of the stranger in the contingent videotape sequence is demonstrated by over 50% of our sample by 9 to 12 months.

In brief, the stages proposed by Amsterdam (1972) and Dixon (1957) are not convincing for several reasons. First, stage was defined as a cluster of behaviors that were most likely to occur at a certain point. There is little evidence for such clustering. For example, sociable behaviors did not decrease in the videotape or picture studies nor in many of the mirror studies; avoidance behaviors were not seen at all in the videotape or picture studies nor in all the mirror studies; and attending to self representations did not drop out with age. Second, some of the developmental sequences hypothesized do not seem to be supported by our data. For example, self-conscious behaviors do not seem to precede mark recognition but develop at the same time.

A problem with all three studies is their failure to look at different representational modes, which has led to the lack of separating featural recognition from knowledge of contingency. As we have concluded, contingency is used quite early in the child's life, but it is the ability to recognize and respond to self, *independent* of contingency, which represents the important developmental milestone in self recognition.

Given these various sequences, we would like to offer the following sequence as summarized in Table 8-1. Confronted with contingent situations—mirrors and contingent videotapes—infants as young as 9 months of age smile, watch themselves intently, imitate and move rhythmically, touch their bodies, and show a wide range of self-directed behaviors. In part, these behaviors change very little over the 9- to 36-month period. These behaviors are exhibited as early as 5 to 6 months of age.

Around 9 to 12 months, there is some indication of self recognition independent of contingency, although this represents the beginning of this ability. Support for this comes from Videotape Study II and Picture Study II of self–other differentiation in the noncontingent situation. At the same time, infants begin to use the mirrors to reach for things, both

TABLE 8-1
Self Recognitory Representations

Age (in months)	Contingency representations	Feature representations
5–8	Play with contingency Body-directed behavior	No self–other differentiation
9–12	Play with contingency Body-directed behavior Use mirror to locate objects	Beginning of self–other differentiation
15–18	Play with contingency Body-directed behavior Mark-directed behavior Self–conscious behavior Use mirror to locate objects	Verbal labeling of self Pointing to self Self–other differentiation
21–24	Play with contingency Body-directed behavior Mark-directed behavior Self–conscious behavior Use mirror to locate objects	Verbal labeling of self Pointing to self Beginning personal pronouns Self–other differentiation
24–36	Play with contingency Body-directed behavior Mark-directed behavior Self–conscious behavior Use mirror to locate objects	Verbal labeling of self Pointing to self Personal pronoun usage

the self (touching the body) and other objects and persons (turning toward a person that is approaching or an object that is dangling overhead).

Around 15 months of age, self- or mark-directed behavior appears in the contingency situation, as does self-conscious behavior. In noncontingency situations, self and other are differentiated, as indicated by contingent play, affect, and attention differences. More importantly, verbal labels begin to appear.

By 20 months, all these trends have become commonplace occurrences; most infants exhibit mark-directed behavior, differentiate between self and other in noncontingent situations, and use their own name. Furthermore, personal pronouns appear.

A stage theory approach has been offered to explain the development of self recognition. As we have pointed out, the stage theory approach finds little support in our data. There are no discrete periods of development, and behaviors seen at earlier ages are still observed at later ages, even when new behaviors appear. In the case of self recognition we find no support for such a developmental pattern, especially if one uses Flavell's (1972) criteria of stages. Recently, Lewis and Starr (1978) discussed the issue of stages of development and the issue of discrete versus continuous theories of development. They concluded that development is by its nature continuous and that stage theories reflect a measurement issue; the caterpillar and butterfly are different and represent discrete development if the measurement is the presence or absence of wings. If the measurement is finer, however, then it is continuous and without discrete points. Thus, from a theoretical point of view, as well as the empirical data from our studies of self recognition, we do not support a stage concept; rather, we prefer to think of self recognition as a continuous process, a slow transformation and addition of new skills into a growing repertoire of behaviors we call self recognition.

INDIVIDUAL DIFFERENCES IN THE DEVELOPMENT OF SELF RECOGNITION

How are we to explain the individual differences in self recognition that have characterized all our studies? Most obvious are the striking developmental trends that have been found. Age is not the only determinant of self recognition, however, as individual differences within age groups have also been found. Perhaps these differences are related to cognitive, social, and experiential variables, as has been hypothesized by Gallup (1977).

Self recognition may be related to mirror experience, since mirrors are the first representational mode with which the infant has experience. Such a relationship has been found for chimpanzees (Gallup, 1970), pretechnological peoples (Kohler, 1927, cited in Amsterdam, 1968), and adults blind from birth (von Senden, 1960). However, we have found no relationship between mirror experience and self recognition in infants. This finding is limited because the data are based on mother's reports, and all infants, at least in our society, have had some prior mirror experience.

Social experience may also affect the expression of self recognition. Mead (1934) and Merleau-Ponty (1964) have suggested that we come to know ourselves through our interactions with others. Indeed, without others, self knowledge would not exist. Gallup (1977) found evidence for this hypothesis in his primate research. Chimpanzees reared in social isolation were unable to exhibit self-directed behavior in a mirror situation even after extensive exposure. As a further test of the importance of social experience, two of the original chimpanzees were given three months of group experience, after which time self recognitory responses began to appear (Hill *et al.*, 1970). Measures of infant social experience have not been found to relate to self recognition as yet.

Cognitive ability and self recognition might be expected to be related, since the ability to infer that a mirror or videotape reflection is a representation of the self implies a notion of distancing and separation. Object permanence has been thought to be especially important in that the notion of permanence theoretically implicates self, other, and object (Lewis & Brooks, 1974; Waite, 1977), and that sensorimotor development subsumes numerous tasks, including object permanence and self recognition (Bertenthal & Fischer, 1978). We have found object permanence and self recognition to be highly related, but this relationship disappears after age is controlled. Bertenthal and Fischer (1978) report an identical finding. Thus, object permanence does not develop earlier than self recognition, nor is the development of the latter dependent upon the former (although in our youngest infants object permanence and imitation were positively related). The ability to process redundant and novel stimuli has also been studied in conjunction with self recognition. Response habituation, the ability to process redundant information, was not related to mark recognition in mirrors, to contingent play in contingent TV representations, nor to imitation in noncontingent videotape representations, although response recovery when a new stimulus was presented was positively related to mark recognition and imitation. Unlike our findings for object permanence, these relationships were significant after age was controlled. Thus, those infants who notice change in inanimate stimuli seem to be those who also notice change in representations of themselves (i.e., unmarked to marked mirror conditions and videotape representations of self and other).

Although affective-cognitive variables, in particular fear of the stranger (Chapter 1) and response recovery, were related to self recognition, cognitive and social variables seem not to be strongly related to self recognition. This is true whether or not age or maturational level is controlled. Thus, the source of individual differences in the onset of self perception remains in question but, theoretically, should be related both to children's other cognitive skills and to the social world in which they live.

CHAPTER 9

Toward a Theory of the Development of Self

Our discussion has centered thus far on self recognition, its representional modes, its developmental course and the individual differences associated with its expression. Our major purpose, however, is to evolve a theory of the development of self. In order to do this, we chose to study self recognition, believing that self recognition is a window on the emerging concept of self—and, by necessity, implies a concept of self. Unfortunately, although self recognition certainly implies a self, its absence may not imply a lack of self. It is possible to consider an organism who possesses a concept of self but is not able to visually recognize self, for example, a person blind from birth. In any case, self recognition may provide clues to how the self develops. In the following discussion, our concept of self as presented in Chapter 1 will be integrated with our findings on self recognition and a general theory of self will be proposed. Specifically, the organizational features of self that lead the child to the discovery of self knowledge, the relationship of self development to other aspects of social knowledge, the principles of social dimensions, and the relationship of the categorical self to social dimensions will be discussed.

SELF DEVELOPMENT

Infants, like children and adults, are attracted to and find pleasing the image of other infants. This attraction may be a reflex of our species (and perhaps other species) to respond to their young. As unlearned behavior, young infants find their reflections interesting from the first, since their own image is an image of an infant. Thus, the first organizing feature of self knowledge may be an unlearned response to behave positively and be attracted to images of young organisms.

In the next step toward self recognition of one's image in the mirror, the infant may notice the means and ends or cause and effect reactions inherent to the mirror. Watching the movement in the mirror, the infant notices that action in one spatial locus affects action in another, movement of the hand *here* results in movement of the hand *there*. Given the overall development of cause and effect taking place in the infant's general cognitive development, the particular cause and effect (self action-reflected outcome) of the mirror serves both as an additional means of developing as well as an organizer for other means. Thus, the second organizing feature may be the cognitive process of the action–outcome pairings associated with means and ends relationships. These two aspects, species-related interest in the young and the cognitive process of means and ends relationships, probably occur in the first three months of life.

One unique feature of the cause and effect relationship in mirrors, one which distinguishes it from all others, is the *identity* of cause and effect actions (behavior, perceptual features, etc.). Usually the cause and the effect have different identities. For example, the head movement that causes the mobile to move involves both head movement and mobile movement, two perceptually different actions. In the case of mirrors, however, the cause and effect have the same identity, as self movement or action is seen in reflected surfaces or is felt in proprioceptive feedback. In this case, the action of hand movement as seen in the mirror *is* hand movement.

Interestingly, our data indicate that self recognition is sustained by this identity of cause and effect in front of the mirror until well into the first year and perhaps even into the second year. Not until sometime after the first year is the infant able to use distinctive features as the basis for self recognition. Rather, self recognition is first sustained and even caused by the identity of behaviors within the cause and effect process.

One further point of interest in terms of identity between action and outcome has to do with social versus nonsocial objects in the infant's world. There is very little similarity between action and outcome in terms of the infant's behavior in the nonsocial world: action of the self and outcome of nonsocial events are highly dissimilar. Nonsocial events are, by definition, different from social ones, with the infant's action and the social world's outcome being more similar than the infant's action and nonsocial world's outcome. For example, the infant's smile followed by the mother's smile is more similar than the infant's movement and the mobile's movement. Thus, the social world, because of its similarity to the infant, plays a greater role in the establishment of self than the nonsocial world. Indeed, the more positive the relationship between infant and caregiver, the more alike and more self recogntioin building will be the result. This is because the positive relationship between child and caregiver has already been defined as the congruency of their responses in interaction (Brazelton *et al.*, 1974; Lewis, 1972b, 1977; Lewis & Freedle, 1973; Lewis & Goldberg, 1969; Stern, 1974).

In fact, from a definitional point of view, it is our strong belief that the first definition or feature of self is the simultaneity and identity of action and outcome. The first epistemological distinction between self and other revolves around this identity and simultaneity. Self is defined from action and reflects the identity of action and outcome in a specific locus in space.

The acquisition of object permanence, and its emergence at eight months, reflects the last organizing feature of self knowledge, specifically, permanence. First, we have postulated a highly interested and positively motivated organism disposed to pay attention to a class of events that includes self. Next, we have a cause and effect relationship that produces the notion of action–outcome pairings and identity, both through infants' action on themselves and, to some degree, their action in the social world. Even given these two features, the perception of self is transient, since it exists in a structure without enduring qualities. This lack of an enduring quality may be a function of memory or storage inadequacies or some other cognitive process immaturity.

Object permanence, the knowledge of an attribute of objects, begins to emerge around the same time self permanence develops, at around eight to nine months of age. Whether object permanence proceeds first from the self outward to other social objects (mother) and then nonsocial objects, or whether it proceeds from nonsocial objects to self, or whether it is a simultaneous development is not clear, although a case can be made for all three positions. In any event, self permanence must be simultaneous with or precede object permanence. We see no logical argument to suggest that knowledge of object existence, independent of one's perception of that object, could occur without first also knowing of the existence of the perceiver of the object. Thus, self permanence emerges as the third important feature necessary for self knowledge.

Only after permanence is achieved can the next organized feature, the characteristics, or the categories of self be achieved. Our data suggest that this occurs around the last quarter of the first year or the first quarter of the second year. Although we cannot demonstrate this process of category acquisition as clearly as we would like, there is every reason to believe that it may occur earlier, or at least some sort of intermediate process occurs, sometime after self permanence.

To recapitulate our discussion on the organizing features of self knowledge: (1) the infant is positively attracted to self as a class of "babyishness"; (2) the infant learns cause and effect and, in particular, one cause and effect—self as both action *and* outcome in the same locus in space; (3) the infant acquires the ability to hold an enduring belief in the existence of objects over time, which must include a self locus in space; and (4) the infant begins to acquire self categories. Thus, to be and to be different from others require that this difference be defined. This definition speaks to what we have called the categorical self, which is seen in the child's ability to recognize himself on the basis of features.

The process of self development has a specific time frame that has parallels with more traditional cognitive and affective aspects of development. As Lewis and Cherry (1977) have tried to demonstrate using language acquisition as a starting point, development is a unitary process involving the simultaneity of development and change across the total organism. The unitary model of development is best exemplified by showing the parallel development between self knowledge, emotional experience, and cognitive growth. Table 9-1 illustrates this parallel development for the four periods outlined for self development. Emotional experience is discussed in greatest detail, as cognitive development was attended to in the previous discussion.

Period One: From Birth to Three Months

This period is characterized by biological determinism and is primarily reflexive in nature. Infants have interest in and positive affect toward social objects, particularly other babies. Differentiation of other social objects and single action–outcome pairings (primary circular reactions) are seen, as well as the beginnings of self as different from other.

Emotional experience (see Lewis & Rosenblum, 1978, and Chapter 7 for a detailed explanation of experience) as such does not exist, since emotional expressions and states are usually produced by strong stimulus changes and can be characterized by reflexive responses to stimuli changes. These unlearned reflexive responses appear to be both simple and complex.

Period Two: Three Months to Eight Months

In this time period social activity and social control of behavior are established. Elaborate action–outcome pairings occur along with means and ends relationships both in the social and nonsocial domains. Mirror contingency becomes of interest as part of the action–outcome behavior, and precursors to self recognition via contingency occurs. The distinction between self and other is consolidated but remains fleeting until the onset of the notion of permanence. In Period Two, emotional experience begins to emerge as learned associations, and past experience begins to affect the expression of emotion. Cognitive growth is rapid, as primary and secondary circular reactions are developed, and as the children learn of their effect on the object and social world.

Period Three: Eight to Twelve Months

The most critical feature of this period is the establishment of permanence which solidifies the self–other distinction and signifies that the self has a location in space which is unique. More complex means and ends relationships are established, and plans and intentionality are demonstrated. Contingent play is of particular interest, as the self–other distinction has been consolidated. Self recognition is established in contingent situations. Given these characteristics, we can see the emergence of a truly social organism, one which knows some things about self as well as others. During this period, early features of a categorical self begin to emerge and self recognition, independent of contingency, appears in its first form.

Period Three has emotional experiences firmly established as clear differentiation emerges. Within the cognitive sphere, this period is characterized by the appearance of object permanence, imitation, and means and ends relationships. The infant's agency emerges as does, through the use of comparison, the beginning of complex intention and plans.

Period Four: Twelve to Twenty-Four Months

The period between 12 and 24 months is best characterized as the beginning of representational behavior, including social representation and the representation of self. During the middle of this period, self recognition becomes less dependent on contingency and increasingly more dependent on feature analysis. The child is now able to recognize himself through the use of features without contingency, i.e., recognizing self in pictures as well as mirrors. At the same time, language acquisition and increased cognitive complexity allow for the development and use of a categorical self. Several dimensions of the early categorical self include gender, age, and efficacy. From this point on, the self as dif-

TABLE 9-1

Development of Self Knowledge, Emotional Experience, and Cognitive Growth

Age	Self knowledge	Emotional experience	Cognitive growth
0–3	Interest in social objects: emergence of self–other distinction	Unconditioned responses to stimulus events (loud noise, hunger, etc.)	Reflexive period, primary circular reactions
3–8	Consolidation of self–other distinction, recognition of self through contingency	Conditioned responses (strangers, incongruity)	Primary and secondary circular reactions
8–12	Emergence of self permanence and self categories; recognition of self through contingency and onset of feature recognition	Specific emotional experiences (fear, happiness, love, attachment)	Object permanence, means-ends, imitation
12–24	Consolidation of basic self categories (age, gender, emergency of efficacy); feature recognition without contingency	Development of empathy, guilt, embarrassment	Language growth; more complex means-ends; symbolic representations

ferent from other is well established, and any change in the self is solely in the categorical realm—a process that will continue throughout the child's lifetime.

In Period Four, more cognitive skills and emotions (e.g., guilt, empathy) emerge. In terms of cognition, language development, complex means–ends, and symbolic representations emerge, facilitating self knowledge and emotional experience. These brief mappings of various functions, as well as the parallel development of self and cognitive knowledge, support our view of the unitary nature of development.

SELF, INTERACTION, AND OTHER: THE ONSET OF SOCIAL COGNITION

In the preceding discussion we elaborated not only on the development of self recognition but also placed this phenomenon in a broader perspective, namely, the development of self. The development of a sense of self is gradual, taking place over the entire first two years of life. It is not an independent phenomenon of development but is part of the total development of the organism (Lewis & Cherry, 1977). As such, self development involves other cognitive, perceptual, affective, and social skill development.

The development of the self within the larger framework of social cognition and development must be considered. In order to do this, it is necessary that three aspects of early social development and knowledge be considered: self, other, and the interaction between them. It is our belief that the study of social cognition involves these three areas of knowing. Indeed, as we have shown, they are not separate aspects of knowledge but are together three aspects of children's commerce with their world.

Social cognition has been defined in a variety of ways: recognition of various emotions exhibited by others, the ability to judge others' emotional states (Bruner & Tagiuri, 1954; Darwin, 1895/1965; Tagiuri, 1969), the reasons a person acts as he does and the perceptions of other's actions (Heider, 1958, Kelly, 1955), in addition to role-taking, empathy (Hoffman, 1978), and person perception (Lewis & Brooks, 1975). There have recently been a number of reviews of the development of social knowledge, which have emphasized its acquisition in the preschool and middle childhood years, while omitting early development (Chandler,

1977; Shantz, 1975; Youniss, 1975). Shantz, for example, has defined early social cognition as "a child's intuitive or logical representations of others, that is, how he [or she] characterizes others and makes references about their covert, inner psychological experiences" (1975, p. 258). Unfortunately, this definition does not include other important aspects of social cognition, such as self knowledge and knowledge of relationships. Youniss (1975) has offered a more inclusive definition, adding a sense of self, knowledge of self vis-à-vis society, and a sense of value and principles, as well as knowledge of others and one's relationship to them. Youniss's definition of social cognition comes close to what we wish to define as the psychological task during the early years of development.

Let us look at these three aspects of the child's knowledge: self, others, and the relationship between self and other(s). Self knowledge has been defined in earlier chapters. Knowledge of others involves knowledge of those who are not the self and of social as opposed to nonsocial objects. Others may refer to a single other, like the mother or father, or others, like groups of people such as the family (Lewis & Feiring, 1979). Relationships refer to direct relationships between self and other (mother and self), or between self and others (such as self and mother and father together), as well as indirect ones (such as self watching the relationship between a mother and father) (Lewis & Feiring, 1979; Lewis & Weinraub, 1976).

In order to define these three features of social knowledge, it is necessary to understand the relationship between them. In fact, children's knowledge of others is developed through their interaction with these others. Without interaction with the social world, there would be little knowledge about it. In addition, through interaction the infant gains knowledge about self as well as knowledge about others. As Merleau-Ponty states, "If I am a consciousness turned toward things, I can meet in things the actions of another and find in them a meaning, because they are themes of possible activity for my own body" (1964, p. 113). Such a view is also taken by Hamlyn (1974) who states, "To understand what a person is . . . involves understanding what sorts of relationships can exist between mere things and between people and things" (p. 7). For us, then, the basic unit out of which knowledge of self and other occurs is the interaction of the organism with others. For us, as for Mead (1934), the interaction between self and other(s) provides meaning for both self and other. It is a parallel process, arriving out of the interaction, in that what I know of another I know of myself and, likewise, what I know about myself I know of the other.

Although interactionalists have been in common agreement that knowledge of the world is derived through interaction with it, they have been remiss in considering the other half of the system. Concerned with what the child knows of the other through interaction—the other usually being physical properties of the environment like weight, height, etc.—interactionalists have not given adequate weight to the fact that knowledge of the other, gained through interaction, must of necessity inform us about ourselves. If I find one object hard and the other soft by reaching and holding them, then not only do I know something about the hardness of objects, but I also know something about the hardness of myself. Because study of the child's social knowledge has been neglected until recently, we have failed to understand the parallel growth of knowledge.

THREE PRINCIPLES OF SOCIAL COGNITION

To better understand early social cognition, we would like to present three underlying principles:

Principle I: Any knowledge gained about the other also must be gained about the self.

Baldwin (1899/1973) understood this principle when he wrote, "My sense of myself grows by imitation of you, and my sense of yourself grows in terms of my sense of myself. Both ego and alter are thus essentially social; each is a socius, and each is an imitative creation" (p. 338).

The parallel development of self and other knowledge is acquired through interaction of the self and other. Thus, interaction becomes the major content of social cognition, since it is through interaction that both self and other knowledge are derived. This is not inconsistent with Youniss (1975) who has also taken the position that "the mental content of social congition is interpersonal relations" (p. 185).

This discussion has direct and specific relevance to our theory of that aspect of self which we have called the categorical self. Not only is the self–other differentiation facilitated by the interaction between the self and others but, what is more important, the first self categories that the child acquires are an outgrowth of interaction with the world and knowledge about the other. Following from this is Principle II:

Principle II: What can be demonstrated to be known about the self can be said to be known about the other and what is known about the other can be said to be known about the self.

This principle can be used to infer early social cognition, specifically, that knowledge which the child possesses about self versus other is a consequence of interaction. In two recent reviews, we have addressed in some detail the cause of knowledge of other, especially from a perceptual-cognitive position (Brooks-Gunn & Lewis, 1979a; Lewis & Brooks, 1975). Knowledge of the other person involves more than the distinction between self and other; it also involves the distinction between social and nonsocial objects. We believe that the distinction between self and other persons, not self and objects, is what is crucial for self knowledge. Piaget also addresses this issue, albeit somewhat obliquely, believing that social objects do have a unique role in the child's development:

> The human being is immersed right from birth in a social environment. Society, even more, in a sense, than the physical environment, changes the very structure of the individual, because it not only compels him to recognize facts, but also provides him with a ready-made system of signs, which modify his thoughts; it presents him with new values and it imposes on him an infinite series of obligations. It is therefore quite evident that social life affects intelligence through the three media of language (signs), the content of interactions (intellectual values) and rules imposed on thought (collective logical and prelogical norms). (p. 156)

Moreover, Piaget has stated:

> if it is clear that the process of sensorimotor causality is due to that of intelligence itself, we must not overlook one circumstance which, though it does not spring from the realm of intellectual mechanisms, certainly accelerates that progress. Just as people doubtless constitute the *first permanent objects* recognized by the baby, so also they are very probably the first objectified *source of causality* because, through imitating someone else, the subject rapidly succeeds in attributing to his models' action an efficacy analogous to his own. Imitating someone else, as Baldwin has shown, is the source of both alter and ego: One may probably go so far as to say that it represents one of the principal occasions for distinguishing between the external world and the

self, and consequently a factor in the substantiation and spatialization of the
world. (p. 360, emphasis added)

Given the importance of knowledge of persons versus objects, what
do we actually know about the infant's ability to differentiate social and
nonsocial objects? The evidence in the first month of life is conflicting
(Fantz, 1963; Fitzgerald, 1968; Hershenson, 1965; Spitz & Wolf, 1946;
Thomas, 1965). However, by two months of age, infants can differentiate easily between social and nonsocial objects (Carpenter, 1973;
Gibson, 1969). The basis of this distinction is not clear, as infants may be
innately predisposed to respond to human features (Bowlby, 1969; Spitz
& Wolf, 1946), social preference may result from progressive learned
differentiation of the physical characteristics of the face (Gibson, 1969),
or differentiation may result from some combination of the two. For
example, the differentiation and preference for social stimuli are determined by the physical properties of the face, such as movement and
contrast, attributes which are known to hold the infant's attention.

Although it is apparent that infants at early ages can differentiate
self from other and at the same time can differentiate social from nonsocial objects, there is very little data on what characteristics of other (and
the self) are acquired by the child. We would like to turn our attention to
some of the social cognitions that appear to be specifically related to the
categorical self.

In any discussion of the categorical self, we are at the same time
considering social knowledge about other. That is, any categories that
are applied to the self can also be applied to the social world. Because of
this parallel, we shall discuss social dimensions, keeping in mind that
they are used for both self and others.

*Principle III: Social dimensions are those attributes of others and self which
can be used to describe people.*

While Piaget and others have greatly increased our knowledge about
some of the dimensions of the nonsocial world (such as weight, length,
and volume), few theorists have attempted to describe the equivalent
social space or social dimensions. The categories of self and others that
emerge from the infant's interaction with the environment allow us to
generate social dimensions which, when applied to the self, form the
basis for the categorical self, as discussed in Chapter 1.

Social Dimensions and the Categorical Self

In the course of our study, both of self recognition, as presented in this volume, and of infants' interactions with their social world (Brooks-Gunn & Lewis, 1979a; Lewis & Brooks, 1974; Lewis & Feiring, 1978; Lewis & Weinraub, 1976; Waite & Lewis, 1978; Weinraub, Brooks, & Lewis, 1977), several factors have emerged. Infants, from the beginning of life, enter into a social world filled with a wide assortment of people. Predisposed to interact with the environment, especially in the social environment, infants enter into and actively participate in a variety of social relationships. In terms of their own social networks, infants learn that they have different relationships with different people and that these relationships differ in terms of the nature of at least the social object, function, and situation (Lewis & Feiring, 1979). From these complex interactons, several categories of self and other emerge. The three, in particular, that we believe come to play a particularly important role in the child's early knowledge are familiarity, age, and gender.

Familiarity

Not only must infants learn to differentiate among social and nonsocial objects they must also differentiate among and respond appropriately to different social objects. The infant comes into contact with a vast array of social objects, including parents, friends, relatives, peers, and strangers. How does the infant go about differentiating among them?

Familiarity has been studied extensively and is obviously one of the first dimensions to be used. Familiarity involves recognition of the caregiver(s) and differentiation between the caregiver(s) and strangers. Both indices of familiarity have been studied under the rubric of attachment (Ainsworth, 1969; Bowlby, 1969) and dependency (Gewirtz, 1972). Usually, differentiation is thought to occur after the infant has an internal representation of the mother that serves as a comparison point. Many studies have shown differentiation of mother and stranger by at least three months of age (cf. Banks & Wolfson, 1967; Bronson, 1972). And recent studies have shown similar early differentiation between father and stranger matched for age and sex (cf. Brooks-Gunn & Lewis, 1979a; Lamb, 1976). Parent–other differentiation is a robust finding, one that has been replicated over a variety of situations and contexts: in the home and in the laboratory; in intrusive and nonintrusive situations; and in novel and peculiar situations, e.g., mother and stranger each wearing a mask (cf. Sroufe, Waters, & Matas, 1974). Infants also differentiate between familiar and strange peers (Lewis *et al.*, 1975) and between siblings and others (Dunn, 1979). Within the familiarity dimension, they respond differently to their mothers and fathers in live situations (Lamb, 1976), in photographs (Lord, Lewis, & Brooks, 1975), and in verbal labeling situations (Chapter 5; Brooks-Gunn & Lewis, in press). Some researchers have suggested studying familiarity as a continuum rather than as a dichotomous function (cf. Rosenthal, 1973). For example, a grandparent may be more familiar than a neighbor or mailman, who are in turn more familiar than the doctor, and so on. Such a framework could be used to study the familiarity dimension with greater precision.

Ontogenetically, familiarity and unfamiliarity are first differentiated immediately following the social and nonsocial differentiation, at least for mother and other comparisons. By three months of age, mothers (Aronson & Rosenbloom, 1971; McGurk & Lewis, 1974) and probably fathers are also being differentiated from others. Familiar and unfamiliar peers, as well as siblings and others, seem to be distinguished quite early. Other familiar persons are differentiated probably around a year of age, although this has not been studied systematically. From the point of view of self as familiar, the young infant's pleasure in playing with contingency in mirrors and early contingent turning, through use of a reflected image, indicates a familiarity with the image in the reflected surface.

Recognition of familiar persons is crucial for the young infant. For example, recognizing the mother is necessary in order for the infant to form a relationship with the mother, to recognize the mother's contingency patterns, and to control the mother's behavior. If she were not recognized, these patterns would be random, being rediscovered at every new encounter. Familiarity is necessary in order to maintain continuity.

Age

Age reflects probably one of the most important social dimensions, since aging is a basic process of human experience universally associated with a wide variety of social activities. The knowledge of age does not have to be associated with knowledge of number, as several obvious and important factors covary with age and have perceptual aspects. These factors include facial change, simple body mo'rement, language usage, and social function. None of these require that the child be able to count, to have seriation, or to understand transitivity. Thus, children under four to five years of age do not understand the concept of number of years old, but they do understand age as a general concept. There is now a body of information, including the studies reported here, showing that infants possess the ability to differentiate different-aged people and use age to categorize the social world quite early. Fagan (1972) found that 6-month-old infants could distinguish between an adult and a baby in 2- and 3-dimensional representations, while we have found that 9- to 12-month-olds could differentiate between photographs of baby and adult faces, with a preference for baby faces. Moreover, in all our studies of stranger approach we have found that infants as young as six months can distinguish between a child, age four to six years, and an adult of parenting age, with infants showing more positive responses toward the approach of the child than toward the adult (Brooks & Lewis, 1976; Greenberg *et al.*, 1973; Lewis & Brooks, 1974). In trying to sort out what physical dimensions facilitated this discrimination, we thought of height and facial configuration. Since, in our studies, neither the adults nor children spoke and since both approached the infant in the same manner, the dimensions of height and facial configuration seemed to be the variables most likely to be utilized in the differentiation. Adults differ from children in height and facial configuration. Thus, the age variable could be reduced to one or more of these featural differences. By using an adult female midget who had the facial features of an adult and the height of a child, we were able to separate the two dimensions in our experiment. If the infants responded to her as they did to adults, then facial features were the cues they were using; if they responded to her as they did to children, then height was the critical dimension. The results showed that they responded to her neither as an adult (gaze aversion) nor as a child (positive affect), but rather with surprise. This response, seen in the youngest infants (7-month-olds), indicates that even by this age the relationship between facial configuration and height may be known and used to make discriminations having to do with "age" (Brooks & Lewis, 1976).

Data on infants' reponses to pictures of different-age children also lend support to our belief that age is an important social dimension which is acquired early. Infants tend to show differential perceptual-affective responses to three classes of pictures of social objects. Toward pictures of other infants, they both attend and show high positive affect; toward pictures of adults, they show attentive behavior but little affect; and toward pictures of children, they show little affect or attention. This three-category system is made up of others (like self), adults, and an in-between category. This same trichotomy of social objects appears again with the onset of the lexicon. As we have pointed out, the earliest words are "baby," which is a peer and self referent, and "mommy" and "daddy," which are adult referents. Referents for older children appear somewhat later. Adults are differentiated early because they care for and interact with infants, peers are differentiated because of the perceived similarity between self and peers, and older children are differentiated probably because the multi-aged peer and sibling groups are a characteristic of infants' social groups (Konner, 1975).

We suspect that age is first differentiated on a physical basis and is reinforced by specific functions performed by specific age groups. For example, Hess (1967) and Lorenz (1943) have suggested that "babyish-ness" may have special properties that evoke specific responses in others. To this physical difference are then added a specific lexicon which differentiates age groups still further. Whatever dimensions are available to young organisms, they are quite capable of making careful differentiations on the basis of age.

To test age knowledge with children as young as three years of age, Edwards and Lewis (1979) asked subjects to classify pictures of heads and shoulders of social objects into four categories: little children, big children, parents, and grandparents. The pictures represented people who ranged in age from 1 to 70 years. The 3-year-olds were capable of carrying out this task of sorting, even though they could not give the exact age (in years). In addition, Edwards and Lewis (1979) found that the children's transition points were remarkably similar to what we as adults consider the difficult age transitions. These young children had the most difficulty categorizing pictures of persons aged 5, 11, and 40 years. The traditional *adult* transitions are from babyhood to childhood (age five), from childhood to adolescence (age 11 to 13), and from adult-hood to middle age (age 40).

Thus, even without the ability to seriate or the knowledge of tran-sitivity, young children have, in some form, a highly developed sense of age. The development of this knowledge of self and other relies first on physical attribution but quickly becomes based on dimensions such as the lexicon and on the activity and behavior of the social objects. In particular, the social activities of others provide a wealth of information related to age (Edwards & Lewis, 1979; Lewis & Feiring, 1979).

Gender

The third social dimension that is acquired early and that can be considered a category of self and other is gender. Although considerable debate continues on the relationship between gender and sex-role behavior, gender is an invariant social dimension transcending culture, history, or location. Across time, gender has been seen as a salient dimension of all cultures. For the most part, infants are socialized differently as a function of their sex through specific caregiver–infant interactions (Goldberg & Lewis, 1969; Lewis, 1972a,b; Lewis & Cherry, 1977; Moss, 1967; Robson, Pederson, & Moss, 1969). Even caregivers themselves respond differentially as a function of their own sex (Lamb, 1976; Weinraub & Frankel, 1977). Thus, infants are cared for differentially, both in terms of the sex of the infant and the sex of the caregiver.

Since biological reproductive differences between men and women may not be noticed by children under three or four years, infants must use such culture-related cues as dress and hair style and such physical cues as height, face, and voice difference to differentiate gender. Gender differentiation has been studied using either photographic representations or live subjects. In general, adults are differentiated on the basis of gender earlier than are children. Infants have been shown to respond differentially to men and women in stranger approach studies, with the men eliciting more negative responses (Benjamin, 1961; Lewis & Brooks, 1974; Morgan & Ricciuti, 1969; Shaffran & Décarie, 1973). These differences appear to be accounted for by height and voice cues (Brooks & Lewis, 1976). Boy and girl children have not been found to elicit different responses (Greenberg et al., 1973; Lewis & Brooks, 1974). Representations of male and female faces yield similar findings. In a series of studies, Fagan (1972) presented 4-, 5-, and 6-month-old infants with representations of adult females, adult males, and infants. In general, the younger infants did not discriminate among conditions, whereas the older ones exhibited gender differentiation. Six-month-olds also differentiated between male and female photographs vis-à-vis vocalizations in a study by Kagan and Lewis (1965). In our work on 9- to 24-month-olds' responses to facial representations, attention and affect were not directed to male and female strangers differentially, but verbal labels were. By 18 months of age, when most of the infants had some utterances in their verbal repertoire, infants labeled adults correctly on the basis of gender 90% of the time, using "mommy" or "lady" for the female adult and "daddy" or "man" for the male adult. Of the infants who had the labels for boy and girl, approximately 80% applied them correctly to the pictures of children (Lewis & Brooks, 1974; Brooks-Gunn & Lewis, in press).

The gender dimension also seems to be relevant for infants themselves. Money and Ehrhardt (1972) report that gender reassignment is possible in the beginning of life without psychological consequences, but that children over 18 months of age often have difficulty with such reassignments. This impressive data argues strongly for children's notion of their own sex, their preference for it, and for their general knowledge of gender. Our own data provide additional support. Recall that for both samples of 15- to 18-month-old infants in Chapter 4, the ability to attend differentially to the self versus another infant was dependent on the self being compared not only with peer but with an opposite-sex peer, suggesting that gender is an important cue used by the child to recognize self in pictorial form.

The origins of social differentiation as a function of gender are not clear. Differences in physical attributes, in culture-related attributes, and in interactions with the social world, as functions of both the sex of the infant and the caregiver, exist. Whatever the basis of the differentiation, infants show gender knowledge by the onset of verbal labeling.

Constructing the Social World

The social cognition acquired by the infant, although impressive from the point of view that children of this age have such knowledge, is still quite limited. We do not know at this time what form that knowledge takes, although we recognize that it must be limited by the child's general cognitive ability and amount of experience. Thus, although infants may demonstrate early gender knowledge, their knowledge is not in the same form as adult knowledge of gender, nor is it fixed. Clearly, with increasing age and cognitive capacity, the concept of gender becomes further articulated, then stable, and finally invariant for both self and for others (Kohlberg, 1966). We hold that the other social dimensions exhibit the same pattern, first being differentiated, then being fur-

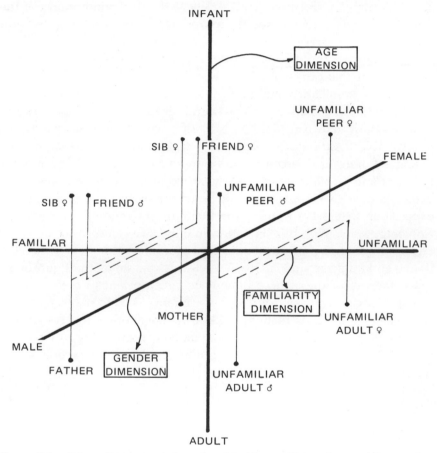

Figure 9-1. Schematic representation of social objects utilizing three social categories: age, gender, and familiarity. The dimensions of familiarity-unfamiliarity and adult–infant are continuous, while the dimension of male–female is dichotomous. However, gender may be perceived as a continuous variable by the young child; for example, a mother may be seen as more female than a 5-year-old girl. On the figure, siblings and parents have been represented as equally familiar, while adult strangers are represented as less familiar than peer strangers. The points are merely illustrative of possible location of persons in a child's social world and may vary depending on the child's perception. From Lewis and Feiring (1978).

ther articulated, then stable, and finally invariant. Unlike others, we believe that the ontogeny of this development occurs from the beginning of life and involves not only knowledge of others but also knowledge of self.

One of the important consequences of the young child's knowledge of these early social dimensions is that the organism is able to "construct" a complex social world. We believe that the primary task of the infant is to adapt to the social environment, which is complex and multi-dimensional (Weinraub, Brooks, & Lewis, 1977). That the infant's world is complex and is peopled by many social objects requires a cognitive structure that can cope with at least three social dimensions. These dimensions—familiarity, age and gender—can be conceptualized in a three-dimensional space as can be seen in Figure 9-1. The space represented is derived by considering familiarity, age, and gender as continuous variables. Although we recognize that gender is not continuous, young children may perceive it to be more continuous (e.g., a mother may be more "female" than a five-year-old girl). Therefore, one might expect gender to become more dichotomous with increasing age, an expectation that is born out in the literature on gender constancy (cf. Kohlberg, 1966). With this limitation in mind, we can turn to the space created through the use of familiarity, age, and gender. Whether the young child utilizes such space is unclear. Even so, as the figure indicates, the use of these three dimensions is sufficient to construct the elaborate social world out of which the infant needs to make sense.

Whatever the construction, the knowledge of other and the knowledge of self are parallel, and the task of understanding early social cognition must be the task of studying self, other, and their interaction, a task we take up in the final chapter.

CHAPTER 10

The Uses of a Theory of Self

In this chapter, we will turn our attention to the contributions of a theory of self. The function of this chapter is to place our theory and our data on self in the larger framework of early social cognition. Just as the self has been divided into two aspects, so this chapter on the uses of self will be divided. First, the existential or subjective self and the role of the self–other differentiation in the social life of the child will be explored. This will include consideration of a sociobiological approach to development, the role of self in cognition, the self–other distinction, self and social relations, and empathy. Second, we shall explore the categorical or the objective self, paying particular attention to friendship and sex-role development.

The Ontogeny of Thought: a Sociobiological Approach

Our view of the development of human organisms is predicated on the belief that development is an active process involving the interaction between the organism and its world. The interaction process itself is the material by which the infant's conceptualization of the world, both social and nonsocial, and of the self develops. Knowledge of self and others, both being aspects of social knowledge, proceeds in a parallel fashion, developing at the same time and from the same material. Moreover, this development has as its source the interaction of the young organism with others—both people and objects. The implication of this is that action within the interaction of the organism and its environment precedes knowledge. Indeed, it is from action that knowledge develops. This implies that the earliest action is not predicated on knowledge, neither knowledge of self or others, nor is it controlled by intention or plan. What, then, might be responsible for this early action and what are the rules that control it? For us, early actions are biologically based, consisting of complex social reflexes. From early reflexes, action within the framework of interaction with others emerges, providing the basic material for knowledge. The sociobiology of early action is predicated on three basic principles: (1) knowledge is a consequence of action, (2) early action is biologically determined, and (3) early action is the material of knowledge.

Implicit in this formulation is the notion that action is converted into knowledge: the young organism, at first controlled by reflexive behavior, becomes increasingly motivated by knowledge and intention. In fact, much of the very early social behavior that has been studied during the 1970s is a type of complex, reflexive social behavior. For example, Condon and Sander (1974) have examined the way in which the adult vocal behavior is able to entrap, that is, to elicit and maintain patterned and synchronous movement in the newborn. Facial expression, eye gaze behavior (Brazelton, Yogman, Als, & Tronick, 1979), as well as movements in space (Bower, 1975; Trevarthen, 1974) are all reflections of complex social reflexes. Early imitation is one such reflexive system which can be elicited by either social objects or by inanimate objects (Jacobson & Kagan, 1978). We will return to imitation since imitation represents a prototypic example of the sociobiological approach to early knowledge. Most, if not all, of the early and complex behavior patterns are probably under biological control at least to some degree.

Reflex systems are not as simple as many have assumed. As Harlow and Mears (1978) have pointed out, not only are reflexes complex, but they must be considered as part of the organism's interactive repertoire. Given the existence of these early reflexive behaviors, their course of development is of some interest, especially if one believes that they are the basic material for knowledge. Like most early reflexive systems, these complex social reflexes should decay with development, giving way to behavior which is motivationally and cognitively based. Early reflexes, such as the Moro or Babinski reflexes, decline (Peiper, 1961/ 1963), their failure to decay indicating central nervous system dysfunction. This may also be true of complex social reflexes. Examples of this decay can be found in the literature. For example, Gewirtz (1965), studying the development of the smiling response across different social situations, found smiling to increase, reaching a peak at around three to four

months. At this point, smiling then declines only to show a slight increase toward the end of the first year. Prior to three months, the smiling
response of the infant was no different as a function of the social milieu,
while after this point, the smiling response becomes increasingly tied
into and dependent on the social environment. Vocalization patterns of
young infants seem to be similarly uninfluenced by the social environment until around the second or third month of life, when the social
environment becomes salient (Lenneberg, Rebelsky, & Nichols, 1965).
Finally, important changes in information processing also appear to
occur around two to three months of age (Lewis & Baldini, 1979).
Taken together, these findings suggest the efficacy of the following
model of sociobiological interaction, as presented in Figure 10-1.

At first, reflexive controls predominate with behavioral expression
chiefly under the control of complex social reflexes. These reflexes function to get the young organism into interaction with the environment.
From this initially reflexive interaction, cognitive and motivational structures emerge which gradually take over the control of behavior. At
around two to three months of age, reflexes and cognitions are of equal
ability in controlling behavior, and after three months, cognitions predominate. The shape of the functions thus described is still hypothet-
ical. Reflexive behavior may not disappear as pictured in Figure 10-1, but
may in fact coexist with cognitive behavior; or development may be
more cyclical, with *each* new level of development recapitulating this
early model, such that at the next reorganization in development, complex reflexive behavior emerges first, providing the material for the next

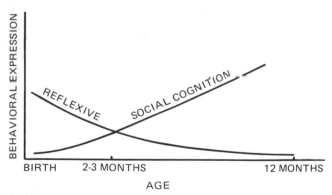

FIGURE 10-1.   The relative influence of complex social reflexes and complex social cognitions upon behavior expression in the first year of life.

level of cognitive behavior. Harlow and Mears (1978) remind us that complex reflexive behavior does not occur only at the beginning of life but may appear throughout the lifetime of the organism. Keeping this caveat in mind, we believe that social knowledge does develop out of early social reflexes that gradually disappear as social cognitions appear, even though we realize that each behavior may exhibit a slightly different trend. However, this notion does not exclude the possibility that some social cognitions may exist from the very beginning of life, although to date no such evidence for this exists.

This model may be useful for conceptualizing early development. Let us consider imitation as an example of the efficacy of our model. The earliest imitation is probably a complex reflexive behavior, a rather valuable one in that it has the effect of matching infants' behavior to that of their caregivers. This should have two functions: on the one hand, such imitation bonds the caregiver more closely to the child; since a similarity between them exists; on the other hand, the child becomes more like the parent. Imitation may be a useful and adaptive reflex, indicating that the newborn is a member of the species—the newborn and the adult being able to notice the similarity. Both see the other as "like myself" (Baldwin, 1899/1973). Imitation is elicited by a class of stimuli; for example, a protruding stick can elicit a tongue protrusion as well as can a protruding tongue (Jacobson & Kagan, 1978). Although the data are scant, there does appear to be a decline in imitative behavior over the first few months of life (Jacobson & Kagan, 1978; Maratos, 1973), which we believe to indicate a decline in the reflexive behavior.[1] At around three months of age, imitative behavior increases again. Although there are no data between 3 and 10 months, there is evidence that imitation increases from 10 to 22 months (Killen & Uzgiris, 1978). Moreover, imitation in 2-year-olds can be deferred for as long as 24 hours (McCall, Parke, & Kavanaugh, 1977) and is dependent on the meaningfulness of the behavior to be imitated (Killen & Uzgiris, 1978). In imitation research, we can observe several phenomena which are of interest

---

[1]Some questions have been raised recently as to whether early reflexive imitation exists. Criticism centers around the inadequate controls for arousal level. Waite and Lewis (1979) have shown that with the proper controls there is little support for the imitation phenomenon; nevertheless, they have shown that the models' gestures do elicit in the 2- and 12-week-old infant a high degree of similar gestures. Given that the caregiver is unlikely to consider base line levels or compare responses across different gestures, it does appear to the caregiver to be imitative behavior. Lewis (1979) has called this subjective imitation since from the point of view of the parent, the infant is imitating their behavior.

to us: first, the early reflexive aspect of this behavior and second, the increasingly important role of the relationship between the imitator and the imitated. These findings are in agreement with our sociobiological model, which provides a useful bridge between the display of similar behavior at two points in time. The model holds that the control of behavior is under the service of two distinct systems: at the earliest time, complex social reflexes and after two to three months, cognitive-motivational structures. Thus, although the neonate and the four-month-old may both show similar behavior, the control and the meaning of that behavior may be quite different.

Social behavior—knowledge of the other, the self, and the relationship of the self to the other—is derived from early social reflexes. Around two to three months of age, social cognitions appear which affect infants' transactions with their environment and allow for the rapid creation of new and more complex cognitive-motivational structures. The central feature of development is the young organisms' interactions with their environment, since it is both the process by which the cognitive-motivational structures are created *and* the material by which the young organism creates social knowledge. In terms of the self, the organism's interactions are, in part, the process by which the self is created: the consistent, synchronous, and responsive environment creates the objective self as well as providing the material of the subjective self.

We have taken the time to discuss early social reflexive behavior not because we do not believe in an active and cognitive organism, but rather because we see little need to posit early complex social knowledge, knowledge which exists from birth. The nativist view of the existence of early cognitive knowledge, or the constructivist view (as outlined to include both a biological and learning position), both arrive at a similar conclusion, and it is this conclusion which, for the sake of our discussion, we hold to be most important. Whatever the process, by about twelve weeks the behavior of the infant appears to be increasingly under the control of cognitive-motivational structures and progressively less under the control of biological forces. Thus, while the early interactions are biologically controlled, subsequent interactions involve organisms that are both competent and active, organisms that, through their immature but functional cognitive-motivational structures, plan, engage, and shape their environment at the same time that they are engaged and shaped by it (Bell, 1974; Lewis & Rosenblum, 1974).

THE ROLE OF SELF IN COGNITION

Psychological inquiry is predicated on various models of human nature (Reese & Overton, 1970). The various paradigms we construct to explain human behavior and which guide the research conducted are not explicated carefully. Nevertheless, two views of human behavior have seemed to predominate through the history of psychology. In the first view, the human is acted upon, whereas in the second, the human acts upon. We have called the former the mechanistic position and the latter, the constructivist position (Lewis & Brooks, 1975).

Mechanistic View

The mechanistic position is best exemplified in the study of perception, in which the information within the stimulus is more important than the act of reconstructing the information according to the organism's cognitions, plans, and needs. The organization, and often the control of behavior, is thought to reside in the stimulus, not in the organism. Although the organism may possess structures for uncovering the stimulus properties, these properties exist in the stimulus itself. Moreover, the organism's structures (when referred to) are passive structures, such as filters, engrams, neural models, etc. Implicit in this view of human behavior is the notion that: (1) a passive organism is being acted upon; (2) behavior is being controlled by the stimulus, and stimulus properties are of a compelling nature; (3) a one-to-one correspondence between the stimulus event and our percepts of that event exists; and, finally (4) that a real world independent of our actions and perceptions exists.

Two examples of such a view come readily to mind. The Gibsons' (E. J. Gibson, 1969; J. J. Gibson, 1963, 1966) view is essentially that of a passive organism absorbing information which is already structured. Although organisms actively seek and attend to information, they do not structure it themselves, that is, "there is a structure in the world and structure in the stimulus, and it is the structure in the stimulus ... that constitutes information about the world" (E. J. Gibson, 1969, pp. 13–14). The theory is stimulus-oriented such that the organism must discover the invariances present in the environment. Learning occurs through the infant's increasing ability to extract information from the environment which is done by learning to differentiate among properties, learning to distinguish patterns, and learning to recognize distinctive features. Representations of these distinctive features are stored, although the information is not actively reconstructed before processing occurs. The lack of central activity in organizing and reorganizing sensory input has been criticized by others, for example, by Gyr (1972). The stimulus-oriented nature of such theories is considered inadequate by congitive theorists who believe that the organism chooses what information is to be extracted and how such material is to be reconstructed (Neisser, 1967). On the surface, the Gibsons' theory is appealing; for example, the development of facial perception is easily explained, as facial features are first distinguished, separated, and then combined to differentiate among persons. Differentiation precedes the development of a schema instead of following it, and the child has little direct or active input into the process of constructing a schema for face (Gibson, 1969).

Lorenz's theory (1943) provides another example of a stimulus compelling an organism to act. In this case, an innate releasing mechanism (IRM) is posited through some as yet undisclosed neural system to predispose the organism to act. Action can be either approach behavior, as in imprinting, or flight behavior as avoiding some predator. These actions are necessary for the survival of the species and are therefore built into the nervous system. Invariant action is produced by the eliciting effect of the stimulus on the organism's nervous system.

Constructivist View

This view of human nature holds that organisms actively construct their world and that, by their actions affect their environment as well as being affected by it. Humans actively seek stimulation and utilize information from the environment as a function of individual plans, personality, and cognitive organization. Such a view suggests that the stimulus event cannot be defined as external to the organism and existing independently of the organism's experience. It is an interactive position and, as such, rejects the notion of a sensory event being independent of the perceiver, or action being independent of the organism's plans, strategies, cognitions, and motives.

The history of constructivism is as old as the mechanistic position. Bartlett (1932), for example, defined a schema as an organized internal structure that is formed by an active process of reconstructing stimulus information. Structures are reorganized because of the interpretation of the incoming information. Thus, structure is defined as originating within the organism, not within the stimulus. Neisser (1967) has elaborated on this theme, suggesting that incoming stimuli are reordered, directed, and developed into percepts by the deliberate action of the organism. This deliberate action is based on past experiences, preferences, and expectations. Thus, there is no one-to-one correspondence between the stored material and the stimulus properties.

Perhaps the outstanding example of the constructivist position is that held by Piaget (1936/1963) which is too familiar to take up in detail. Like Bartlett, Piaget holds to a constructivist position and rejects a passive copy theory. Development occurs through the interaction of the organism's internal structures (these themselves built from interaction) and the external world. Through the dual processes of assimilation and accommodation, cognitive structures for organizing the world are formed and are constantly being reconstructed. With age and experience, the structures are altered; the orderly progression of structural change is the focus of genetic epistemology (Piaget, 1936/1963). Lewis (1972b) and Sameroff and Chandler (1975), among others, have elaborated on the interactive or transactional nature of development.

An active organism, one whose structures are determined by past experience and current abilities, including plans, motives, and cognitive skills, is the model to which we adhere in our discussion of self. The relationship between self and action is crucial. Consider, for example, early means and ends behaviors (Piaget, 1936/1963); their existence implies that infants plan, test hypotheses, and alter their behavior as a consequence of outcomes. These behaviors, in turn, are quite compatible with the notion of agency, which is a feature of self. Such examples lead us to believe that if one holds to a model of active cognition, one must logically hold to a belief in the self. It does not appear logical to believe in plans, intentions, and hypothesis testing without a belief in the organism's possession of some notion of self. How can an organism make a plan or test a hypothesis without also having an agency of the plan or a tester of the hypothesis? "I wish" or "I think" or "Do I see a circle or square?" all imply some agency of these actions. Moreover, this agency has as one of its dominant features a specific locus in space, yet another feature of self. To see a red circle over there and a blue one next to it implies an observer who is not in the same isomorphic space as these objects. As we suggested in Chapter 9, to perceive "there" implies a perceiver "here."

Thus, to hold to a constructivist model of cognition is at one and the same time to hold to an implicit belief in self knowledge. A mechanistic model makes no such premise—machines have no self—and, therefore, we would argue that the *sine qua non* of cognitive theory is the notion of self.

THE SELF–OTHER DISTINCTION

Self–Other Duality

The active organism derives information from its action in the world, providing through its actions both the questions and answers. This does not mean that reinforcement, modeling, or observation play no role in development, but rather that the organism itself makes use of the information provided by the reinforcement or imitation. Unless the organism is ready or capable of using that information, concepts such as these have little meaning. Even social learning theorists like Mischel (1973) state that "the impact of any stimulus depends on the organism that experiences it" (p. 262) and "clearly different persons may group and encode the same events and behaviors in different ways. At a molar level, such individual differences are especially evident in the personal constructs individuals employ and in the kinds of information to which they selectively attend" (pp. 267–268). The use of an active model necessitates that we view the child as central to all information processing and that this information has meaning only as the child gives it meaning.

Counter to this is the idea that there exist classes of events (stimuli) that act independently of the organism. Such events would not have to be defined by the organism and would cause action independently of the child. An example of this is the existence of innate releasing mechanisms, such as the human face, for a young infant. Spitz and Wolf's (1946) classical work on the smiling response to a human face is an example of such a phenomenon. In a somewhat different context, William James (1890/1950), in discussing attention, makes reference to two classes of events: those he calls immediate, passive, sensorial attention events and those terms associated attention events. In the former, these events cause us to attend independently of our will or past history; a loud noise will get us to start and turn, interrupting the most active engagement. The latter events cause attending through their association with our past experience. James's discussion is particularly apt:

> Such an empiricist writer as Mr. Spencer, for example, regards the creature as absolutely passive clay, upon which 'experience' rains down. The clay will be impressed most deeply where the drops fall thickest, and so the final shape of the mind is moulded. Given time enough, and all sentient things ought, at this rate, to end by assuming an identical mental constitution—for 'experience,' the sole shaper, is a constant fact, and the order of its items must end by being exactly reflected by the passive mirror which we call the sentient organism. If such an account were true, a race of dogs bred for generations, say in the Vatican, with characters of visual shape, sculptured in marble, presented to their eyes, in every variety of form and combination, ought to discriminate before long the finest shades of these peculiar characters. In a word, they ought to become, if time were given, accomplished *connoisseurs* of sculpture. Anyone may judge of the probability of this consummation. Surely an eternity of experience of the statues would leave the dog as inartistic as he was at first, for the lack of an original interest to knit his discriminations on to. Meanwhile the odors at the bases of the pedestals would have organized themselves in a consciousness of this breed of dogs into a system of 'correspondences' to which the most hereditary caste of *custodi* would never approximate, merely because to them, as human beings, the dog's interest in those smells would for ever be an inscrutable mystery. These writers have, then, utterly ignored the glaring fact that subjective interest may, by laying its weighty index-finger on particular items of experience, so accent them as to give to the least frequent associations far more power to shape our thought than the most frequent ones possess. The interest itself, though its genesis is doubtless perfectly *natural, makes* experience more than it is made by it. (p. 403)

That such a class of events exists in human experience, therefore, is not to be denied; nonetheless, the conclusions drawn from this fact are vast. The sociobiological view presented earlier suggests that although such events do occur, their action (the organism's passive behavior) is nothing more than the material for constructing cognitive structures. *It is not the passive action which is important but rather the interpretation of that action.* The study of human development is, therefore, not merely the study of that action but the child's interpretation of the meaning of the event, an event that is now defined as the relationship between two acts, as, for example, between the loud noise and a head turn. Further support for such a position can be found in examination of particular behaviors which have an identical structural form but which have vastly different meaning. For example, in ethnology, the same signal may have different effects on different perceivers. The "long call" of black-headed gulls attracts unmated females and repels rivals. And again, "head to sound" posture repels neighbors but attracts females (see Manley, 1960, cited in Eibl-Eibesfeldt, 1970). Heider (1958) has articulated this position from the perspective of interpersonal relations when he says:

> One might say psychological processes such as motives, intentions, sentiments, etc., are the core processes which manifest themselves in overt behavior and expression in many variable ways. The manifestations are then directly grasped by p, the observer, in terms of these psychological core processes; they would otherwise remain undecipherable. By looking through the mediation, p perceives the distal object, the psychological entities that bring consistency and meaning to the behavior; *p's reaction is then to this meaning not to the overt behavior directly.* (p. 34)

The developmental task for a young organism—it is also the task for developmental psychology—is to make sense of the variety of events which occur, some of which are external and internal events, both others' behavior and one's own behavior. In Chapter 7 we have shown this task in respect to affective experience and expression; the task is no different for cognitive and social events as well. The task of perceiving, ordering, and interpreting events involves the self. As we have discussed earlier, knowledge requires the interaction of the self and other, other being both social and nonsocial. In fact, we have argued for the duality of knowledge of self and other. In Chapter 9 we saw that to know of a thing is to know of ourselves. This duality of knowledge can be approached either from our knowledge of self extended to others— what we know of self is what we know of others—or from our knowledge of others extended to self—what we know of others is what we know of self. In all likelihood, such knowledge acquisition is bidirectional, the discovery of self informing us about other and the discovery of other telling us about self. In a recent chapter on the child's construing of self, Bannister and Agnew (1977) presented a similar analysis:

> The ways in which we elaborate our construing of self must be essentially those ways in which we elaborate our construing of others, for we have not a concept of self but *a bipolar construct of self—not self or self-others.* (p. 99, italics added)

This self–other or self–not-self structure of knowledge takes many forms. Bannister and Agnew, in discussing this duality, make reference to person processes in terms of *"relating to–not relating to, destroying– creating, flowing to–flowing from, constituting–being no part of, SELF"* (p. 99).

The final aspect of our discussion pertains to knowledge of other persons. Since people (unlike other objects) are like us, it is necessary to consider the topic of social versus nonsocial knowledge and the distinction between them. Although most knowledge is embedded in a social context, whether or not infants perceive a difference between social and nonsocial objects is open to debate. We believe that they are different, both because of some basic attributes of objects and the organism's differential interaction with them. Movement, an attribute children use to distinguish between living and nonliving, may be used by the infant to organize its world of stimuli. For example, the neonate is not able to track moving objects easily although tracking skills increase rapidly, especially when stimuli move slowly. Through such tracking experiences, the infant probably learns to distinguish figure from ground. The consistency of an object, independent of its background, may be the mechanism whereby objects begin to attain object constancy (not permanence, which is a later development). The important role of tracking in the infants' early gross ability to perform this action is compensated by the parent's willingness to move slowly across the child's field and to attract and hold the infant's attention. Thus, prior to the child's ability to track objects actively, persons aid the child in this ability through their active movement across the child's field of vision. Since tracking may be responsible for organizing stimuli into larger units, the willingness of the social world to facilitate this and related abilities lays the ground work for the self–other distinction. Other attributes of social stimuli have to do with IRMs associated with the face and body. Hess's (1967) notion of babyishness and Spitz and Wolf's (1946) work with ovals and dark spots suggest that the human face and face-like features have a certain prewired attraction for the babies, causing them to act differently to social and nonhuman stimuli. Finally, and possibly of most importance, is the fact that social stimuli—humans and human-like objects—have intention and therefore are able to organize their behavior in interaction with the child. Other attributes and behaviors of humans, such as synchrony of behavior, responsivity of the environment, and imitation, are all behaviors which are facilitated by the intention of the adult and which help organize the infant's knowledge of the social world into a reciprocal and synchronous interplay between infant and other humans. Natural outcomes of this process are action–outcome pairings, agency, and spatial location. The nonsocial world does not possess these features or result in these outcomes.

The interaction with the social world, which is most adaptive and which occurs from the beginning of life, supplies the material for the construction of knowledge and self. The cognitive rule the child uses in finally distinguishing between the social and nonsocial, based on the infant's earlier experience, is that the former implies a similarity between the perceived and the perceiver, namely, the self, while the latter does not (Hamlyn, 1974; Tagiuri, 1969). Thus, not only is the development of self facilitated by the social world, but, by interactions with it, the child is better able to distinguish social from nonsocial. Social experience, social knowledge, and self are tied into the same process, each feeding from the development of the other.

The amount of knowledge the infant acquires about the social world in the first months of life—one way in which this process can be explored experimentally—is impressive. As we saw earlier, the child is capable of distinguishing social and nonsocial objects by two months of age. Although Brazelton *et al.* (1979) have argued for differentiation between mother and stranger or between mother and father even earlier, the data are not clear on this point. Haith, Bergman, and Moore (1977) have presented impressive evidence that the child does not attend to the inside of human face until after five to seven weeks of age, suggesting that the differentiation of social objects cannot occur until around the two month period. Social knowledge is, however, much more extensive than that, even excluding the work in self recognition that we have presented in detail earlier. Disruption of the mother's face–voice relationship results in distress and attention in four-month-old infants and possibly in some one-month-olds (Aronson & Rosenbloom, 1971; Carpenter, 1973; McGurk & Lewis, 1974). The complex social interaction in which the three-month-old infant regulates interactions with the social environment is another example (Brazelton, Koslowski, & Main, 1974; Lewis & Freedle, 1973; Stern, 1974). The importance of such interaction is most clear in impaired children, as impairments such as blindness can lead to serious problems in the social realm (Fraiberg, 1974). Knowledge of others has been studied in the research on person perception and fear. We have shown repeatedly that children are more wary of adult strangers than of child strangers, and that infants as young as seven months of age have an understanding of the face–body relationship (Brooks & Lewis, 1976; Lewis & Brooks, 1974; Lewis *et al.*, 1975). Bronson (1975) has found some infants to be capable of recognizing strangers as early as three months of age.

A last issue involves the timing of the acquisition of social and

nonsocial knowledge. Since nonsocial objects may be less complicated—
that is, are less variable and more predictable—the infant might first
acquire knowledge about them that is generalized later to deal with
animate objects. This view reflects the overwhelming predominance
given to the nonsocial domain, both because of Piaget's interest and the
ease with which it is studied. Piaget did consider social knowledge,
and recently a number of other investigators have become concerned
with it. Although Piaget himself equivocates on the issue of whether or
not the child's nonsocial cognitive structures are the basis for social
structures, most of those following him have taken this position (cf.
Lee, 1975). The danger in this position is that much evidence, as documented in this and previous chapters, is omitted or ignored. Moreover, the fact that interactions with the nonsocial world are highly
variable and that nonsocial objects have no intentions suggests that the
social world can organize and simplify the infant's task through the use
of plans. Thus, means and ends are more easily achieved when the
social object tends to be responsive than when infants have to find
contingency between their action and outcome, a less-than-certain
likelihood. Notwithstanding these arguments, it is to the social world
that the child needs to adapt, with even the elaborate reflexive behaviors
found at birth being directed to social interaction, for example, holding
onto (Moro and Darwinian reflexes) and eating (sucking and rooting
reflexes).

The empirical data on this question are quite scant. Although Bell
(1970) and Décarie (1965) have shown that person permanence precedes
object permanence, others have argued that this is not the case (Jackson,
Campos, & Fischer, 1978). The latter investigators believe that when
social and nonsocial objects behave similarly, permanence is acquired at
the same time. While this may be true, we must remember that social
and nonsocial objects do *not* act similarly: when people act like people
rather than objects, permanence occurs earlier (Bell, 1970; Décarie,
1965). In line with this argument, social knowledge is acquired before
object knowledge.

By centering around the study of feature detection (Caron, Caron,
Caldwell, & Weiss, 1973; Fantz, 1965; Haaf & Bell, 1967; Kagan *et al.*,
1966; Lewis, 1969), the study of social knowledge has been limited to
passive models of social cognition. Toward a consideration of social
knowledge, we have offered three propositions as well as the social

categories by which the child comes both to view itself and others, these including age, gender, and familiarity (Chapter 9). Although certainly not exhaustive, these dimensions provide us with an opportunity to explore the self–other distinction.

To conclude our discussion of the self–other knowledge, we quote again Baldwin (1899/1973) who has pointed out that "My sense of myself grows by imitation of you, and my sense of yourself grows in terms of my sense of myself" (p. 338).

The Self–Other in Social Relations

Although we have attempted to explicate self–other knowledge, it is possible to consider the self–other distinction from a social relationship point of view. This is probably more useful since self knowledge, at least as tested in the more traditional sense, requires a verbal organism. Given our concern with the opening years of life, these verbal measures of self knowledge have not been available to us. Thus, the development of self–other knowledge might be best approached and studied from a consideration of the self–other relation. The subsequent discussion will hold to the proposition that all but very young infants utilize knowledge of self to guide their behavior with others. Self knowledge can be observed or inferred from self–other relationships. Kelly (1955, p. 131) makes use of a similar conclusion, but in another context: "When the person begins to use himself as a datum in forming constructs... he finds that the constructs he forms operate as rigorous controls upon his behavior. *His behavior* in *relation* to other people is particularly affected. . . . Thus, much of his social life is controlled by the comparisons he has come to see *between himself and others.*"

Kelly's view (1955) is similar to ours, especially as we consider the task of the infant to be comparable to that of the scientist Kelly, too, held to the view that all humans function as psychologists—all actively engaged in constructing events and generating personal theories to predict, control, and understand their own behavior, the behavior of others, and their interactions. The title of his first book, *The Psychology of Personal Constructs,* mirrors Kelly's central theme: "a person's processes are psychologically channelized by the ways in which he anticipates events" (1955, p. 46). The way people construe events for discerning meaning and the way they are able to anticipate events, form memories, and determine the course of action is through the use of a cognitive model involving personal constructs.

The construct systems of individuals are hierarchically ordered, with core constructs being those that are the fundamental beliefs and values a person holds. Given that Kelly described a personality theory, his emphasis on cognition and of an active organism is particularly important, especially for considering the self and social cognition. The role of the self as agent, as well as the self as construct, is vital and gives us some hint as to how it might develop. The importance of Kelly's theory for development should not be overlooked. As Kelly points out:

> the self is, when considered in the appropriate context, a proper concept or construct [for both the child and the experimenter]. It refers to a group of events which are in a certain alike way and, in that same way, necessarily different from other events. The way in which the events are alike is the self. That also makes the self an individual, differentiated from other individuals. (1955, p. 131).

Indeed, the use of personal constructs in interaction has importance for any cognitive-motivational theory of development. Actions, both internal and external, are actively construed by the infant and child as they go about learning through constructing their world. Two examples of how they utilize their own past and experience in interaction with external events illustrate this point. First, consider the various theories pertaining to attention distribution. The more passive models, those using a simple match-mismatch view (Cohen & Gelber, 1975; Sokolov, 1963), also called discrepancy (McCall & McGhee, 1977), have argued that the child attends when there is a mismatch between an already constructed model and a new event. Lewis (1971) has argued that the plans of the organism and its intentions are necessary in order to understand its attention distribution. Although mismatch between an expectation and an event can lead to attention, it is also the case that match is equally likely to produce this effect. When ten-month-old infants see their mother, certainly a match between internal representation and external event, their attention is drawn and captured by her. Second, the ordering of social objects cannot be determined independent of the child's personal constructs. Categories of social events are dependent on the active process of the organism. Consider three social objects: a female stranger, a mother, and a father. If the young child constructs a concept of gender, then the two females are similar and father is different; if, however, family (or familiarity) is the construct, then mother and father are similar and the female stranger is not. The experimenter is unable to determine which two of these three persons go together at any point in time since the infant is actively constructing the pairing. In a study where attention is elicited by discrepancy, it is impossible for the experimenter to know *a priori* which two of these three events constitute a discrepancy from the other; that cognitive activity belongs to the construct the child decides to use. In the same manner, in the study of categories or classes, it is the child's personal constructs that are of importance.

Thus, the self as construct and the self as the agent for the creation of all other constructs points to the duality of the self and its role, both as the subject of social cognition and the source of that cognition. In a recent article by Epstein (1973) on the self concept, a similar view is taken:

> What it is that consists of concepts that are hierarchically organized and internally consistent; that assimilates knowledge, yet, itself, is an object of knowledge; ... that is necessary for solving problems in the real world; ... The answer, by now should be evident.... *The self-concept is a self-theory....* Accordingly, there are major postulate systems for the *nature of the world, for the nature of self, and for their interaction.* (p. 407)

SELF AND INTERACTION

Epstein's use of the world, self, and their interaction brings us back to the three basic features that we believe define social cognition. Although we have spent considerable time discussing the self and other, relatively little effort has been given to the interaction between self and other. Interaction between self and other is important, because it is from this interaction that both self and other are formed. It is also important because once self and other are formed, at least in some rudimentary way, the self is utilized in the interaction with the other. The clearest example of this is in the concept of empathy.

Self and Empathy

Much of what has been discussed under social knowledge and social relationships could also be considered under the heading of empathy. To begin with, let us define empathy as a response to another's situation. It includes awareness of what another may be experiencing, perceiving, thinking, or feeling. Thus, empathy is the ability to be able to put oneself in another's place and to imagine what the other is experiencing. True empathetic responses, therefore, do not necessitate our experiencing or having experienced the other's experience, rather, only that we be able to imagine (in the absence of direct indication of) what the other must be experiencing. As an example of empathy without direct experience, A writes to B of A's experience and B experiences A's experience without being or having been there. This ability to empathize with others is the basis of adult social knowledge and relationships, and, as such, is the core process by which we are able to maintain adult social relations. Heider (1958) uses this as a central theme in his work on interpersonal relations. At one point, describing social perception, he says:

> Social perception in general can best be described as a process between the center of one person and the center of another person, from life space to life space. When A observes B's behavior, he "reads" it in terms of psychological entities (and his reactions, being guided by his own sentiments, expectations, and wishes, can again be understood only in terms of psychological concepts). A, through psychological processes in himself, perceives psychological processes in B. (p.33)

This extension and allocation of our psychological experience to take in the other is profoundly important for and refers only to social objects. When I perceive a rock or tree, it is not necessary for me to consider any psychological fact about the rock or tree (not so for children at play, for they do evoke such a state in me). Nor do I believe that the rock or tree elicits from me a psychological response. The children may elicit such a state from me, as the more I know of the children, the more likely I am to believe that such a state is evoked in them by me. It may be safe to conclude that the more one knows of any other, the more likely one is to believe that reciprocal states of empathy are present. This would not be surprising in light of Hamlyn's (1974) statement that to know of A is to know the possible interaction with A.

Asch (1952) also picks up on this theme as a potential difference between our social and nonsocial interactions:

> The paramount fact about human interactions is that they are happenings that are *psychologically represented in each* of the participants. In our relation to an object, perceiving, thinking and feeling take place on one side,

whereas in relations between persons these processes take place on both
sides and in dependence upon one another. (p. 142)

Asch goes on to include not only the cognitive point of view but
includes the emotional aspects of empathy which we shall consider
shortly:

> We (humans) interact with each other not as the paramecium does by
> altering the surrounding medium chemically, nor as the ants do by smell, but
> via emotions and thoughts that are capable of taking into account the emo-
> tions and thoughts of others. (p. 142)

Although we have stressed the social cognition aspect of empathy,
Hoffman (1978) has placed particular emphasis on the fact that empathy
is an affective state. That is, the experience of A produces through its
perceptual and cognitive mediation an affect in B. This affect or arousal
state has motivational properties, as in the case of the empathic arousal
of distress wherein the distressed condition of A produces an empathic
distress in B. It does not seem necessary that all social cognitions pertaining to the perceived state of another evoke an arousal or affective state in
the perceiver. Therefore, it may be productive to have two terms for the
process: (1) the social cognition (sometimes referred to as role-taking)
of another's experience in the absence of arousal or affect; and (2) empathy, which includes social cognition, arousal, and affective experience. In any case, the presence or absence of affective state is not ger-
mane to our discussion of self and empathy.

Empathy is central to the flow of human interaction. Given the
existence of two classes of stimuli, shared and unshared events, empathy may be necessary. Shared events are those which A can verify
with B. Thus, if A says, "Look at that black and white bird," B can look
at what A is looking at and can verify A's experience. Unshared events
are those which have to do with A's feeling and cognitive states. These
events are not verifiable, as A cannot say, "Look at my feeling or thinking." That is because these events are internal, belonging only to A.
Toward a similar point, Heider quotes Ichheiser:

> The counterpart of the collectively perceivable world is the world of our
> individual (private) experiences. The desk on which I am writing is an object
> which can be perceived by myself, by you, and by anyone else, as something
> which is "located" in the interpersonal, collective world. By contrast, my
> feeling of being happy, or my conviction of being right, is perceived and can
> be directly perceived, as this particular feeling or conviction, only by me.
> (1958, p. 62)

Empathy is the bridge between the internal events of people; since cognitions and feelings are so important in human interaction, some form of verification is necessary. The ability of humans to be empathic, therefore, becomes critical to the communication between them. Thus, empathy is not just a pleasant addition to human interaction but is absolutely essential for interpersonal relations. As such, it may be under the control of strong selective factors, a point made recently by Trivers (1971) in his discussion of the evolution of reciprocal altruism. In exploring this problem, Asch has referenced to the mutually shared environment and, in a delightful phrase, captures the empathic experience: "The tree that I see others see too; what I hear they hear" (1952, p. 128).

Empathy, the ability to share indirectly the experience of another by placing oneself in the position of the other is, of course, a central feature and attribute of self. Even more, it is both the material out of which self is derived and, at the same time, one of the uses of self. Empathy is probably derived from the shared reciprocal nature of the earliest social exchanges in which adult caregivers cater to the infant's needs and, through their action, "inform" the child that they know how he/she feels and at the same time behave in a way to relieve or share the feeling of the child. Thus, in a distress empathy situation, the caregiver is "moved" (aroused, feels unhappy, or worried) by the infant's cues and acts to relieve the child's distress. In like manner, they make the child smile and then reinforce the child's smile through their similar action. Their imitation and elaboration of the child's action is the basis of the behavioral manifestation of empathy, informing the infant of their concern. The same behaviors in the same situations also facilitate the development of self, since a reciprocal, shared, and responsive environment is the material out of which self and self–other differentiation develops. This interplay between parent and child produces a shared space between them. This shared space is constructed of the shared past experience.

The situational context is another important element. Lewis and Freedle (1973, 1977) have shown that the situational or perceptual elements constitute the early forms of meaning in that they provide the elements of differentiation as well as provide contextual associations. The intentions, affects, and cognitions of the caregiver and the need satisfaction of the infant are still additional elements of the interaction. These provide a framework for shared space and shared meaning, that is, the beginnings of empathy between the child and the caregiver. It is like a conversation between two people who know each other well and who have spoken of the subject many times before. Because of the shared space, much is said but little spoken. Merleau-Ponty (1964) makes reference to such experiences between adults in conversation, although it could be said for parent and child:

> A common ground constitutes itself between the other one and myself, my thought and his make up a single tissue, my words and his are called out by the phase of the discussion, they insert themselves in a common operation of which neither one of us is the sole creator. A double being comes about, . . . we are, one for the other, collaborators in a perfect reciprocity, our perspectives guide one into the other, we coexist within the same world. (p. 407)

Given the early acquisition of self and the nature of interactions, empathic behavior would seem to be possible in the second year of life. The emergence of a self and a self–other differentiation, the experiencing of empathic-like states should occur, although they may not be evidence of true empathic behavior. As Hoffman (1975) has argued, the child has to be able to take the other's perspective, to be able to see that others have inner states, thoughts, perceptions, and feelings. Originally, it was believed that not until seven or eight years of age did egocentric behavior give rise to social behavior (Piaget, 1932). However, children as young as 2-½ years of age have been able to show simple role-taking (Fishbein, Lewis, & Keiffer, 1972; Masangkay et al., 1974), and even younger children are capable of role-taking, provided they are highly motivated and they occur in the more natural setting such as the home. Hoffman (1975) reports two examples of this and Borke (1972) suggests this is possible in an 18-month-old infant. Given this recent evidence, as well as our work on self recognition, empathy, in all likelihood, has its beginnings in the second year of life, emerging with and providing support for the child's emerging concept of self.

One last word on empathy. Empathy may be the root of all prosocial behavior, and its support and encouragement are essential for the well-being of the child as well as the species. Its development is to be found in the nature of the early caregiver–child interaction and, as such, provides support for the importance of that relationship on social experience. The milieu for its proper development is in the adult–child relationship rather than the peer–peer relationship (Bowlby, 1961; Harlow & Harlow, 1965; Lewis et al., 1975): since the adult–child relationship is predicated on the altruism of the adult toward the child, the child is able to learn that his or her needs are recognized, attended to, and are felt by the other. This learning should provide the material for the child's own empathic responses. Moreover, the verbal exercises of feeling or thought expression should serve as a stimulus for those classes of events that are not perceptually available to the child. Thus, in order to facilitate the development of empathy, verbalization of feelings and cognition states and the response to the experiences of others should be encouraged. Whether empathy can be encouraged after the opening years of life remains in question; nonetheless, its possible implementation within a more traditional, educational experience should be encouraged. Even so, the nature of empathic training requires interpersonal interaction between adult and child, one that is fostered rarely outside the family (e.g., in school settings).

In the discussion of social knowledge and social relationships, the role of the self has been shown to be central in understanding human behavior. From a theoretical perspective, the self, vis-à-vis social knowledge and relationships, stands as part of the phenomenon itself. Nowhere is this clearer than in the role of self in empathic experiences, since knowledge of both self–other differentiation and self–other similarity is necessary for empathy. Thus, being able to empathize means being able to place *oneself* in the role of the other, and this implies a notion of *oneself*.

Self and Friendship

In studying friendship, we must focus our attention on two aspects of the self: the subjective and the objective. In the first, we ask what levels of social cognition are necessary in order for children to be friends. In the second, we focus our attention on the relationship of friendship to aspects of the self—that is, how does the use of the self influence friendship.

The issue of friendship was taken up most seriously by Piaget (1926) in relation to egocentrism. In studying children's language, Piaget reported a high incidence of dyadic speech which did not have any relationship to the speech of the other, where responses to previous statements were not appropriate and where soliloquies or monologues substituted for interactive patterns. Such social interactions were labeled *egocentric* by Piaget, who believed that not until six or seven years of age was the child able to interact in a nonegocentric fashion. Several important social-cognitive skills were believed necessary for true social behavior; without them the child was not mature socially. These skills include differentiation of self–other, what we have called the existential self; personal identity, referred to as the categorical self; empathy; and finally, role- or perspective-taking. Without these skills, true social behavior, including friendship, was not possible. We do not deny that these skills are necessary for some social interactions or that their presence facilitates social exchange; nevertheless, friendship may be possible even in the absence of or in premature forms of these skills.

That social behavior is dependent on a sophisticated set of cognitive skills is obvious, but as we have tried to indicate, cognitive skills may make their appearance and develop through social behavior. Thus, although a cognitive skill as measured in certain ways may be absent, it may not be absent when measured in other ways. For example, role-taking ability varies as a function of measurement and situation. Role-taking, in terms of Piaget's specific task, appears much later when children are asked to hold up an object in order to take a picture of it. Very young children hold it in the direction of the experimenter, indicating perspective-taking ability (Marvin, 1972). In addition, as we have seen, there are unlearned, complex, reflexive behaviors that facilitate complex social behavior. For example, Hess (1967) has argued for "babyishness" of the face as an innate releaser of certain affective behaviors. If the faces of children are such a releaser for adults, it may have the same effect on other children, thus eliciting peer-affective behavior. Finally, it has been amply demonstrated that infants from the beginning of life engage in a positive and highly satisfying affective relationship with a wide variety of adults, including mother, father, friends, and relatives (Lewis & Rosenblum, 1979). Given these complex relationships—wanting to be near, positive affect (liking), shared experiences—it would seem that friendship may be possible even without the cognitive aspects we have mentioned previously.

Even so, let us consider the set of social-cognitive skills that are necessary for more sophisticated social relationships, for although social relations may be possible from the earliest of times, the acquisition of social cognitions should facilitate and deepen these relationships. We have listed several aspects of social behavior which are probably necessary for complex social relations such as friendship: self–other differentiation, self identity, empathy, and role- or perspective-taking. We have already spoken to the issues of self–other differentiation under the rubric of the existential self, and we have discussed self identity in terms of early social dimensions—age, gender, and familiarity. Empathy and its role in perspective-taking have also been alluded to in the present chapter and are discussed in detail elsewhere (Chandler & Greenspan, 1972; Masangkay *et al.*, 1974; Selman, 1971). Role-taking, like the other aspects, seems to occur quite early (Borke, 1972), involves multiple skills (Selman, 1971), increases with age (Miller, Kessel, & Flavell, 1970), and increases the successfulness of peer communication (Garvey & Hogan, 1973; Maratos, 1973; Mueller, 1972; Mueller & Lucas, 1975). Although there are examples of egocentric speech in seven-year-old children, these may be counter-examples; Bates, Camaioni, and Volterra (1975) found that infants 11 through 16 months of age "were able to augment and/or recombine their preverbal signals if adults failed to understand their commands" (Bates, 1975). Halliday (1973) describes role-taking behavior in his 18-month-old son and Borke (1971, 1972) has also presented similar cases. The data on this issue are not clear, although it seems that the simpler the role-taking task, the more related to perceptual cues, the more natural the occurrence, and finally, the more familiar the people, the more likely the young child is to show role-taking behavior.

Given that children within the second year of life show at least primitive examples of all these social skills, it is reasonable to argue that they can engage in friendships with their peers (Garvey & Hogan, 1973; Maratos, 1973; Mueller, 1972; Mueller & Lucas, 1975). If we consider unequal age peers where some of the social facilitation of the relationship is borne by the older child, friendships between infants are possible. That unequal age peer relationships exist has been well documented by others (e.g., Hartup, 1976; Konner, 1975; Lewis *et al.*, 1975).

Just as the self contributes to empathy, so is the self concept necessary in talking about friendship. To discuss the use of self in friendship, we first need to present two principles of a general cognitive-motivational system which makes use of the self. First, the self is used in statements pertaining to social attraction; thus, the cognitive role is based on the comparison of self to other. Second, a motivational component is used that operates on the principle that "like me" attracts, while "not like me" repels: where attraction is synonymous with approach behavior, including positive affect, friendship, imitation, and attention; and repulsion is synonymous with avoidance, including negative affect, avoidance behaviors and ignoring, etc. The notion of a motivational component based on attraction to similarity has received some attention, especially in social psychology. Byrne (1971) has shown the effects of "like me" on the attraction between people. Given these two principles, the role of the use of self in social development can be stated. In social situations in which social relations are possible, A compares self to B, and if A considers himself like B, will be attracted toward B. To examine this process in preverbal children, A may be given a choice between B and C, in which B and A are alike on a salient dimension, but C and A are not. If A chooses B and not C, we may be able to say that the cognitive-motivational system of self is at work. Such an example may be found in the social relation literature. In three of our own studies (Lewis & Brooks, 1974; Brooks & Lewis, 1976; Lewis et al., 1975), we have shown that an infant or young child, A, prefers—both in attention and approach behavior—other children, B, to adults, C. Although other explanations are possible, we have suggested that it is A's cognition that B is "like me," which results in the attraction to B and not C. A more impressive example can be found in some of the recent work on the relationship of social objects and social functions. Edwards and Lewis (1979) studied whether young children 3 to 5 years of age were able to apply age dimensions to a set of pictures of people's faces from 1 to 70 years of age. Children were asked to place the pictures into four piles which were labeled, "little children," "big children," "parents," and "grandparents," which they were able to do easily. Although the children could not apply numerical age labels to faces, they were able to order faces according to age. The children were then asked to decide with which of three persons (as represented by pictures) they would like to do the following things: play with, learn from, share, and receive help. The three pictures were of a 3-, 7-, and 20-year-old. Of interest here are their responses when asked, "With whom would you like to play?" In general, the children 3 to 5 years of age preferred to play with a child of like age, approximately 3 years old. There were, however, children who preferred to play with the 7-year-old. When the children were asked which picture they were most like, it was found that those children who wished to play with the 7-year-old were those who were more likely to have reported that they were like the 7-year-old, whereas those who reported they wished to play with the 3-year-old were more likely to have reported they were like the 3-year-old. The child's choice was a function of the similarity of self to B or C and suggests that the self plays a role in social relations.

Our notion of the use of self offers a cognitive-motivational explanation to very young children's behavior and, as such, releases us from explanatory models which defer either to biological or simple reinforcement principles, both of which fail to utilize the active nature of the child's actions. That is, we are suggesting that the role of self is required in all social actions. Such a position would not be at variance with notions of modeling or imitation with older children, which have shown that a relationship between the model and the imitator facilitates modeling or imitation (Bandura, 1978), or Kohlberg's (1966) notion of the function of similarity for older children. Our data suggest much earlier use of social cognition and a cognitive-motivational system which utilizes self information in social action.

This model has many practical implications, for example, for education. The teacher, wishing the student to have a set of skills or information, may find it necessary to share something in common with the student, to be like one another. Being like one another must have salience to the particular goal the teacher and student have in mind and, further, the commonality they share must be perceived by the student. If these conditions are met, we would think that there exists a greater likelihood of information exchange than under the condition where teacher and student share nothing with each other. The mother of the young infant satisfies this "like me" requirement with a variety of behaviors, a common and shared past, a reciprocal and responsive interaction. Children may satisfy the "like me" rule, since the infant and other child are both young and small. Since we think that age is a cogent dimension in children's lives, they may utilize "like me" statements in the formation of friendships or for teaching. Given this as the case, educational systems are likely to succeed to the degree that they match teacher and pupil characteristics. Thus, Kagan (1964) found that school-age boys did better on reading skills when they had a male teacher than when they had a female one, and there is anecdotal evidence that older siblings are better teachers than parents. Finally, the work of Suomi and Harlow (1975) and Novak and Harlow (1975) indicates that primate peers (especially younger ones) are more effective teachers or therapists than adults. The large-scale treatment of alcohol or drug addiction points to the most successful treatment procedures being those in which people with *like problems,* alcohol or drug addiction, treat others with a similar disorder! This type of data point up once again that the self, actually used as an object among other objects, has the capacity to determine social behavior.

Sex-Role Development

Another example of the utilization of an objective self has to do with the child's acquisition of sex-role behavior. The conceptualization of sex-role development traditionally has centered around rather separate and distinct theories; these being biological, social reinforcement, and cognitive.

The biological theories consider that sex-role development is biologically tied to gender—people's sex roles, in large part, are determined by their gender; thus, boys behave like boys because they are males. The focus of study for such theories is on hormonal differences, which are held to account for the sexual dimorphism. The animal literature is replete with examples of the role of hormones on sex-typed behavior (Goy, 1970). The work of Money and Ehrhardt (1972) and Erhardt and Baker (1974) has helped illuminate the role of hormonal factors in temperamental, attitudinal, and behavioral sex differences. Money and Ehrhardt studied progestin-induced hermaphroditism and fetally-androgenize females. These girl children's social behavior was compared to a matched sample of girls, and it was found that for attitude preference and behavior, these female children tended to be more masculine than did the controls. They were more likely to be tomboys, they showed increased energy levels in play, they preferred cars, trucks, and building material over dolls, they showed little interest in clothing, hairdos, and jewelry, and they were more likely to think about careers in their future (Ehrhardt & Baker, 1974; Money & Ehrhardt, 1972). This, then, is the type of evidence, although there are some methodological difficulties, that is marshalled for the argument linking gender and sex-role preferences.

Less clear are those arguments that are biologically based and whose evidence rests on very early differences between children as a function of sex (Hutt, 1972). In this argument, the very early sex differences are used as evidence for the proposition of psychological and physical sex differences as a function of biological differences. This approach does carry with it some confusion, for as early as we can observe differential infant behavior, we can, at the same time, observe differential parental behavior. We and others have reported that infant girls as young as 12 weeks of age show greater attention to auditory stimuli than do the same-aged boys (Lewis, 1972a; Watson, 1969). However, parent–infant interaction data on the same age infants show that girls are talked to more than boys by their mothers, and when a girl vocalizes, her mother is more apt to respond with a vocalization than when a boy vo-calizes (Lewis, 1972b). This being the case, are girls more attentive to auditory signals because of some biological difference? Perhaps the bio-logical differences influence the mother's behavior—is she more likely to talk to someone who is "interested" than one who is not? On the other hand, it could also be the case that the differential maternal behavior is influencing the infant behavior: mothers who talk more to their children have children who become more interested in auditory stimuli. It is clear that, among humans, sexual dimorphism exists and that some sex dif-ferences are influenced by biology. Whether these differences influence sex-role behavior remains in some question.

Those interested in the environmental determinants of sex role hold that sex-role behavior is learned by the child and that this learning is primarily the consequence of the differentially rewarded behavior of the child by the adult. Such views hold that people's sex-role behavior is, to a large degree, learned by the reinforcement patterns of the adults (and other children) to the child's gender. The case here has been widely made for children of all ages, from infants to adults. The evidence for such a proposition is enormous and has been reviewed too often to bear repeating here (Mischel, 1966). Nevertheless, we will touch on several examples from the infancy literature to make our point and to show how such a theory provides explanatory evidence for its view.

Brooks and Lewis (1974), as part of a larger study on the mother–infant relationships, observed the dress of seventeen pairs of one-year-old, opposite-sex twins brought into our laboratory. Opposite-sex twins were observed in order to hold maternal differences constant and, there-fore, to look at intrafamilial differences as a function of the child's gen-der. The differential dressing patterns these mothers of one-year-olds used clearly marks out their differential sex-role reinforcement. Of these seventeen pairs, only one pair was dressed in identical outfits. Nine sets were wearing overalls, but sex could be identified by the color of the clothing—the girls wore pink, red, or yellow, the boys wore blue, green, or brown. The other seven pairs were dressed so that the boys wore pants and the girls wore dresses. Thus, sex-role appropriate behavior was reinforced early, by one year of age. By affecting the color and type of clothes, these mothers of both girls and boys were differentially re-warding sex role behavior in a concrete and meaningful fashion.

The differential behavior of mothers (and fathers) to their children as a function of gender has been well documented (Lamb, 1976; Lewis,

1972a; Moss, 1967; Thoman, Leiderman, & Olson, 1972). Although it is assumed that this differential behavior on the part of significant others is responsible for the differential sex-role behavior, there is little direct evidence for this being the case. For example, Goldberg and Lewis (1969) reported that a mother's touching of her child at 6 months was related to how much the child touched her at one year. Explicit in this relationship is the belief that the early differential behavior exhibited to the sexes is, in fact, responsible for the later sex role differences observed. Unfortunately, a direct test of this proposition is lacking. That no one has directly tested this theory is puzzling in light of its many proponents. However, it may be understandable that a rejection of social learning theory has in the past implied an acceptance of a biological position.

There is, of course, an alternative to both environmental and biological theories of sex-role development, what have been called cognitive theories (Lewis & Weinraub, 1979). In both the environmental and biological theories, the role of the child is rather passive: in the first, passive vis-à-vis its biological gender; and in the second, passive vis-à-vis the differential reinforcement patterns of others. In both views, the child is acted upon by external forces and behavior is passively shaped by these same forces. In contrast to these two passive views of sex-role acquisition, the cognitive theories of sex-role development have, as a model, an active organism, one which participates in, is influenced by, and who influences those forces which help determine development (Kohlberg, 1966).

Such a model utilizes the child's cognition—its ability to make plans, to ask questions, and to test hypotheses. In particular, children's growing social cognition enables them to determine how to act under certain conditions. This social cognition, as we have attempted to show, centers around knowledge of self—in this case, children's gender and their knowledge of others' gender. It is important here to state that children acquire information about others as well as themselves through the observation of the interactions of others which *do not* involve the self. Thus, I learn about myself, others, their relationships, and my relationship to them, both by interacting with them and by watching them interact. Lewis and Feiring (1978) have called the interaction between self and other *direct* effects, and the interaction between two others *indirect* effects. Bronfenbrenner (1977) has called them primary and secondary effects. Children do learn through indirect means, that is, by watching the interactions of others. The differential reinforcement patterns, like differential behavior as a function of some undefined biological phenomenon, provide the information for the child to construct whatever appropriate behaviors are required, that is, how to act in a sex-role appropriate manner. These events, like those of watching how others behave, provide the material the children use to construct the schema necessary to generate appropriate sex-role behavior.

This construction requires first that the child actively interacts with the world; second, that the child be able to differentiate between others on the basis of their gender, using such physical properties as size, hair length, facial features, and clothes. Finally, the child must be able to obtain knowledge about the cultural or familial behaviors which are deemed appropriate for the particular gender. This cognitive information requires a duality of self–other knowledge. Thus, children acquire knowledge about their own gender at the same time that they acquire knowledge about the gender of others. We believe these cognitive abilities are acquired early, and our data on attention and labeling seem to bear this out.

We would agree, however, that the form of this knowledge is certainly not the same as that for an adult. As Kohlberg (1966) and Emmerich, Goldman, Kirsh, and Sharabany (1977) have shown, the young child's concept of gender is not constant and is easily confused. That the child fails to maintain conservation of gender in the face of a set of transformations (for example, by adding long hair or a dress) is no reason to reject the view that the child has acquired knowledge of gender and sex-role behavior; only that this knowledge, like other aspects of knowledge at this age, is not mature and is easily manipulated. However, the child's knowledge of gender, even in its immature form, becomes an active generator of appropriate sex-role behavior. Money, Hampson, and Hampson (1957) report that after 18 months of age, sex reassignment leads to significant emotional and behavior adjustment problems. Utilizing such information as physical properties, language ("You are just like your father"), and reinforcement activities, children construct their own behavior, just as they do for friendship. Children label themselves—call it alpha—and determine that there are alphas and betas in the environment. Given the cognitive-motivational properties of the self, we hold that the child moves toward other alphas and away from betas. That is, it is the child who realizes what gender he or she is, and in what behaviors he or she should engage. Although the child must utilize a great amount of information, the child probably distinguishes between the sexes in terms of one or two particularly salient dimensions. At first, hair length, for example, may be the critical dimension for gender differentiation; only later would the large (and more important) set of gender differences be discovered. The differentiation on relatively little information, most probably on physical dimensions, allows children to distinguish between the sexes at an early age. After early differentiation between the sexes, the child may be attracted to those like the self (see also Kohlberg, 1966). Once making the differentiation, the movement toward like-self objects provides additional information about self and other which, in turn, produces greater differentiation and attraction. Thus, the process is additive in nature, not requiring a complete gender knowledge on the part of the child in order to begin the process.

Such a theory of sex-role development incorporates several features which are of particular importance. Besides the early acquisition and active nature of the construction of sex roles, the environmental and biological influences are relatively unimportant in the child's learning. Social learning theories argue that if the environment only ceased in reinforcing sex-role behavior, a more unisex culture could be created. Although reinforcement and differentiation of the environment are important factors in our theory of sex-role development, they are not essential. In fact, the major source of sex-role behavior is the child's cognition; as such, the elimination of specific reinforcements may not be sufficient to eliminate sex-role behavior. Cognitions of "like me" are easily formed, and since they require outside factors, they are self generating and a product of the mental apparatus of the child. Given that there are at least physical differences among the sexes (Tanner, 1970), this may be sufficient for children to label themselves as alpha or beta. We believe that gender knowledge, based if nothing more than on physical characteristics differences, may be a natural occurrence in the mental and social development of humans. Not that gender roles are anything more than culturally specific; nonetheless, behaviors, whatever their nature, based on some gender difference, may be a psychological truth which, because of its dependency on mental structures, cannot be eliminated. Thus, our energy may be better spent eliminating sex-role behaviors which do injustice to one or another of the sexes instead of trying to eliminate sex-role behavior entirely.

If the role of each of the factors—biological, gender, social reinforcement, and cognition—should not be overlooked, it is to the last factor, the active construction through cognition, that we consider the most likely explanation for sex-role behavior. For us, development, in general, and sex role behavior, in particular, are the interactions of a variety of forces that coalesce around the child's cognitive ability and, specifically, around the child's social cognition, knowledge of self and other, and the personal identity associated with that differentiation.

The utilization of the self for social action is now widely accepted for adult behavior (Kelly, 1955). What we have attempted to show is that this process occurs from the beginning of life and has relevance for any theory of development. Moreover, the use of such a theory of self provides us, through the cognitive-motivational theory we have outlined, with the processes that could be used by an organism in active interaction with its environment. As we tried to demonstrate earlier, the belief in an active organism, one who influences and is influenced by its environment and one who has cognitions, motives, and feelings, requires that we utilize the concept of self. The developmental perspective we have constructed must utilize such a notion if it is not to rest on forces external to the organism.

References

ABEL, H., & SAHINKAYA, R. Emergence of sex and race friendship preferences. *Child Development*, 1962, *33*, 939–943.

ABELY, P. Le signe du miroir dans les psychoses et plus spécialement dans la démence précoce. *Annales Médico-Psychologiques*, 1930, *88*, 28–36.

ABELSON, R. Script processing in attitude formation and decision making. In J. S. Carroll & J. Payne (Eds.), *Cognition and Social Behavior*. Hillsdale, N. J.: Erlbaum, 1976.

ABLON, G. U. Comparison of the characteristics of the play of young mildly retarded and average children, with mother present and absent. Unpublished doctoral dissertation. Cleveland, Ohio: Case Western Reserve University, 1967.

AINSWORTH, M. D. Object relations, dependency, and attachment: A theoretical review of the infant–mother relationship. *Child Development*, 1969, *40*, 969–1026.

AMES, L. B. The sense of self of nursery school children as manifested by their verbal behavior. *Journal of Genetic Psychology*, 1952, *81*, 193–232.

AMSTERDAM, B. K. Mirror behavior in children under two years of age. Unpublished doctoral dissertation. Chapel Hill: University of North Carolina, 1968.

AMSTERDAM, B. K. Mirror self-image reactions before age two. *Developmental Psychology*, 1972, *5*, 297–305.

AMSTERDAM, B. & GREENBERG, L. M. Self-conscious behavior of infants: A videotape study. *Developmental Psychobiology*, 1977, *10*, 1–6.

ARONSON, E., & ROSENBLOOM, S. Space perception in early infancy: Perception with a common auditory-visual space. *Science*, 1971, *172*, 1161–1163.

ASCH, S. E. *Social psychology*. Englewood Cliffs, N.J.: Prentice-Hall, 1952.

BALDWIN, J. M. *Handbook of psychology: Feeling and will*. New York: Holt, 1894.

BALDWIN, J. M. *Social and ethical interpretations in mental development*. New York: Arno, 1973. (Originally published, 1899.)

BANDURA, A. The self system in reciprocal determinism. *American Psychologist*, 1978, *33*, 344–358.

BANDURA, A., & WALTERS, R. H. *Social learning and personality development*. New York: Holt, Rinehart & Winston, 1963.

BANKS, J. H., & WOLFSON, J. H. *Differential cardiac response of infants to mother and stranger*. Paper presented at the Eastern Psychological Association meetings. Boston, April 1967.

BANNISTER, D., & AGNEW, J. The child's construing of self. In J. Cole (Ed.), *Nebraska symposium on motivation, 1976*. Lincoln: University of Nebraska Press, 1977.

BARD, P. Emotion: I. The neuronormal basis of emotional reactions. In C. Murchinson (Ed.), *Handbook of general experimental psychology*. Worcester, Mass.: Clark University Press, 1934.

BARTLETT, F. C. *Remembering*. Cambridge: Cambridge University Press, 1932.

BATES, E. Peer relations and the acquisition of language. In M. Lewis & L. Rosenblum (Eds.), *Friendship and peer relations: The origins of behavior* (Vol. 4). New York: Wiley, 1975.

BATES, E., CAMAIONI, L., & VOLTERRA, V. The acquisition of performatives prior to speech. *Merrill-Palmer Quarterly*, 1975, *21*, 205–226.

BAYLEY, N. *Bayley scales of infant development*. New York: The Psychological Corporation, 1969.

BELL, R. Q. Contributions of human infants to caregiving and social interaction. In M. Lewis & L. Rosenblum (Eds.), *The effect of the infant on its caregiver: The origins of behavior* (Vol. 1). New York: Wiley, 1974.

BELL, S. M. The development of the concept of object as related to infant–mother attachment. *Child Development*, 1970, *41*, 291–311.

BENHAR, E. E., CARLTON, P. L., & SAMUEL, D. A search for mirror-image reinforcement and self-recognition in the baboon. In S. Kondo, M. Kawai, & A. Ehara (Eds.), *Contemporary primatology: Proceedings of the Fifth International Congress of Primatology*. Basel, Switzerland: Karger, 1975.

BENJAMIN, J. D. Some developmental observations relating to the theory of anxiety. *Journal of the American Psychoanalytic Association*, 1961, *9*, 652–668.

BERTENTHAL, B. I., & FISCHER, K. W. Development of self-recognition in the infant. *Developmental Psychology*, 1978, *14*, 44–50.

BIGELOW, A. *A longitudinal study of self-recognition in young children*. Paper presented at the meetings of the Canadian Psychological Association, Quebec, June 1975.

BLOOM, L., LIGHTBOWN, P., & HOOD, L. Structure and variation in child language. *Monographs of the Society for Research in Child Development*, 1975, *40*(2, serial no. 160).

BOND, E. K. Perception of form by the human infant. *Psychological Bulletin*, 1972, *77*, 225–245.

BORKE, H. Interpersonal perception of young children: Egocentrism or empathy. *Developmental Psychology*, 1971, *5*, 263–269.

BORKE, H. Chandler and Greenspan's "Ersatz egocentrism": A rejoinder. *Developmental Psychology*, 1972, *7*, 107–109.

BOULANGER-BALLEYGUIER, G. Premiers réactions devant le miroir. *Enfance*, 1964, *1*, 51–67.

BOWER, T. G. R. Infant perception of the third dimension and object concept development. In L. B. Cohen & P. Salapatek (Eds.), *Infant perception: From sensation to cognition* (Vol. 2). New York: Academic, 1975.

BOWLBY, J. Separation anxiety: A critical review of the literature. *Journal of Child Psychology and Psychiatry*, 1961, *1*, 251–269.

BOWLBY, J. *Attachment and loss* (Vol. 1), *Attachment*. New York: Basic, 1969.

BOWLBY, J. *Attachment and loss* (Vol. 2), *Separation: Anxiety and anger*. New York: Basic, 1973.

BRACKBILL, Y. Extinction of the smiling response in infants as a function of reinforcement schedule. *Child Development*, 1958, *29*, 115–124.

BRAZELTON, T. B. Neonatal behavioral assessment scale. *Clinics in developmental medicine*, No. 50, Spastics International Medicine Publications. Philadelphia: Lippincott, 1973.

BRAZELTON, T. B., KOSLOWSKI, B., & MAIN, M. The origins of reciprocity: The early mother–infant interaction. In M. Lewis & L. Rosenblum (Eds.), *The effect of the infant on its caregiver: The origins of behavior* (Vol. 1). New York: Wiley, 1974.

BRAZELTON, T. B., YOGMAN, M. W., ALS, H., & TRONICK, E. The infant as a focus for family reciprocity. In M. Lewis and L. Rosenblum (Eds.), *The child and its family: The genesis of behavior* (Vol. 2). New York: Plenum, 1979.

BROMAN, S. H., NICHOLS, P. L., & KENNEDY, W. A. *Preschool IQ: Prenatal and early developmental correlates*. New York: Wiley, 1975.

BRONFENBRENNER, U. Toward an experimental ecology of human development. *American Psychologist*, 1977, *32*, 513–531.

BRONSON, G. W. Infants' reactions to unfamiliar persons and novel objects. *Monographs of the Society for Research in Child Development*, 1972, *47*(3, serial no. 148).

BRONSON, W. C. Developments in behavior with age-mates during the second year of life. In M. Lewis & L. Rosenblum (Eds.), *Friendship and peer relations: The origins of behavior* (Volume 4). New York: Wiley, 1975.

BROOKS, J., & LEWIS, M. Attachment behavior in thirteen-month-old, opposite-sex twins. *Child Development*, 1974, *45*, 243–247.

BROOKS, J., & LEWIS, M. Infants' responses to strangers: Midget, adult and child. *Child Development*, 1976, *47*, 323–332.

BROOKS-GUNN, J., & LEWIS, M. Early social knowledge: The development of knowledge about others. In H. McGurk (Ed.), *Childhood social development*. London: Methuen, 1979. (a)

BROOKS-GUNN, J., & LEWIS, M. The effects of age and sex on infants' playroom behavior. *Journal of Genetic Psychology*, 1979, *134*, 99–105. (b)

BROOKS-GUNN, J., & LEWIS, M. Why Mama and Papa: The development of social labels. *Child Development*, in press.

BROWN, W. L., McDOWELL, A. A., & ROBINSON, E. M. Discrimination learning of mirrored cues by rhesus monkeys. *Journal of Genetic Psychology*, 1965, *106*, 123–128.

BRUNER, J. S., & TAGIURI, R. The perception of people. In G. Lindzey (Ed.), *Handbook of social psychology* (Vol. 2). Cambridge, Mass.: Addison-Wesley, 1954.

BUHLER, C. *The first year of life*. New York: John Day, 1930.

BYRNE, D. *The attraction paradigm*. New York: Academic, 1971.

CAIRNS, R. B. Attachment behavior of mammals. *Psychological Review*, 1966, *73*, 409–426. (a)

CAIRNS, R. B. Development maintenance, and extinction of social attachment behavior in sheep. *Journal of Comparative and Physiological Psychology*, 1966, *62*, 298–306. (b)

CAIRNS, R. B. Attachment and dependency: A psychobiological and social-learning synthesis. In T. L. Gewirtz (Ed.), *Attachment and dependency*. Washington, D. C.: Winston, 1972.

CARON, A. J., CARON, R. F., CALDWELL, R. C., & WEISS, S. J. Infant perception of the structural properties of the face. *Developmental Psychology*, 1973, *9*, 385–400.

CARPENTER, G. C. *Mother–stranger discrimination in the early weeks of life*. Paper presened at the biennial meeting of the Society for Research in Child Development, Philadelphia, March 1973.

CATTELL, P. *The measurement of intelligence of infants and young children*. New York: The Psychological Corporation, 1940.

CHANDLER, M. J. Social cognition: A selective review of current research. In W. F. Overton & J. M. Gallagher (Eds.), *Knowledge and development* (Vol. 1), *Advances in research and theory*. New York: Plenum, 1977.

CHANDLER, M. J., & GREENSPAN, S. Ersatz egocentrism: A reply to H. Borke. *Developmental Psychology*, 1972, *7*, 104–106.

CHARLESWORTH, W. R. Cognition in infancy: Where do we stand in the mid-sixties? *Merrill-Palmer Quarterly*, 1968, *14*, 25–46.

CLARK, E. U. What's in a word? On the child's acquisition of semantics in his first language. In T. E. Moore (Ed.), *Cognitive development and the acquisition of language*. New York: Academic, 1973.

COHEN, L. B. Attention-getting and attention-holding processes of infant visual preferences. *Child Development*, 1972, *43*, 869–879.

COHEN, L. B., & GELBER, E. R. Infant visual memory. In L. B. Cohen & P. Salapatek (Eds.), *Infant perception: From sensation to cognition* (Vol. 1). New York: Academic, 1975.

COLLER, A. R. The assessment of "self-concept" in early childhood education. ERIC Clearinghouse on Early Childhood Education. Urbana: University of Illinois, 1971.

CONDON, W. S., & SANDER, L. W. Neonate movement is synchronized with adult speech: International participation and language acquisition. *Science*, 1974, *183*, 99–101.

COOLEY, C. H. *Human nature and the social order*. New York: Scribner's, 1912.

COOLEY, C. H. *Social organization: A study of the larger mind*. New York: Schocken, 1962. (Originally published, 1909.)

CORNIELSON, F. S., & ARSENIAN, I. A study of the responses of psychotic patients to photographic self image experience. *Psychiatric Quarterly*, 1960, *34*, 1–8.

DARWIN, C. A biographical sketch of an infant. *Mind*, 1877, *2*, 285–294.

DARWIN, C. *The expression of emotions in man and animals*. Chicago: University of Chicago Press, 1965. (Originally published, 1895.)

DÉCARIE, T. G. *Intelligence and affectivity in early childhood*. New York: International Universities, 1965.

DELMAS, F. A. Le signe du miroir dans la démence précoce. *Annales Médico-Psychologiques*, 1929, *87*, 227–233.

DEUTSCH, M., & KRAUSS, R. *Theories in social psychology*. New York: Basic Books, 1965.

DICKIE, J. R., & STRADER, W. H. Development of mirror image responses in infancy. *Journal of Psychology*, 1974, *88*, 333–337.

DIGGORY, J. C. *Self-evaluation*. New York: Wiley, 1966.

DIXON, J. C. Development of self recognition. *Journal of Genetic Psychology*, 1957, *91*, 251–256.

DUNN, J., & KENDRICK, C. Interaction between young siblings in the context of family relationships. In M. Lewis & L. Rosenblum (Eds.), *The child and its family: The genesis of behavior* (Vol. 2). New York: Plenum, 1979.

ECKERMAN, C. O., WHATLEY, J. L., & KUTZ, S. L. Growth of social play with peers during the second year of life. *Developmental Psychology*, 1973, *9*, 207–212.

EDWARDS, C. P., & LEWIS, M. Young children's concepts of social relations: Social functions and social objects. In M. Lewis & L. Rosenblum (Eds.), *The child and its family: The genesis of behavior* (Vol. 2). New York: Plenum, 1979.

EHRHARDT, A. A., & BAKER, S. S. Fetal androgens human central nervous system differentiation and behavior sex differences. In R. Friedman & R. Vandeville (Eds.), *Sex differences in behavior*. New York: Wiley, 1974.

EIBL-EIBESFELDT, I. *Ethology: The biology of behavior*. New York: Holt, Rhinehart & Winston, 1970.

EKMAN, P. Universals and cultural differences in facial expressions of emotion. In J. K. Cole (Ed.), *Nebraska symposium on motivation* (Vol. 19). Lincoln: University of Nebraska Press, 1971.

EMDE, R. N., KLIGMAN, D. H., REICH, J. H., & WADE, T. D. Emotional expression in infancy: I. Initial studies of social signaling and an emergent model. In M. Lewis & L. Rosenblum (Eds.), *The development of affect: The genesis of behavior* (Vol. 1). New York: Plenum, 1978.

EMMERICH, W., GOLDMAN, K. S., KIRSH, B., & SHARABANY, R. Evidence for a transitional phase in the development of gender constancy. *Child Development*, 1977, *48*, 930–936.

EPSTEIN, S. The self-concept revisited, or a theory of a theory. *American Psychologist*, 1973, *28*, 404–416.

ERIKSON, E. H. *Childhood and society*. New York: Norton, 1937.

ESCALONA, S. K., & CORMAN, H. H. *Albert Einstein scales of sensory-motor development*. Unpublished manuscript, 1968.

FAGAN, J. F. Infants' recognition memory for faces. *Journal of Experimental Child Psychology*, 1972, *14*, 453–476.

FANTZ, R. L. Pattern vision in newborn infants. *Science*, 1963, *140*, 296–297.

FANTZ, R. L. Visual perception from birth as shown by pattern selectivity. *Annals of the New York Academy of Science*, 1965, *118*, 793–814.

FAURE, H. L'investissement délirant de l'image de soi. *Evolution Psychiatrique*, 1956, *3*, 545–577.

FISHBEIN, H. D., LEWIS, S., & KEIFFER, K. Children's understanding of spatial relations. *Developmental Psychology*, 1972, *7*, 21–33.

FITZGERALD, H. E. Autonomic pupillary reflex activity during early infancy and its relation to social and nonsocial visual stimuli. *Journal of Experimental Child Psychology*, 1968, *6*, 470–482.

FLAVELL, J. H. An analysis of cognitive-developmental sequences. *Genetic Psychology Monographs*, 1972, *86*, 279–350.

FLAVELL, J. H. The genesis of our understanding of persons: Psychological studies. In T. Mischel (Ed.), *Understanding other persons*. Totowa, New Jersey: Rowman & Littlefield, 1974.

FRAIBERG, S. Blind infants and their mothers: An examination of the sign system. In M. Lewis & L. Rosenblum (Eds.), *The effect of the infant on its caregiver: The origins of behavior* (Vol. 1). New York: Wiley, 1974.

FRENKEL, R. E. Psychotherapeutic reconstruction of the traumatic amnesic period by the mirror image projective technique. *Journal of Existentialism*, 1964, *17*, 77–96.

FREUD, S. *The interpretation of dreams*. New York: Basic, 1954. (Originally published, 1900).

FREUD, S. Instincts and their vicissitudes. *Collected papers*. New York: Basic, 1959. (Originally published, 1915.)

FREUD, S. *New introductory lectures on psychoanalysis*. New York: Norton, 1965.

FULLARD, W., & REILING, A. M. An investigation of Lorenz's "babyness." *Child Development*, 1976, *47*, 1191–1193.

GALLUP, G. G., JR. Mirror image reinforcement in monkeys. *Psychonomic Science*, 1966, *5*, 39–40.

GALLUP, G. G., JR. Mirror image stimulation. *Psychological Bulletin*, 1968, *70*, 782–793.

GALLUP, G. G., JR. Chimpanzees: Self-recognition. *Science*, 1970, *167*, 86–87.

GALLUP, G. G., JR. *Towards an operational definition of self-awareness*. Paper presented at the IXth International Congress of Anthropological and Ethnological Sciences, Chicago, 1973.

GALLUP, G. G., JR. Self-recognition in primates: A comparative approach to the bidirectional properties of consciousness. *American Psychologist*, 1977, *32*, 329–338.

GALLUP, G. G., JR. Self-recognition in chimpanzees and man: A developmental and comparative perspective. In M. Lewis and L. Rosenblum (Eds.), *The child and its family: The genesis of behavior* (Vol. 2). New York: Plenum, 1979.

GALLUP, G. G., JR. & McCLURE, M. K. Preference for mirror-image stimulation in differentially reared rhesus monkeys. *Journal of Comparative and Physiological Psychology*, 1971, *75*, 403–407.

GALLUP, G. G., JR., McCLURE, M. K., HILL, S. D., & BUNDY, R. A. Capacity for self-recognition in differentially reared chimpanzees. *Psychological Record*, 1971, *21*, 69–74.

GARVEY, C., & HOGAN, R. Social speech and social interaction: Egocentrism revisited. *Child Development*, 1973, *44*, 562–568.

GESELL, A. *Infancy and human growth*. New York: Macmillan, 1928.

GESELL, A., & THOMPSON, N. *Infant behavior: Its genesis and growth*. New York: McGraw-Hill, 1934.

GESELL, A., & THOMPSON, H. *The psychology of early growth*. New York: Macmillan, 1938.

GEWIRTZ, J. L. A learning analysis of the effects of normal stimulation, privation, and deprivation on the acquisition of social motivation and attachment. In B. Foss (Ed.), *Determinants of infant behavior*. New York: Wiley, 1961.

GEWIRTZ, J. L. The course of infant smiling in four child-rearing environments in Israel. In B. M. Foss (Ed.), *Determinants of infant behavior* (Vol. 3). New York: Wiley, 1965.

GEWIRTZ, J. L. Mechanisms of social learning: Some roles of stimulus and behavior in early human development. In D. A. Goslyn (Ed.), *Handbook of socialization theory and research*. Chicago: Rand McNally, 1969.

GEWIRTZ, J. L. Attachment, dependence and a distinction in terms of stimulus control. On the selection and use of attachment and dependence indices. In J. Gewirtz (Ed.), *Attachment and dependency*, Washington: Winston, 1972, 139–215.

GEWIRTZ, J. L. The attachment acquisition process as evidenced in the maternal condition of cued infant responding (particularly crying). *Human Development*, 1976, *19*, 143–155.

GIBSON, E. J. *Principles of perceptual learning and development*. New York: Appleton-Century-Crofts, 1969.

GIBSON, J. J. The useful dimensions of sensitivity. *American Psychologist*, 1963, *18*, 1–15.

GIBSON, J. J. *The senses considered as perceptual systems*. Boston: Houghton Mifflin, 1966.

GOLDBERG, S., & LEWIS, M. Play behavior in the year-old infant: Early sex differences. *Child Development*, 1969, *40*, 21–31.

GOODALL, J. *In the shadow of man*. Boston: Houghton Mifflin, 1971.

GOULET, J. The infant's conception of causality and his reactions to strangers. In T. G. Décarie (Ed.), *The infant's reactions to strangers*. New York: International Universities, 1974.

GOY, R. W. Early hormonal influences on the development of sexual and sex-related behavior. In F. O. Schmitt (Ed.), *Neurosciences: Second Study Program*. New York: Rockefeller University Press, 1970.

GREENBERG, D. J., HILLMAN, D., & GRICE, D. Infant and stranger variables related to stranger anxiety in the first year of life. *Developmental Psychology*, 1973, *9*, 207–212.

GRIFFITHS, R. *The abilities of babies*. London: University of London, 1954.

GUARDO, C. J. Self revisited: The sense of self identity. *Journal of Humanistic Psychology*, 1968, *8*, 137–142.

GUARDO, C. J., & BOHAN, J. B. Development of a sense of self identity in children. *Child Development*, 1971, *42*, 1909–1921.

GYR, J. W. Is a theory of direct visual perception adequate? *Psychology Bulletin*, 1972, *77*, 246–261.

HAAF, R. A., & BELL, R. O. The facial dimension in visual discrimination by human infants. *Child Development*, 1967, *38*, 893–899.

HAITH, M. M., BERGMAN, T., & MOORE, M. J. Eye contact and face scanning in early infancy. *Science*, 1977, *198*, 853–855.

HALL, C. S., & LINDZEY, G. *Theories of personality*. New York: Wiley, 1970.

HALLIDAY, M. A. K. *Early language learning: A sociolinguistic approach*. Paper presented for the Ninth International Congress of Anthropological and Ethnological Sciences, Chicago, 1973.

HAMLYN, D. W. Person perception and our understanding of others. In T. Mischel (Ed.), *Understanding other persons*. Totowa, N. J.: Rowman & Littlefield, 1974.

HARLOW, H. F., & HARLOW, M. K. The affectional systems. In A. M. Schrier, H. F. Harlow, & F. Stollnitz (Eds.), *Behavior of nonhuman primates* (Vol. 2). New York: Academic, 1965.

HARLOW, H. F., & MEARS, C. The nature of complex, unlearned responses. In M. Lewis &

L. Rosenblum (Eds.), *The development of affect: The genesis of behavior* (Vol. 1). New York: Plenum, 1978.

HARRIS, L. P. Self-recognition among institutionalized profoundly retarded males: A replication. *Bulletin of the Psychonomic Society*, 1977, *9*, 43–44.

HARTUP, W. W. Cross-age versus same-age peer interaction: Ethological and cross-cultural perspectives. In V. Allen (Ed.), *Children as teachers*. New York: Academic, 1976.

HAVILAND, J., & LEWIS, M. *Infants' greetings to strangers*. Paper presented at the Human Ethology session of the Animal Behavior Society meeting, Wilmington, N. C., May 1975. *Research Bulletin 76–2*, Princeton, N. J.: Educational Testing Service, 1976.

HAYES, K. J., & NISSEN, C. H. Higher mental functions in a home-raised chimpanzee. In A. M. Schrier & F. Stollnitz (Eds.), *Behavior of nonhuman primates* (Vol. 3). New York: Academic, 1971.

HEIDER, F. *The psychology of interpersonal relations*. New York: Wiley, 1958.

HERSHENSON, M. *Form perception in the human newborn*. Paper presented at the Second Annual Symposium, Center for Visual Science, University of Rochester, June 1965.

HESS, E. H. Ethology. In A. M. Freedman & H. I. Kaplan (Eds.), *Comprehensive textbook of psychiatry*. Baltimore: Williams & Wilkins, 1967.

HESS, E. H. Ethology and developmental psychology. In P. Mussen (Ed.), *Carmichael's manual of child psychology* (Vol. 1). New York: Wiley, 1970.

HILL, S. D., BUNDY, R. A., GALLUP, G. G., JR., & McCLURE, M. K. Responsiveness of young nursery-reared chimpanzees to mirrors. *Proceedings of the Louisiana Academy of Sciences*, 1970, *33*, 77–82.

HOFFMAN, M. L. Developmental synthesis of affect and cognition and its implications for altruistic motivation. *Developmental Psychology*, 1975, *11*, 607–622.

HOFFMAN, M. L. Toward a theory of empathic arousal and development. In M. Lewis & L. Rosenblum (Eds.), *The development of affect: The genesis of behavior* (Vol. 1). New York: Plenum, 1978.

HOLLINGSHEAD, A. B. *Two-factor index of social position*. New Haven, Conn.: Author, 1957.

HUTT, C. *Males and females*. United Kingdom: Nichols, 1972.

IZARD, C. *The face of emotion*. New York: Appleton-Century-Crofts, 1971.

JACKLIN, C. N. *Peer interaction in boys and girls*. Paper presented in a Symposium on Same and Cross-Sex Interaction: Peers and Parents at the Society for Research in Child Development meetings, San Francisco, March 1979.

JACKSON, E., CAMPOS, J., & FISCHER, K. The question of decalage between object performance and person performance. *Developmental Psychology*, 1978, *14*, 1–10.

JACOBSON, S. W., & KAGAN, J. *Release responses in early infancy: Evidence contradicting selective imitation*. Paper presented at the International Conference on Infant Studies, Providence, March 1978.

JAMES, W. *The principles of psychology*. New York: Holt, 1950. (Originally published, 1890.)

JAMES, W. *Psychology: The briefer course*. Edited by G. Allport. New York: Harper & Row, 1961. (Originally published, 189?)

JAYNES, J. *The origins of consciousness in the breakdown of the bicameral mind*. New York: Houghton Mifflin, 1977.

KAGAN, J. The child's sex role classification of school objects. *Child Development*, 1964, *35*, 1051–1056.

KAGAN, J. Reflectivity, impulsivity and reading ability in primary grade children. *Child Development*, 1965, *36*, 609–628.

KAGAN, J. Discrepancy, temperament, and infant distress. In M. Lewis & L. Rosenblum (Eds.), *The origins of fear: The origins of behavior* (Vol. 2). New York: Wiley, 1974.

KAGAN, J. The uses of cross-cultural research in early development. In P. H. Leiderman, S.

R. Tulkin, & A. Rosenfeld (Eds.), *Culture and infancy: Variations in the human experience.* New York: Academic, 1977.

KAGAN, J. On emotion and its development: A working paper. In M. Lewis & L. Rosenblum (Eds.), *The development of affect: The genesis of behavior* (Vol. 1). New York: Plenum, 1978.

KAGAN, J., HENKER, B., HEN-TOV, A., LEVINE, J., & LEWIS, M. Infants' differential reactions to familiar and distorted faces. *Child Development,* 1966, *37,* 519–532.

KAGAN, J., & LEWIS, M. Studies of attention in the human infant. *Merrill-Palmer Quarterly,* 1965, *11,* 95–127.

KAYE, K., & MARCUS, J. Imitation over a series of trials without feedback: Age six months. *Infant Behavior and Development,* 1978, *1,* 141–155.

KELLY, G. *Theory of personality: The psychology of personal constructs.* New York: Norton, 1955.

KILLEN, M., & UZGIRIS, I. C. *Imitation of actions with objects: The role of social meaning.* Paper presented at the International Conference on Infant Studies, Providence, R. I., March 1978.

KOHLBERG, L. A cognitive-developmental analysis of children's sex-role concepts and attitudes. In E. E. Maccoby (Ed.), *The development of sex differences.* Stanford: Stanford University Press, 1966.

KOHLER, W. *The mentality of apes.* Translated by E. Winter. New York: Harcourt, 1927.

KONNER, M. Relations among infants and juveniles in comparative perspective. In M. Lewis & L. Rosenblum (Eds), *Friendship and peer relations: The origins of behavior* (Vol. 4). New York: Wiley, 1975.

KREUTZER, M. A., & CHARLESWORTH, W. R. *Infants' reactions to different expressions of emotions.* Paper presented at the meetings of the Society for Research in Child Development, Philadelphia, March 1973.

LAMB, M. Fathers: Forgotten contributors to child development. *Human Development,* 1975, *18,* 245–266.

LAMB, M. (Ed.). *The role of the father in child development.* New York: Wiley, 1976.

LANGLOIS, J. H., GOTTFRIED, N. W., & SEAY, B. The influence of sex of peer on the social behavior of preschool children. *Developmental Psychology,* 1973, *8,* 93–98.

LEE, L. C. Toward a cognitive theory of interpersonal development: Importance of peers. In M. Lewis & L. Rosenblum (Eds.), *Friendship and peer relations: The origins of behavior* (Vol. 4). New York: Wiley, 1975.

LENNEBERG, E. H., REBELSKY, F. G., & NICHOLS, I. A. The vocalizations of infants born to deaf and to hearing parents. *Human Development,* 1965, *8,* 23–37.

LENSSEN, B. Infants' reactions to peer strangers. Unpublished doctoral dissertation, Stanford University, 1973.

LESTER, B. M., KOTELCHUCK, M., SPELKE, E., SELLER, M. J., & KLEIN, R. E. Separation and protest in Guatemalan infants: Cross-cultural and cognitive findings. *Developmental Psychology,* 1974, *10,* 79–85.

LETHMATE, J. & DÜCKER, G. Untersuchungen zum Selbsterkennen im Spiegel bei Orangutans und einigen anderen Affenarten. *Zeitschrift für Tierpsychologie,* 1973, *33,* 248–269.

LEWIS, M. *Mother–infant interaction and cognitive development: A motivational construct.* Paper presented at the National Institute of Child Health and Human Development, Symposium on *Issues in Human Development,* Philadelphia, November 1967. Also in Victor C. Vaughan (Ed.), *Issues in human development.* Washington, D.C.: U. S. Government Printing Office, 1967.

LEWIS, M. Infants' responses to facial stimuli during the first year of life. *Developmental Psychology,* 1969, *1,* 75–86.

LEWIS, M. Individual differences in the measurement of early cognitive growth. In J. Hellmuth (Ed.), *Exceptional infant* (Vol. 2). New York: Brunner/Mazel, 1971.

LEWIS, M. Parents and children: Sex-role development. *School Review,* 1972, *80,* 229–240. (a)

LEWIS, M. State as an infant–environment interaction: An analysis of mother–infant interaction as a function of sex. *Merrill-Palmer Quarterly,* 1972, *18,* 95–121. (b)

LEWIS, M. *The meaning of fear.* Paper presented at a symposium, The Origins of Joy and Fear: The Development of Affect Systems in Infancy, at the Society for Research in Child Development meetings, Denver, April 1975.

LEWIS, M. (Ed.). *The origins of intelligence: Infancy and early childhood.* New York: Plenum, 1976.

LEWIS, M. *The infant and its caregiver: The role of contingency.* Paper presented at a conference on Infant Intervention Programs, The University of Wisconsin, Milwaukee, June 1977. Also in, *Allied Heath and Behavioral Sciences, 1*(4), in press.

LEWIS, M. *Issues in the study of imitation.* Paper presented at the Symposium on Imitation in Infancy: What, How and When, at the Society for Research in Child Development Meetings, San Francisco, March 1979.

LEWIS, M., & BALDINI, N. Attentional processes and individual differences. In G. Hale and M. Lewis (Eds.), *Attention and cognitive development.* New York: Plenum, 1979.

LEWIS, M., & BROOKS, J. Self, other, and fear: Infants' reactions to people. In M. Lewis & L. Rosenblum (Eds.), *The origins of fear: The origins of behavior* (Vol. 2). New York: Wiley, 1974.

LEWIS, M., & BROOKS, J. Infants' social perception: A constructivist view. In L. Cohen & P. Salapatek (Eds.), *Infant perception: From sensation to cognition* (Vol. 2). New York: Academic, 1975.

LEWIS, M., & BROOKS, J. Self knowledge and emotional development. In M. Lewis & L. Rosenblum (Eds.), *The development of affect: The genesis of behavior* (Vol. 1). New York: Plenum, 1978.

LEWIS, M., & BROOKS-GUNN, J. *Visual attention at three months as a predictor of cognitive functioning at two years of age.* Manuscript in preparation.

LEWIS, M. & CHERRY, L. Social behavior and language acquisition. In M. Lewis & L. Rosenblum (Eds.), *Interaction conversation and the development of language: The origins of behavior* (Vol. 5). New York: Wiley, 1977.

LEWIS, M., & FEIRING, C. The child's social world. In R. M. Lerner & G. D. Spanier (Eds.), *Contributions of the child to marital quality through the life-span.* New York: Academic, 1978.

LEWIS, M., & FEIRING, C. The child's social network: Social object, social functions and their relationship. In M. Lewis & L. Rosenblum (Eds.), *The child and its family: The genesis of behavior* (Vol. 2). New York: Plenum, 1979.

LEWIS, M., & FREEDLE, R. Mother–infant dyad: The cradle of meaning. In P. Pliner, L. Krames, & T. Alloway (Eds.), *Communication and affect: Language and thought.* New York: Academic, 1973.

LEWIS, M., & FREEDLE, R. The mother and infant communication system: The effects of poverty. In H. McGurk (Ed.), *Ecological factors in human development.* Amsterdam: North-Holland, 1977.

LEWIS, M., & GOLDBERG, S. The acquisition and violation of expectancy: An experimental paradigm. *Journal of Experimental Child Psychology,* 1969, *7,* 70–80.

LEWIS, M., & LEE-PAINTER, S. An interactional approach to the mother–infant dyad. In M. Lewis & L. Rosenblum (Eds.), *The effects of the infant on its caregiver: The origins of behavior* (Vol. 1). New York: Wiley, 1974.

LEWIS, M., McGURK, H., SCOTT, E., & GROCH, A. Infant attentional distribution across two modalities. Unpublished manuscript, 1973.

LEWIS, M., & ROSENBLUM, L. (Eds.). *The origins of fear: The origins of behavior* (Vol. 2). New York: Wiley, 1974.

LEWIS, M., & ROSENBLUM, L. (Eds.). *Friendship and peer relations: The origins of behavior* (Vol. 4). New York: Wiley, 1975.

LEWIS, M., & ROSENBLUM, L. (Eds.). *The development of affect: The genesis of behavior* (Vol. 1). New York: Plenum, 1978.

LEWIS, M., & ROSENBLUM, L. (Eds). *The child and its family: The genesis of behavior* (Vol. 2). New York: Plenum, 1979.

LEWIS, M., & SCOTT, E. *A developmental study of infant attentional distribution within the first two years of life.* Paper presented at the XX International Congress of Psychology, Symposium on Learning in Early Infancy, Tokyo, August 1972.

LEWIS, M., & STARR, M. Developmental continuity. In J. Osofsky (Ed.), *Handbook of infant development.* New York: Wiley, 1978.

LEWIS, M., & WEINRAUB, M. Sex of parent × sex of child: Socioemotional development. In R. C. Friedman, R. M. Richart, & R. L. Vande Wiele (Eds), *Sex differences in behavior.* Huntington, N. Y.: Krieger, 1974.

LEWIS, M., & WEINRAUB, M. The father's role in the infant's social network. In M. Lamb (Ed.), *The role of the father in child development.* New York: Wiley, 1976.

LEWIS, M., & WEINRAUB, M. Origins of early sex role development. *Sex Roles,* 1979, *5*(2), 135–153.

LEWIS, M., BROOKS, J., & HAVILAND, J. Hearts and races: A study in the measurement of emotion. In M. Lewis & L. Rosenblum (Eds.), *The development of affect: The genesis of behavior* (Vol. 1). New York: Plenum, 1978.

LEWIS, M., GOLDBERG, S., & CAMPBELL, H. A developmental study of information processing within the first three years of life: Response decrement to a redundant signal. *Monographs of the Society for Research in Child Development,* 1969, *34,* (9, Serial No. 133).

LEWIS, M., GOLDBERG, S., & RAUSCH, M. Attention distribution as a function of novelty and familiarity. *Psychonomic Science,* 1967, *7,* 227–228.

LEWIS, M., KAGAN, J., KALAFAT, J., & CAMPBELL, H. The cardiac response as a correlate of attention in infants. *Child Development,* 1966, *37,* 63–71.

LEWIS, M., WEINRAUB, M., & BAN, P. *Mothers and fathers, girls and boys: Attachment behavior in the first two years of life.* Paper presented at the Society for Research in Child Development meetings, Philadelphia, March 1973. *Research Bulletin 72-60.* Princeton, N. J.: Educational Testing Service, 1972.

LEWIS, M., WILSON, C. D., & BAUMEL, M. Attention distribution in the 24-month-old child: Variations in complexity and incongruity of the human form. *Child Development,* 1971, *42,* 429–438.

LEWIS, M., YOUNG, G., BROOKS, J., & MICHALSON, L. The beginning of friendship. In M. Lewis & L. Rosenblum (Eds.), *Friendship and peer relations.* New York: Wiley, 1975.

LINDEN, E. *Apes, men, and language.* New York: Penguin, 1974.

LINDSLEY, D. Emotion. In S. S. Stevens (Ed.), *Handbook of experimental psychology.* New York: Wiley, 1951.

LISSMAN, H. W. Die Umwelt des Kampffisches (*Betta splendens* Regan). *Zeitschrift für Vergleichende Physiologie,* 1932, *18,* 62–111.

LORD, S., LEWIS, M., & BROOKS, J. *Person perception: Infants' responses to pictures.* Paper presented at the Eastern Psychological Association meetings, New York, April 1975.

LORENZ, K. Z. Die angeborenen Formen möglicher Erfahrung. *Zeitschrift für Tierpsychologie,* 1943, *5,* 235–409.

MACCOBY, E. E., & FELDMAN, S. S. Mother-attachment and stranger-reactions in the third year of life. *Monographs of the Society for Research in Child Development,* 1972, *37* (1, Serial No. 146).

MAHLER, M. S. *On human symbiosis and the vicissitudes of individuation* (Vol. 1). *Infantile psychosis.* New York: International Universities, 1968.

MAHLER, M. S., & GOSLINER, B. J. On symbiotic child psychosis: Genetic, dynamic, and restitutive aspects. In *The psychoanalytic study of the child* (Vol. 10). New York: International Universities, 1955.

MAHLER, M. S., PINE, F., & BERGMAN, A. *The psychological birth of the infant.* New York: Basic, 1975.

MANS, L., CICCHETTI, D., & SROUFE, L. A. Mirror reactions of Down's Syndrome infants and toddlers: Cognitive underpinnings of self-recognition. *Child Development,* 1978, *49,* 1247–1250.

MARATOS, O. *The origin and development of imitation in the first six months of life.* Paper presented to the British Psychological Society, Liverpool, 1973.

MARVIN, R. Attachment behavior cooperation and communication skills in 2, 3, and 4 year olds. Unpublished doctoral thesis, University of Chicago, 1972.

MASANGKAY, Z. S., McCLUSKEY, K. A., McINTYRE, C. W., SIMS-KNIGHT, J., VAUGHN, B. E., & FLAVELL, J. H. The early development of inferences about the visual percepts of others. *Child Development,* 1974, *45,* 357–366.

McCALL, R., & McGHEE, P. The discrepancy hypothesis of attention and affect. In F. Weizmann & I. Uzgiris (Eds.), *The structuring of experience.* New York: Plenum, 1977.

McCALL, R. B., PARKE, R. D., & KAVANAUGH, R. D. Imitation of live and televised models by children one to three years of age. *Monographs of the Society for Research in Child Development,* 1977, *22*(5, Serial No. 173).

McGURK, H., & LEWIS, M. Space perception in early infancy: Perception within a common auditory-visual space? *Science,* 1974, *186,* 649–650.

McLEAN, P. D. Mirror display in the squirrel monkey. *Science,* 1964, *146,* 950–952.

MEAD, G. H. *Mind, self, and society: From the standpoint of a social behaviorist.* Chicago: University of Chicago Press, 1934.

MELTZOFF, A. N., & MOORE, M. K. Imitation of facial and manual gestures by human neonates. *Science,* 1977, *198,* (4312), 75–78.

MELVIN, K. B., & ANSON, J. E. Image-induced aggressive display: Reinforcement in the paradise fish. *The Psychological Record,* 1970, *20,* 225–228.

MERLEAU-PONTY, M. *Primacy of perception.* J. Eddie (Ed.), & W. Cobb (trans.), Evanston: Northwestern Universities Press, 1964.

MILLER, P., KESSEL, F., & FLAVELL, J. Thinking about people thinking about people thinking about people . . . A study of cognitive-social development. *Child Development,* 1970, *41,* 613–625.

MISCHEL, W. A social-learning view of sex differences in behavior. In E. E. Maccoby (Ed.), *The development of sex differences.* Stanford: Stanford University Press, 1966.

MISCHEL, W. Toward a cognitive social learning reconceptualization of personality. *Psychological Review,* 1973, *80,* 252–283.

MONEY, J., & EHRHARDT, A. *Man and woman, boy and girl.* Baltimore: The Johns Hopkins University Press, 1972.

MONEY, J., HAMPSON, J., & HAMPSON, J. Imprinting and the establishment of gender role. *Archives of Neurology and Psychiatry,* 1957, *72,* 333–336.

MORGAN, G. A., & RICCIUTI, H. N. Infants' responses to strangers during the first year. In B. M. Foss (Ed.), *Determinants of infant behavior* (Vol. 4). London: Methuen, 1969.

MOSS, H. A. Sex, age, and state as determinants of mother–infant interaction. *Merrill-Palmer Quarterly,* 1967, *13,* 19–36.

MUELLER, E. The maintenance of verbal exchanges between young children. *Child Development,* 1972, *43,* 930–938.

MUELLER, E. Toddlers + toys = an autonomous social system. In M. Lewis & L. Rosenblum (Eds.), *The child and its family: The genesis of behavior* (Vol. 2). New York: Plenum, 1979.

MUELLER, E., & LUCAS, L. A developmental analysis of peer interaction among toddlers. In M. Lewis & L. Rosenblum (Eds.), *Friendship and peer relations: The origins of behavior* (Vol. 4). New York: Wiley, 1975.

NEISSER, U. *Cognitive psychology.* New York: Appleton, 1967.

NOVAK, M. A., & HARLOW, H. F. Social recovery of monkeys isolated for the first year of life: Rehabilitation and therapy. *Developmental Psychology,* 1975, *11,* 453–465.

ORBACH, J., TRAUB, A. C., & OLSON, R. Psychophysical studies of body-image: II. Normative data on the adjustable body-distorting mirror. *Archives of General Psychiatry,* 1966, *14,* 41–47.

OSTANCOW, P. Le signe du miroir dans la démence précoce. *Annales Médico-Psychologiques,* 1934, *92,* 787–790.

PAPOUŠEK, H. & PAPOUŠEK, M. Mirror-image and self-recognition in young human infants: I. A new method of experimental analysis. *Developmental Psychobiology,* 1974, *7,* 149–157.

PARSONS, T., & BALES, K. E. *Family socialization and interaction process.* Glencoe, Illinois: Free Press, 1955.

PEIPER, A. *Cerebral function in infancy and childhood.* New York: Consultants Bureau Enterprises, 1963. (Originally published, 1961.)

PIAGET, J. *The language and thought of the child.* New York: Harcourt, Brace, 1926.

PIAGET, J. *The moral judgment of the child.* New York: Harcourt, Brace, & World, 1932.

PIAGET, J. *The construction of reality in the child.* Translated by M. Cook. New York: Basic, 1954. (Originally published, 1937.)

PIAGET, J. *The psychology of intelligence.* Translated by M. Piercy and D. E. Berlyne. Paterson, N. J.: Littlefield, Adams, 1960. (Originally published, 1947.)

PIAGET, J. *Play, dreams, and imitation in childhood.* New York: Norton, 1962.

PIAGET, J. *The origins of intelligence in children.* Translated by M. Cook. New York: Norton, 1963. (Originally published, 1936.)

PIAGET, J. The mental development of the child: In J. Piaget (Ed.), *Six psychological studies.* New York: Vintage, 1967. (Originally published, 1940.)

PIAGET, J. Piaget's theory. In P. H. Mussen (Ed.), *Carmichael's manual of child psychology* (3rd ed.). New York: Wiley, 1970.

PREYER, W. *Mind of the child* (Vol. 2). *Development of the intellect.* New York: Appleton, 1893.

REBELSKY, F. *Infants' communication attempts with mother and stranger.* Paper presented at the Eastern Psychological Association meetings, New York, April 1971.

REESE, H., & OVERTON, W. Models of development and theories of development. In L. R. Goulet & P. B. Baltes (Eds.), *Life span developmental psychology: Research and theory.* New York: Academic, 1970.

RHEINGOLD, H. L. *Some visual determinants of smiling infants.* Unpublished manuscript, 1971.

RHEINGOLD, H. L., & ECKERMAN, C. O. *Fear of the stranger: A cultural examination.* Paper presented at the Society for Research in Child Development meetings, Minneapolis, April 1971.

RHEINGOLD, H. L., & ECKERMAN, C. O. Fear of the stranger: A critical examination. In H. W. Reese (Ed.), *Advances in child development and behavior.* (Vol. 8). New York: Academic, 1973.

RHEINGOLD, H. L., GEWIRTZ, J. L., & ROSS, H. W. Social conditioning of vocalizations in the infant. *Journal of Comparative Physiological Psychology*, 1959, 52, 68–72.

RITTER, W. E., & BENSON, S. B. "Is the poor bird demented?" Another case of "shadow boxing". *Auk*, 1934, 51, 169–170.

ROBSON, K. S., PEDERSON, F. A., & MOSS, H. A. Developmental observations of diadic gazing in relation to the fear of strangers and social approach behavior. *Child Development*, 1969, 40, 619–627.

ROSENTHAL, M. K. Attachment and mother–infant interaction: Some research impasse and a suggested change in orientation. *Journal of Child Psychology and Psychiatry*, 1973, 14, 201–207.

SAGI, A., & HOFFMAN, M. L. Empathic distress in the newborn. *Developmental Psychology*, 1976, 12, 175–176.

SAMEROFF, A. J. Can conditioned responses be established in the newborn infant: 1971? *Developmental Psychology*, 1971, 5, 1–12.

SAMEROFF, A. J., & CHANDLER, M. J. Reproductive risk and the continuum of caretaking. In F. Horowitz (Ed.), *Review of child development research*. Chicago: University of Chicago Press, 1975.

SCARR, S., & SALAPATEK, P. Patterns of fear development during infancy. *Merrill-Palmer Quarterly*, 1970, 16, 53–90.

SCHACTER, S., & SINGER, J. E. Cognitive, social and physiological determinants of emotional state. *Psychological Review*, 1962, 69, 379–399.

SCHAEFFER, H. R. The onset of fear of strangers and the incongruity hypothesis. *Journal of Child Psychology and Psychiatry*, 1966, 7, 95–106.

SCHANK, R. C., & ABELSON, R. P. *Scripts, plans, goals, and understanding*. Hillsdale, N. J.: Erlbaum, 1977.

SCHLOSBERG, H. The description of facial expression in terms of two dimensions. *Journal of Experimental Psychology*, 1952, 44, 229–237.

SCHMIDT, M. Beobachtungen am Orang-Utan. *Zoologische Garten*, 1878, 19, 230–232.

SCHULMAN, A. H., & KAPLOWITZ, C. Mirror-image response during the first two years of life. *Developmental Psychobiology*, 1977, 10, 133–142.

SELMAN, R. L. Taking another's perspective: Role-taking development in early childhood. *Child Development*, 1971, 42, 1721–1734.

SERAFICA, F. C., & CICCHETTI, D. Down's Syndrome children in a strange situation: Attachment and exploration behaviors. *Merrill-Palmer Quarterly*, 1976, 22, 137–150.

SHAFFRAN, R., & DÉCARIE, T. *Short-term stability of infants' responses to strangers*. Paper presented at The Society for Research in Child Development meetings, Philadelphia, March 1973.

SHAIN, R. A. A study of selected factors in separation distress during the last half of the first year of life. Unpublished doctoral dissertation, Temple University, 1976.

SHANTZ, C. U. *The development of social cognition*. Chicago: University of Chicago Press, 1975.

SHENTOUB, S. A., SOULAIRAC, A., & RUSTIN, E. Comportement de l'enfant arrière devant le miroir. *Enfance*, 1954, 7, 333–340.

SIGEL, I., & COCKING, R. Cognition and communication: A dialectic paradigm for development. In M. Lewis & L. Rosenblum (Eds), *Interaction, conversation and the development of language: The origins of behavior* (Vol. 5). New York: Wiley, 1977.

SIMNER, M. L. Newborn's response to the cry of another infant. *Developmental Psychology*, 1971, 5, 136–150.

SOKOLOV, E. N. *Perception and the conditioned reflex*. New York: Macmillan, 1963.

Spelke, E., Zelazo, P., Kagan, J., & Kotelchuck, M. Father interaction and separation protest. *Developmental Psychology,* 1973, *9,* 83–90.

Spitz, R. A. Infantile depression and the general adaptation syndrome. On the relation between physiologic model and psychoanalytic conceptualization. In P. Hoch & J. Zubin (Eds.), *Depression.* New York: Grune & Stratton, 1954.

Spitz, R. A., & Wolf, K. M. The smiling response: A contribution to the ontogenesis of social relations. *Genetic Psychology Monographs,* 1946, *34,* 57–125.

Sroufe, L. A. Wariness of strangers and the study of infant development. *Child Development,* 1977, *48,* 731–746.

Sroufe, L. A., Waters, E., & Matas, L. Contextual determinants of infant affective response. In M. Lewis & L. Rosenblum (Eds.), *The origins of fear: The origins of behavior* (Vol. 2). New York: Wiley, 1974.

Stern, D. N. The goal and structure of mother–infant play. *Journal of the American Academy of Child Psychiatry,* 1974, *13,* 402–421.

Stoller, F. H. Group psychotherapy on television: An innovation with hospitalized patients. *American Psychologist,* 1967, *22,* 158–162.

Stone, L. J., Smith, H. T., & Murphy, L. B. (Eds). *The competent infant.* New York: Basic, 1973.

Stutsman, R. *Mental measurement of preschool children.* Yonkers: World, 1931.

Suomi, S. J., & Harlow, H. F. The role and reason of peer relationships in rhesus monkeys. In M. Lewis & L. Rosenblum (Eds.), *Friendship and peer relations: The origins of behavior* (Vol. 4). New York: Wiley, 1975.

Tagiuri, R. Person perception. In G. Lindzen & E. Aronson (Eds.), *The handbook of social psychology.* Reading, Mass.: Addison-Wesley, 1969.

Tanner, J. M. Physical growth. In P. H. Mussen (Ed.), *Carmichael's manual of child psychology.* New York: Wiley, 1970.

Taylor, E. M. *Psychological appraisal of children with cerebral defects.* Cambridge: Harvard University Press, 1961.

Thoman, E. B., Leiderman, P. H., & Olson, J. P. Neonate–mother interaction during breast-feeding. *Developmental Psychology,* 1972, *6,* 110–118.

Thomas, H. Visual-fixation responses of infants to stimuli of varying complexity. *Child Development,* 1965, *36,* 629–638.

Thompson, T. I. Visual reinforcement in Siamese fighting fish. *Science,* 1963, *141,* 55–57.

Tinklepaugh, O. L. An experimental study of representational factors in monkeys. *Journal of Comparative Psychology,* 1928, *8,* 197–236.

Tolman, C. W. Feeding behavior of domestic chicks in the presence of their own mirror image. *Canadian Psychologist,* 1965, *6,* 227(Abstract).

Tomkins, S. S. *Affect, imagery, consciousness* (Vol. 1), *The positive affects.* New York: Springer, 1962.

Tomkins, S. S. *Affect, imagery, consciousness* (Vol. 2), *The negative affects.* New York: Springer, 1963.

Townes-Rosenwein, L., & Lewis, M. *Normal and discrepant face–voice integration in early infancy.* Paper presented at the Eastern Psychological Association meetings, Philadelphia, April 1974.

Traub, A. C., & Orbach, J. Psychophysical studies of body-image: The adjustable body-distorting mirror. *Archives of General Psychiatry,* 1964, *11,* 53–66.

Trevarthen, C. Conversations with a two-month-old. *New Scientist,* 1974, 230–233.

Trivers, R. L. The evolution of reciprocal altruism. *Quarterly Review of Biology,* 1971, *46,* 35–37.

TURNURE, C. Response to voice of mother and stranger by babies in the first year. *Developmental Psychology*, 1971, 4, 182–190.

UZGIRIS, I. C. The many faces of imitation in infancy. In L. Montado (Ed.), *Fortschritte der Entwicklungs psychologie*. Stuttgart: W. Kuhlhammer. Gmbh., in press.

UZGIRIS, I. C., & HUNT, J. McV. *Assessment in infancy: Ordinal scales of psychological development*. Chicago: University of Illinois Press, 1976.

VON SENDEN, M. *Space and sight: The perception of space and shape in the congenitally blind before and after operation*. Glencoe, Ill. Free Press, 1960.

WAHLER, R. Infant social attachments, a reinforcement theory: Interpretation and investigation. *Child Development*, 1967, 38, 1079–1088.

WAITE, L. H. *Theoretical perspectives on social cognition during the first two years of life*. Paper presented at the Seventh Annual Symposium of the Piaget Society, Philadelphia, May 1977.

WAITE, L. H., & LEWIS, M. *Inter-modal person schema in infancy: Perception within a common auditory-visual space*. Paper presented at the Eastern Psychological Association meetings, Boston, April 1977.

WAITE, L. H., & LEWIS, M. *Maternal report on social imitation development during the first year*. Paper presented at the Eighth Annual Symposium of the Piaget Society, Philadelphia, May 1978.

WAITE, L. H., & LEWIS, M. *Early imitation with several models: An example of socio-affective and socio-cognitive development*. Paper presented at the Society for Research in Child Development Meetings, San Francisco, March 1979.

WALLON, H. *Les origines du caractère chez l'enfant; les précludes du sentiment de personalité*. (2nd Ed.) Paris: Presses Universitaires de France, 1949.

WATSON, J. S. Operant conditioning of visual fixation in infants under visual and auditory reinforcement. *Developmental Psychology*, 1969, 1, 408–416.

WEINRAUB, M. *Children's responses to brief periods of maternal absence: An experimental intervention study*. Final report to the Foundation for Child Development, 1976.

WEINRAUB, M., & FRANKEL, J. Sex differences in parent–infant interactions during free play departure and separation. *Child Development*, 1977, 48, 1240–1249.

WEINRAUB, M., & LEWIS, M. The determinants of children's responses to separation. *Monographs of the Society for Research in Child Development*, 1977, 42(4, serial number 172).

WEINRAUB, M., BROOKS, J., & LEWIS, M. The social network: A reconsideration of the concept of attachment. *Human Development*, 1977, 20, 31–47.

WHITE, B. L. *Human infants: Experience and psychological development*. Englewood Cliffs, N. J.: Prentice-Hall, 1971.

WHITE, R. W. Motivation reconsidered: The concept of competence. *Psychological Review*, 1959, 66, 297–323.

WOLFF, P. H. Observations on the early development of smiling. In B. M. Foss (Ed.), *Determinants of infant behavior* (Vol. 2). New York: Wiley, 1963.

WOODWORTH, R. S., & SCHLOSBERG, H. *Experimental psychology* (Rev. ed.). New York: Holt, 1954. (Originally published, 1938.)

WYLIE, R. C. *The self concept*. Lincoln: University of Nebraska Press, 1961.

WYLIE, R. C. The present status of self theory. In E. F. Borgatta & W. E. Lambert (Eds.), *Handbook of personality: Theory & research*. Chicago: Rand McNally, 1968.

YOUNG, G., & LEWIS, M. *Friends and strangers: Peer relations in infancy*. Paper presented at the Human Ethology Session of the Animal Behavior Society meeting, Wilmington, N. C., May 1975.

YOUNISS, J. Another perspective on social cognition. In A. D. Pick (Ed.), *Minnesota symposium on child psychology* (Vol. 9). Minneapolis: University of Minnesota Press, 1975.

ZAJONC, R. B. Family configuration and intelligence: Variations in scholastic aptitude scores, parallel trends in family size and the spacing of children. *Science,* 1976, *192,* (4236), 227–236.

ZAJONC, R. B. *The birth order puzzle.* Paper presented at a conference, The origins of behavior: The social network of the developing infant, Princeton, N. J., December 1977.

ZAZZO, R. Images du corp et conscience du soi. *Enfance,* 1948, *1,* 29–43.

Author Index

Italic numbers indicate pages where complete reference citations are given.

Abel, H., 138, *273*
Abelson, R., 27, *273, 285*
Abely, P., 16, *273*
Ablon, G. U., *273*
Agnew, J., 251, *273*
Ainsworth, M. D., 233, *273*
Als, H., 242, 253, *274*
Ames, L. B., 59, 161, 203, 212, *273*
Amsterdam, B. K., 17, 23, 24, 25, 29, 44, 60, 61, 62, 63, 64, 67, 70, 105, 106, 108, 109, 110, 111, 171, 181, 182, 204, 205, 206, 208, 209, 210, 211, 212, 215, 216, 217, 220, *273*
Anson, J. E., 18, *283*
Aronson, E., 18, 234, 253, *273*
Arsenian, I., 16, *276*
Asch, S. E., 258, 259, 260, *273*

Baker, S. S., 267, *276*
Baldini, N., 180, 243, *281*
Baldwin, J. M., 230, 244, 255, *273*
Bales, K. E., 4, *284*
Ban, P., 138, *282*
Bandura, A., 266, *273*
Banks, J. H., 9, 233, *273*
Bannister, D., 251, *273*
Bard, P., 186, *273*
Bartlett, F. C., 247, 248, *273*

Bates, E., 264, *274*
Baumel, M., 201, *282*
Bayley, N., 21, 22, *274*
Bell, R. O., 254, *278*
Bell, R. Q., 245, *274*
Bell, S. M., 3, 168, 170, 254, *274*
Benhar, E. E., 19, *274*
Benjamin, J. D., 138, 237, *274*
Benson, S. B., 17, *285*
Bergman, A., 14, 15, 253, *278, 283*
Bertenthal, B. I., 63, 109, 110, 179, 180, 202, 204, 210, 217, 220, *274*
Bigelow, A., 70, 105, 202, 209, 211, *274*
Bloom, L., 161, *274*
Bohan, J. B., 10, *278*
Bond, E. K., 25, *274*
Borke, H., 261, 264, *274*
Boulanger-Balleyguier, G., 204, 205, *274*
Bower, T. G. R., 242, *274*
Bowlby, J., 5, 232, 233, 261, *274*
Brackbill, Y., 10, 111, *274*
Brazelton, T. B., 224, 242, 253, *274*
Broman, S. H., *274*
Bronfenbrenner, U., 269, *275*
Bronson, G. W., 9, 233, *275*
Bronson, W. C., 60, 138, 253, *275*

Brooks (-Gunn), J., 5, 25, 60, 107, 112, 115, 119, 136, 137, 138, 186, 192, 193, 194, 195, 201, 220, 228, 231, 233, 234, 235, 237, 238, 240, 246, 253, 261, 264, 265, 268, *275, 281, 282, 287*
Brown, W. L., 18, *275*
Bruner, J. S., 228, *275*
Buhler, C., 21, 22, *275*
Bundy, R. A., 19, 182, 220, *277, 279*
Byrne, D., 265, *275*

Cairns, R. B., *275*
Caldwell, R. C., 254, *275*
Camaioni, L., 264, *274*
Campbell, H., 167, 169, *282*
Campos, J., 180, 254, *279*
Carlton, P. L., 19, *274*
Caron, R. F., 254, *275*
Carpenter, G. C., 232, 253, *275*
Cattell, P., 21, 22, *275*
Chandler, M. J., 228, 248, 264, *275, 285*
Charlesworth, W. R., 111, *275, 280*
Cherry, L., 225, 228, 237, *281*
Cicchetti, D., 178, *283, 285*
Clark, E. U., 163, *275*
Cocking, R., 179, *285*
Cohen, L. B., 169, 256, *276*

Coller, A. R., 11, 276
Condon, W. S., 242, 276
Cooley, C. H., 9, 11, 12,
     13, 19, 276
Corman, H. H., 276
Cornielson, F. S., 16,
     276

Darwin, C., 5, 12, 20,
     24, 59, 185, 204, 228,
     276
Décarie, T. G., 3, 138,
     237, 254, 276, 285
Delmas, F. A., 16, 276
Deutsch, M., 12, 276
Dickie, J. R., 23, 61, 63,
     204, 205, 206, 276
Diggory, J. C., 276
Dixon, J. C., 23, 24, 59,
     60, 62, 67, 110, 111, 204,
     205, 215, 216, 217, 276
Dücker, G., 19, 280
Dunn, J., 234, 276

Eckerman, C. O., 60, 107,
     138, 192, 276, 284
Edwards, C. P., 4, 236, 237,
     265, 276
Eibl-Eibesfeldt, I., 137,
     251, 276
Ehrhardt, A. A., 238, 267,
     276, 283
Ekman, P., 185, 276
Emde, R. N., 195, 276
Emmerich, W., 270, 276
Epstein, S., 257, 276
Erikson, E. H., 9, 276
Escalona, S. K., 276

Fagan, J. F., 136, 138, 235,
     237, 277
Fantz, R. L., 232, 254, 277
Faure, H., 16, 277
Feiring, C., 4, 229, 233,
     236, 237, 269, 281
Feldman, S. S., 282
Fischer, K., 63, 109, 110,
     179, 180, 202, 204, 210,
     217, 220, 254, 274,
     279
Fishbein, H. D., 261, 277

Fitzgerald, H. E., 232, 277
Flavell, J. H., 66, 157, 208,
     219, 261, 264, 277, 283
Fraiberg, S., 253, 277
Frankel, J., 237, 287
Freedle, R., 182, 224, 253,
     260, 281
Frenkel, R. E., 16, 277
Freud, S., 9, 13, 14, 15,
     27, 277
Fullard, W., 137, 277

Gallup, G. G., 16, 17, 18,
     19, 23, 24, 29, 60, 61,
     62, 63, 65, 106, 177, 181,
     182, 204, 206, 207, 208,
     220, 277, 279
Garvey, C., 264, 277
Gelber, E. R., 256, 276
Gesell, A., 21, 22, 23, 59,
     60, 155, 202, 203, 212,
     277
Gewirtz, J. L., 10, 233, 242,
     278, 285
Gibson, E. J., 232, 246, 247,
     278
Gibson, J. J., 246, 247, 278
Goldberg, S., 10, 167, 183,
     224, 237, 269, 278, 281,
     282
Goldman, K. S., 270, 276
Goodall, J., 17, 278
Gosliner, B. J., 14, 283
Gottfried, N. W., 138, 280
Goulet, J., 278
Goy, R. W., 267, 278
Greenberg, D. J., 115, 136,
     138, 201, 235, 237, 278
Greenberg, L. M., 24, 25,
     70, 105, 209, 210, 211,
     273
Greenspan, S., 264, 275
Grice, D., 115, 136, 138,
     201, 235, 237, 278
Griffiths, R., 21, 22, 278
Groche, A., 281
Guardo, C. J., 10, 278
Gyr, J. W., 247, 278

Haaf, R. A., 254, 278
Haith, M., 253, 278

Hall, C. S., 8, 278
Halliday, M. A. K., 264,
     278
Hamlyn, D. W., 229, 253,
     258, 278
Hampson, J., 270, 283
Harlow, H. F., 5, 242, 244,
     261, 266, 278, 284, 286
Harlow, M. K., 5, 261,
     278
Harris, L. P., 16, 279
Hartup, W. W., 264, 279
Haviland, J., 139, 186, 193,
     194, 279, 282
Hayes, K. J., 20, 182, 279
Heider, F., 13, 238, 251,
     258, 259, 279
Henker, B., 254, 280
Hen-Tov, A., 254, 280
Hershenson, M., 232, 279
Hess, E. H., 137, 236, 252,
     263, 279
Hill, S. D., 19, 182, 220,
     277, 279
Hillman, D., 115, 136, 138,
     201, 235, 237, 278
Hoffman, M. L., 137, 139,
     228, 259, 261, 279, 285
Hogan, R., 264, 277
Hollingshead, A. B., 30, 48,
     72, 116, 125, 142, 150,
     169, 192, 279
Hood, L., 161, 274
Hunt, J., 287
Hutt, C., 267, 279

Izard, C., 185, 279

Jacklin, C. N., 138, 279
Jackson, E., 180, 254, 279
Jacobson, S. W., 242, 244,
     279
James, W., 11, 12, 28, 185,
     186, 249, 250, 279
Jaynes, J., 187, 279

Kagan, J., 138, 169, 197,
     238, 242, 244, 254, 266,
     279, 280, 282, 286
Kalafat, J., 169, 282

Kaplowitz, C., 23, 60, 62, 204, 205, 206, 208, 285
Kavanaugh, R. D., 244, 283
Kaye, K., 280
Keiffer, K., 261, 277
Kelly, G., 28, 228, 255, 256, 272, 280
Kendrick, C., 276
Kennedy, W. A., 274
Kessel, F., 264, 283
Killen, M., 244, 280
Kirsh, B., 270, 276
Klein, R. E., 280
Kligman, D. H., 195, 276
Kohlberg, L., 239, 240, 266, 269, 270, 271, 280
Kohler, W., 181, 220, 280
Konner, M., 236, 264, 280
Koslowski, B., 224, 253, 274
Kotelchuck, M., 138, 280, 286
Krauss, R., 276
Kreutzer, M. A., 111, 280
Kutz, S. L., 60, 138, 276

Lamb, M., 138, 233, 234, 268, 280
Langlois, J. H., 138, 280
Lee, L. C., 254, 280
Lee-Painter, S., 281
Leiderman, P. H., 269, 286
Lenneberg, E. H., 243, 280
Lenssen, B., 60, 280
Lester, B. M., 280
Lethmate, J., 19, 280
Levine, J., 254, 280
Lewis, M., 4, 5, 10, 25, 20, 60, 75, 87, 107, 111, 112, 115, 119, 136, 137, 138, 139, 167, 169, 178, 180, 182, 183, 185, 186, 191, 192, 193, 194, 195, 197, 201, 211, 219, 220, 224, 225, 226, 228, 229, 231, 233, 234, 235, 236, 237, 238, 240, 243, 244, 245, 246, 248, 253, 254, 256,

Lewis, M. (cont.)
260, 261, 263, 264, 265, 267, 268, 269, 275, 276, 278, 279, 280, 281, 282, 283, 286, 287
Lewis, S., 261, 277
Lightbown, P., 161, 274
Linden, E., 182, 282
Lindsley, D., 186, 282
Lindzey, G., 8, 278
Lissman, H. W., 17, 282
Lord, S., 234, 282
Lorenz, K. Z., 137, 236, 247, 282
Lucas, L., 60, 264, 284

Maccoby, E. E., 282
Mahler, M. S., 14, 15, 283
Main, M., 224, 253, 274
Mans, L., 178, 283
Maratos, O., 244, 264, 283
Marcus, J., 280
Marvin, R., 263, 283
Masangkay, Z. S., 66, 157, 208, 261, 264, 283
Matas, L., 195, 234, 286
McCall, R., 244, 256, 283
McClure, M. K., 18, 19, 182, 220, 277, 279
McCluskey, K. A., 66, 157, 208, 261, 264, 283
McDowell, A. A., 18, 275
McGhee, P., 256, 283
McGurk, H., 5, 234, 253, 281, 283
McIntrye, C. W., 66, 157, 208, 261, 264, 283
McLean, P. D., 18, 283
Mead, G. H., 9, 11, 12, 13, 19, 182, 220, 229, 283
Mears, C., 242, 244, 278
Meltzoff, A. N., 109, 283
Melvin, K. B., 18, 283
Merleau-Ponty, M., 7, 15, 179, 182, 220, 229, 261, 283
Michalson, L., 5, 60, 136, 234, 253, 261, 264, 265, 282
Miller, P., 264, 283
Mischel, W., 249, 268, 283

Money, J., 238, 267, 270, 283
Moore, M. K., 109, 253, 278, 283
Morgan, G. A., 138, 192, 194, 237, 283
Moss, H. A., 237, 269, 283, 285
Mueller, E., 5, 60, 264, 283, 284
Murphy, L. B., 8, 286

Neisser, U., 247, 248, 284
Nichols, I. A., 243, 280
Nichols, P. L., 274
Nissen, C. H., 20, 182, 279
Novak, M. A., 266, 284

Olson, J. P., 269, 286
Olson, R., 16, 284
Orbach, J., 16, 284, 286
Overton, W., 246, 284
Ostancow, P., 16, 284

Papoušek, H., 24, 25, 70, 105, 113, 209, 211, 214, 284
Papoušek, M., 24, 25, 70, 105, 113, 209, 211, 214, 284
Parke, R. D., 244, 283
Parsons, T., 4, 284
Pederson, F. A., 237, 285
Peiper, A., 242, 284
Piaget, J., 1, 3, 8, 9, 15, 28, 166, 168, 169, 180, 189, 231, 232, 248, 254, 261, 262, 263, 284
Pine, F., 14, 15, 283
Preyer, W., 5, 20, 24, 59, 62, 108, 204, 205, 284

Rausch, M., 167, 282
Rebelsky, F., 9, 243, 280, 284
Reese, H., 246, 284
Reich, J. H., 195, 276
Reiling, A. M., 137, 277

Rheingold, H. L., 10, 24, 107, 110, 113, 192, 211, 214, *284, 285*
Ricciuti, H. N., 138, 192, 194, 237, *283*
Ritter, W. E., 17, *285*
Robinson, E. M., 18, *275*
Robson, K. S., 237, *285*
Rosenbloom, S., 234, 253, *273*
Rosenblum, L., 4, 111, 112, 185, 186, 192, 197, 226, 245, 263, *282*
Rosenthal, M. K., 234, *285*
Ross, H. W., 10, *285*
Rustin, E., 16, *285*

Sagi, A., 137, 139, *285*
Sahinkaya, R., 138, *273*
Salapatek, P., 192, 194, *285*
Sameroff, A. J., 137, 248, *285*
Samuel, D., 19, *274*
Sander, L. W., 242, *276*
Scarr, S., 192, 194, *285*
Schacter, S., 186, *285*
Schaeffer, H. R., 194, *285*
Schank, R. C., 27, *285*
Schlosberg, H., 201, *285, 287*
Schmidt, M., 17, *285*
Schulman, A. H., 23, 60, 62, 204, 205, 206, 208, *285*
Scott, E., 167, *281, 282*
Seay, B., 138, *280*
Seller, M. J., *280*
Selman, R. L., 264, *285*
Serafica, F. C., *285*
Shaffran, R., 138, 237, *285*
Shain, R. A., *285*
Shantz, C. U., 229, *285*
Sharabany, R., 270, *276*
Shentoub, S. A., 16, *285*

Sigel, I., 179, *285*
Simner, M. L., 137, 139, *285*
Sims-Knight, J., 66, 157, 208, 261, 264, *283*
Singer, J. E., 186, *285*
Smith, H. T., 8, *286*
Sokolov, E. N., 256, *285*
Soulairac, A., 16, *285*
Spelke, E., 138, *280, 286*
Spitz, R. A., 9, 14, 232, 249, 252, *286*
Sroufe, L. A., 178, 195, 234, *283, 286*
Starr, M., 219, *282*
Stern, D. N., 224, 253, *286*
Stoller, F. H., 16, *286*
Stone, L. J., 8, *286*
Strader, W. H., 23, 61, 63, 204, 205, 206, *276*
Stutsman, R., 21, 23, 155, *286*
Suomi, S. J., 266, *286*

Tagiuri, R., 228, 253, *275, 286*
Tanner, J. M., 139, 271, *286*
Taylor, E. M., 66, *286*
Thoman, E. B., 269, *286*
Thomas, H., 232, *286*
Thompson, H., 212, *277*
Thompson, N., 21, 59, 60, *277*
Thompson, T. I., 18, *286*
Tinkelpaugh, O. L., 18, *286*
Tolman, C. W., 17, 206, *286*
Tomkins, S. S., 186, 191, *286*
Townes-Rosenwein, L., *286*
Traub, A. C., 16, *284, 286*
Trevarthen, C., 242, *286*
Trivers, R. L., 260, *286*

Tronick, E., 242, 253, *274*
Turnure, C., 9, *287*

Uzgiris, I. C., 109, 244, *280, 287*

Vaughn, B. E., 66, 157, 208, 261, 264, *283*
Volterra, V., 264, *274*
von Senden, M., 220, *287*

Wade, T. D., 195, *276*
Wahler, R., 9, *287*
Waite, L. H., 28, 220, 233, 244, *287*
Wallon, H., 9, 15, *287*
Walters, R. H., *273*
Waters, E., 195, 234, *286*
Watson, J. S., 267, *287*
Weinraub, M., 4, 138, 197, 229, 233, 237, 240, 269, *282, 287*
Weiss, S. J., 254, *275*
Whatley, J. L., 60, 138, *276*
White, B. L., 2, *287*
White, R. W., *287*
Wilson, C. D., 201, *282*
Wolf, K. M., 9, 232, 249, 252, *286*
Wolff, P. H., 9, 111, *287*
Wolfson, J. H., 9, 233, *273*
Woodworth, R. S., 201, *287*
Wylie, R. C., 8, 11, *287*

Yogman, M. W., 242, 253, *274*
Young, G., 5, 60, 136, 234, 253, 261, 264, 265, *282, 287*
Youniss, J., 229, 230, *288*

Zajonc, R. B., 4, *288*
Zazzo, R., 20, 24, 105, 202, *288*
Zelazo, P., 138, *286*

Subject Index

Action–outcome pairing, 9, 164, 183,
  222–226, 252. *See also* Contingency
Affect, 36, 42, 75, 76, 81–85, 87,
  98–101, 105–107, 111–114,
  117–141, 184, 205, 207, 213, 215,
  219, 225
  differential, 85, 101
Age. *See* Social category; Stranger
Agency, 2, 183, 188, 189, 227, 248,
  252
  definition of, 188
Agent, 184
Altruism, reciprocal, 260
Apes, great (chimpanzees), 19, 65, 177,
  181, 182, 220
Attachment, 233
Attention, 32, 36, 42, 60, 61, 73, 76, 86,
  87, 91, 105, 106, 111–114, 132,
  179, 180, 209, 219, 249, 256, 264

Behavior
  imitative, 32, 44, 50, 73, 108, 112, 165,
    193, 195, 196, 212
  mark-directed, 19, 34, 39, 45, 46, 50,
    53, 55, 56, 59, 64, 67, 69, 105,
    168–172, 175, 178, 181, 193, 195,
    196, 207, 208, 214, 216, 217, 219
  mirror directed, 17, 18, 32, 33, 36, 37,
    40, 42–44, 50, 52, 54, 55, 60, 61,
    68, 193, 206, 218
  other-directed, 20, 21, 23, 38, 61,
    68, 106
  self-directed (body directed), 16–20,
    23, 26, 29, 32–34, 36–40, 42, 43,
    50–55, 58, 60–63, 65, 66, 68, 69,
    105, 106, 165, 171, 174, 181, 194,
    195, 207, 208, 212–214, 218–220
  social, 166, 245, 261

Categorical self. *See* Self
Cause and effect, 223, 225
Chimpanzees. *See* Apes, great
Circular reaction, 1, 70, 183, 206, 211,
  214
  primary, 2, 225, 226, 227
  secondary, 189, 226, 227
Cognitive-motivational structures,
  245, 264–266, 270, 272
  theory of development, 139, 256
  two principles of, 264
Constructivist view, 245–249
Contingency, 9, 25, 27, 28, 69–71, 75,
  78, 80–114, 183, 209, 211, 214,
  216, 219, 226, 227, 254. *See also*
  Action–outcome pairing
  knowledge of, 218
  mirror, 24, 226
Contingency feedback, 9, 10, 61, 71,
  123, 133, 178, 180, 200, 209
Contingent play. *See* Play
Contingent self. *See* Self

Development, unitary nature of, 228
Differentiation, 80, 86, 104, 105, 111,
  119
  age, 115
  familiar–unfamiliar, 197, 233–234
  gender. *See* Social category
  object–people, 197
  of inner and outer world, 13
  parent–other, 233
  self–other. *See* Self–other
    differentiation
  social–nonsocial, 234, 238
Dimensions, saliency of, 97, 113, 114,
  141
Distinctive feature. *See* Feature

293

Duality
 of the self, 8, 257
 subject–object, 3

Egocentrism, 262, 264
Emotion
 definition of, 184
 development (ontogenesis) of, 184–197
Emotional experience (emotional feeling),
  28, 184, 185, 189–191, 196, 197,
  225–227
 definition of, 190
 ontogenesis of, 189, 190
Emotional expression, 185, 191, 192, 197,
  226
Emotional state, 185, 190, 193, 226
Empathy, 15, 28, 187, 188, 241, 257–264
 definition of, 258, 260
Ethnology, 250
Event
 definition of, 250, 259
 external, 198, 251
 internal, 198, 251, 259
 shared, 259
 unshared, 259
Existential self. See Self

Facial recognition, 15
Familiarity. See Social category
Fear, 187, 190, 192, 253. See also Stranger
 development of, 191
Feature, 97, 137, 227, 235
 distinctive, 223
 perceptual, 70, 114
Friendship, 5, 28, 137, 241, 262–264

Gender. See Social category
Gender differentiation. See
  Differentiation, gender
Genetic epistomology, 9, 15, 26, 248

Imitation, 28, 32, 33, 36, 37, 40, 42, 52,
  54, 55, 58, 60–62, 74, 76, 79, 87,
  105, 106, 109, 169, 171, 175, 180,
  207, 210, 215, 221, 226, 227, 230,
  231, 242, 249, 252, 260, 264, 266
 definition of, 169
 reflexive, 244
 subjective, 244
Imprinting, 5

Individual differences, 59, 165–183,
  198, 219, 221, 222
Information processing, 249
Innate releasing mechanism (innate
  releaser), 247, 249, 252, 263
Intentionality, 2, 167, 183, 226, 227,
  242, 251, 252, 254, 256, 260
Interactive nature of development. See
  Transactional nature
Internal representation. See
  Representation
Interpersonal relations, 251, 258, 262

Knowledge
 of other, 7, 11, 13, 15, 166, 197,
   228–231, 239–241, 245
 of relationship (self to other), 228–230,
   238–240, 245, 251, 255
 of self, 7, 11, 13, 15, 166, 225,
   228–230, 239–245, 269. See also
   Self knowledge
 social/nonsocial. See Social knowledge

Language
 acquisition (onset of), 198, 225, 227
 comprehension, 142, 152–154, 158,
   160, 161, 164, 203, 212
 development, 12, 28, 227
 personal pronoun usage, 147, 148, 150,
   154–156, 161–163, 203, 212, 213,
   215, 219
 production, 142, 151, 153, 154,
   161, 164, 203, 212
 "Like me" ("Like myself"), 141, 242,
   264–266, 271. See also Similarity
Like-self objects, 271
Linguistic-symbolic representation. See
  Representation
Locus in space (location in space), 10, 187,
   225, 226, 248, 252, 259

Maternal behavior, differential, 268–270
Means–end relationship, 2, 3, 183,
   211, 214, 223, 226, 227, 248,
   254
Mechanistic position (mechanistic view
   of behavior), 246–247, 249
Metatheory, 198

Nativist position (nativist view), 245
Noncontingent self. See Self

Nonsocial knowledge. *See* Social
   knowledge
Nonsocial object. *See* Object

Object
   nonsocial, 223, 224, 231, 232
   social, 4, 213, 223–225, 227, 231–233,
      236, 240

Peers, 5, 28, 116, 122–125, 127, 129–132,
      134–141
Perception, 239, 246
   person, 253
Permanence
   object, 3, 4, 10, 26, 166, 168, 170,
      172–174, 179–181, 184, 197, 220,
      221, 224, 226, 227, 231, 252, 254
   person, 3, 4, 179, 197, 254
   self, 4, 10, 164, 179, 189, 224, 226,
      227
Personal construct, 249, 255–257
Personal identity, 263, 272
Perspective-taking. *See* Role-taking
Phenomenology, 8, 10
Play, 11, 67
   contingent, 74, 77, 79, 90–92,
      108–114, 165, 169, 170–174,
      176–178, 181, 210, 213, 215,
      218, 219, 221, 226
Psychoanalysis, 9, 13

Reflex, 222
   physical, 242–244
   social, 242–245
Reflexive behavior, 226, 242, 254
Reflexive control, 243
Representation, 2, 213, 214
   complexity of, 107
   facial, 7, 238
   familiarity of, 107
   immediate, 24
   internal, 233, 256
   linguistic–symbolic, 6
   modes of, 172, 178, 179, 198, 214, 215,
      217, 222
      mirror, 16, 28, 105, 107, 165, 200,
         204, 209, 226
      picture, 16, 27, 28, 115–141, 165,
         199, 200, 201, 209

Representation (*cont.*)
   modes of (*cont.*)
      videotape, 16, 28, 72, 104–114, 165,
         200
      nonimmediate, 24
   of self. *See* Self representation
   symbolic, 227
Role-taking, 12, 263, 264

Schizophrenia, 16
Self
   and action, 224
   as agent, 256
   as construct, 139, 256
   as object, 5, 8, 11
   as subject, 5, 8, 11
   categories of, 225, 231
   categorical/objective, 8, 11, 27, 115,
      141, 163, 222, 225, 227, 230, 232,
      241, 262, 263
   contingent/noncontingent, 90
   existential/subjective, 8, 11, 27, 28, 115,
      141, 163, 241, 262–264
   origins of, 1–27, 166
   visual knowledge of, 113
Self action, 26
Self awareness (awareness of self), 19, 23,
      26, 27, 63, 65, 67, 136, 171, 185,
      188–190, 196, 203, 206, 212, 214,
      216
Self concept (concept of self), 5, 11, 28,
      165, 166, 183, 187, 188, 198, 222,
      264
   development of, 11, 12
Self consciousness, 203, 213. *See also*
      Behavior
Self development (development of self),
      9, 12, 28, 166, 178, 181, 183, 189,
      198, 199, 222–240, 253
Self identity, 10, 14, 15, 263, 264
Self knowledge, 6, 26, 27, 109, 164, 178,
      182, 184, 185, 189–191, 197, 199,
      203, 220, 222–224, 227–230, 249,
      255
Self recognition, 6, 16, 17, 19, 20, 27,
      28, 35, 44, 46, 48, 53, 62–68, 70,
      80, 115, 146, 147, 158, 161, 162,
      166, 171–182, 184–198, 201, 203,
      207, 208, 212, 213, 215–217,
      220–222, 224, 226, 227, 233, 240,
      261

Self recognition (cont.)
and social behavior, 27
development of, 23, 67, 110, 224, 226, 228
mirror, 191, 223, 227
operational definition of, 204
pictorial, 25, 140
visual, 15, 21, 23, 24, 59, 69, 133, 140, 165, 189, 196, 198, 199, 214, 227
Self referents, 21, 26, 156, 163, 202, 210
Self representation, 29–69, 87, 179, 198–221, 227
contingent/noncontingent, 104, 105, 107–109, 179, 214
recognition of, 106
Self–other differentiation, 9, 14, 15, 71, 96, 110, 112–114, 119, 127, 136, 183, 199, 202, 211, 214, 215, 218, 219, 226, 227, 230–232, 237, 238, 241, 252, 255, 260–263
development of, 10, 225, 226, 270, 271
direct–indirect effects, 269, 270
primary–secondary effects, 269–270
self–opposite sex, 202
self–same sex, 202
verbal knowledge of, 150
Self–other duality, 249, 270
Sensorimotor stage, 3, 220, 231
Separation anxiety, 191
Separation–individuation, 14
Sex-role behavior, 237, 267–272
acquisition of, 241, 267
differential, 268, 269
Sex-role development, 28, 241, 267–272
three theories of, 267
Similarity, 224, 242, 253, 257, 265.
See also "Like me"
self-other, 236, 262
Social behavior. See Behavior
Social category (social dimension), 232–240, 255
age, 71, 77, 78, 86, 96–101, 103, 104, 108, 111, 112, 114–116, 119–134, 142, 156, 159, 164, 177, 200, 220,

Social category (social dimension) (cont.)
age (cont.)
227, 234–237, 239, 240, 264, 266
familiarity, 69, 133, 164, 233–234, 239, 240, 257, 264, 267
gender, 11, 71, 97–99, 108, 115, 116, 119–142, 146, 156, 160, 164, 166, 199, 200, 227, 237–240, 257, 264, 267–272
Social cognition, 4, 5, 7, 8, 27, 28, 228, 230–232, 238, 244, 245, 254, 257, 259, 262, 263, 271, 272
Social development, 181
Social experience, 178, 182
Social knowledge, 7, 222, 229, 252–254, 257, 258, 262
acquisition of, 253, 254
three features of, 229
Social network, 4, 233
Social object. See Object
Social perception, 258
Social reinforcement, 10
Social reflexes. See Reflex
Social world, 5, 13, 223–224
Socialization, 187
Sociobiological approach to development, 241–246, 250
three principles of, 242
Sociological theories, 11, 243
Stimuli
external, 187
internal, 187
Stranger, 88, 90, 91, 97–99, 119, 126–130, 135, 202, 227
adult, 89, 93, 115, 253
age of, 127, 133–141, 144
approach, 71, 90, 138
child, 115, 253
fear, 5, 107, 190, 197, 221, 253
Symbolic representation. See Representation

Transactional nature of development, 248
Transitivity, 236